RICHMOND BURNING

RICHMOND BURNING

THE LAST DAYS OF
THE CONFEDERATE CAPITAL

NELSON LANKFORD

VIKING

VIKING

Published by the Penguin Group

Penguin Putnam Inc., 375 Hudson Street, New York, New York 10014, U.S.A.

Penguin Books Ltd, 80 Strand, London WC2R 0RL, England

Penguin Books Australia Ltd, 250 Camberwell Road, Camberwell,
    Victoria 3124, Australia

Penguin Books Canada Ltd, 10 Alcorn Avenue, Toronto,
    Ontario, Canada M4V 3B2

Penguin Books India (P) Ltd, 11 Community Centre, Panchsheel Park,
    New Delhi–110 017, India

Penguin Books (N.Z.) Ltd, Cnr Rosedale and Airborne Roads, Albany,
    Auckland, New Zealand

Penguin Books (South Africa) (Pty) Ltd, 24 Sturdee Avenue, Rosebank,
    Johannesburg 2196, South Africa

Penguin Books Ltd, Registered Offices:
Harmondsworth, Middlesex, England

First published in 2002 by Viking Penguin,
a member of Penguin Putnam Inc.

10   9   8   7   6   5   4   3   2   1

LIBRARY OF CONGRESS CATALOGING-IN-PUBLICATION DATA

Lankford, Nelson D.
    Richmond burning : the last days of the Confederate capital / Nelson D. Lankford.
        p.   cm.
    Includes bibliographical references (p.) and index.
    ISBN 0-670-03117-8
    1. Richmond (Va.)—History—Siege, 1864–1865.   2. Richmond (Va.)—History—
Civil War, 1861–1865.   I. Title
E477.61 .L36 2001
973.7'38—dc21   2001056845

This book is printed on acid-free paper. ∞

Printed in the United States of America
Set in Aldus
Designed by Carla Bolte

For Harry, Olivia, and Maggie

CONTENTS

PROLOGUE

April 15, 1865

I have fought a good fight, I have finished my course, I have kept the faith.

—II Timothy 4:7

From a black sky the rain came down in hissing torrents and churned the road into a river of mud. The rider, head bent against the storm, wore a slouch hat stained from travel like his uniform. He was careworn, fatigued, soaked to the skin, but he had almost reached his destination. Six days after Appomattox, Robert E. Lee was coming back to Richmond.

It was Holy Saturday, the day after Good Friday and one of the most somber of the Christian year. For the Episcopal churches of the occupied city, there would be no Easter Sunday in 1865. The local Federal military commander ordered them shut because their liturgy called for prayers for the Confederate president, and the words could not be altered without consent of the bishop, who was out of touch somewhere in Canada. If they would not pray for the president of the United States, they would not be allowed to pray at all.

William Hatcher, a Baptist minister, recognized the rider passing his house in Manchester, the community directly across the James River from the capital. Hatcher later watched Ulysses S. Grant's sol-

1

diers march past his house, with regimental colors flying and bands playing. Good Confederate that he was, though, he treasured the memory not of the resplendent northern army but of this earlier, more modest procession that passed his doorway in the driving rain. His words took on an almost biblical cadence when the clergyman described the scene: "I saw another sight in connection with Richmond's fall. . . . What I saw was a horseman. His steed was bespattered with mud, and his head hung down as if worn by long travelling. . . . my own, my peerless chieftain, Robert E. Lee."[1]

Just beyond Hatcher's house, past the last street before the river, the vista opened to an unobstructed view of the city set on the hills of the opposite bank. Before the war, this vantage point offered travelers an arresting sight. Slender church spires and public buildings rose in terraced ranks above the commercial precincts crowding the riverfront. Towering over all stood the chaste white colonnaded portico of the Capitol that housed Virginia's legislature.

Now this place gave Lee his first sight of Richmond after the war that had rent the young American republic and sowed destruction on a colossal scale, but nowhere more terribly than in the Virginia capital. No matter how he may have steeled himself against the sight, it must have been a shock.

In front of him and upstream to the left, where the toll bridge and the two railroad trestles had spanned the James, now only fire-blackened stone piers marched across the river. Union army engineers had thrown a line of pontoons over the gap as soon as they occupied the city twelve days before. That rough structure offered the only way to cross. The Capitol survived, but it now looked down on the utter ruin that war had brought to the southern citadel, and over it the Stars and Stripes waved for the first time since the internecine nightmare had begun.

Tottering brick chimneys and piles of rubble stretched all along the waterfront. Richmond's industrial and commercial might lay in ashes. For days the fires continued to smolder, springing to life here and there among the gutted ruins long after the danger to the rest of the city had passed. By some accounts, even as late as this wet Saturday, nearly two weeks after the fire, the rain had not yet put out the last of the smoking embers. To his left, Lee could see the sprawling workshops and furnaces of the Tredegar ironworks, which had forged cannon for his army. Those buildings had escaped the fire, but they would fashion no more artillery pieces for the South.

In all, eight hundred buildings had burned, maybe more. Nine-tenths of its commercial heart had died with Confederate Richmond. In the words of an eyewitness describing the boundary of the fire, "The pencil of the surveyor could not have more distinctly marked out the business portion of the city."[2] Now it was gone: the Henrico County Courthouse, where the records of other counties had been stored for safekeeping, the General Court of Virginia and all of its documents, railroad depots, every bank and many law offices, green-grocers and dry goods stores, brokerage houses, slave markets, the offices of commission merchants, giant flour mills, most of the newspapers and their print shops, saloons, livery stables, warehouses, tobacco factories, machine shops.

Buildings could be replaced, but other losses were more costly. Hardly a household in Richmond escaped untouched after four years of war. An uncle killed in action, a brother who succumbed to camp fever, a father who died of pneumonia toiling as an impressed slave to build earthworks, a consumptive sister who worked herself into an early grave on the home front—each left an empty chair at the family dinner table. For decades to come, the awkward gait of the veteran hobbling down the street on an ill-fitting prosthesis would remind those who survived of the thousands who did not. When more than three-quarters of southern white males of military age saw service, and when the casualties from wounds and disease exceeded a third of the total, to speak of the loss of a generation was hardly an exaggeration.

The country would be brought under one government again, but the toll of deaths on both sides, perhaps most especially on the losing side, would weigh heavily on the broken hearts of the survivors for as long as they lived. Indeed, the loss would embitter and aggrieve for generations to come.

As he peered through sheets of rain at the grim sight laid out before him, Lee may have remembered earlier visits. It lacked only a week of being the fourth anniversary of the day he went up to the Capitol to accept command of Virginia's army. That had been a time of barely suppressed emotions, as the reticent professional soldier publicly pledged himself "to the service of my native State, in whose behalf alone will I ever again draw my sword."[3] Did he recall that event, as he surveyed the devastation? Did he think about his earlier decision to decline command of the Union's army?

When Lee cast his lot, the juggernaut of civil war had already begun to roll. The passions that had incited Americans to demonize one another over slavery and states' rights now drove them to kill one another. Four years of bloodletting lay before them. By genius, luck, and the irresolution of his opponent, Lee saved Richmond for the South in 1862. Against a stronger and more worthy adversary, he parried the blow again in 1864. By then Richmond had become not just the capital, it had become the Confederacy itself.

But he had saved it for what? Only to be laid waste in the extremity of the Confederate cause? And what would be the fate of those who led the effort for southern independence, an effort that, in defeat, the world would brand treason?

Before Lee crossed the pontoon bridge, the rest of his party caught up with him. They drove a caravan of tattered wagons that a magnanimous victor had permitted the general and his little entourage to keep in order to carry their personal belongings home from the surrender. Among their papers was a signed and countersigned parole giving Federal protection to "the undersigned, prisoners of war." Heading the list was the neat, crisp signature of "R E Lee Genl."[4]

The general, accompanied by his son Rooney, a nephew, and others of his headquarters staff, did not cross the river unobserved. They had been expected. Word coursed through the city when they appeared in the rain at the far end of the temporary bridge. The procession of tired horses and men clattered across the pontoons and through slippery cobblestone streets, hemmed in on all sides by piles of rubble that scavengers had begun picking over even while the bricks were still hot to the touch.

With each block the horsemen passed, more Richmonders came out to see the general. "As soon as his approach was whispered," wrote Judith McGuire, a devoutly Confederate refugee from northern Virginia, "a crowd gathered in his path, not boisterously, but respectfully."[5] Some accounts say that people began to cheer and that he acknowledged their praise by repeatedly lifting his hat to them. These people, at least, did not blame him. On the contrary. They pressed forward to shake his hand, to touch him. But his adjutant, Walter Taylor, who rode at his side, remembered that "no demonstration attended General Lee's return."[6] A hostile northern reporter said the onlookers "satisfied themselves with quietly waving their hats and their hands," but even he had to concede that a few cheers arose as the cavalcade neared the Lee house.[7] There the general refused to make a speech and went inside the rented red-brick town house on Franklin Street, two blocks from Capitol Square, where his invalid wife waited.

Though eyewitnesses disagreed on whether any blue-coated soldiers also cheered, one Union officer who saw Lee that Saturday remembered him kindly. Capt. George Bruce, 13th New Hampshire Regiment, recalled that "as I looked into his face the shadow of Appomattox was upon it," the same famous look of weary nobility that Mathew Brady's camera captured for posterity a week later.[8] Bruce made that comment in later years when the passage of time had cast the soft light of forgiveness over his recollection. Two weeks before the time about which the Yankee captain wrote, however, he held a different opinion. Then he considered Lee the master of a still-dangerous army that had come close to killing the United States of America in a misbegotten attempt to set up a separate republic built on human chattel slavery.

The physical toll on Lee was apparent. Gone were the trim black mustache and clean-shaven chin of 1861, replaced by a beard as white as the hair on his head. He had aged a generation in four years. When he shut the door behind him, he ended this final, unscheduled but public, corporate ceremony in the life of Confederate Richmond. That brief sight of the general gave a fleeting lift to those who came out to watch, at least to the majority who had supported the cause. But it also gave a frisson of long-delayed pleasure to the minority of Unionists who had endured Confederate rule and then rejoiced to see the old flag restored. Confederate or Unionist, few of them had the luxury to dwell on the general's return, for their parlous circumstances dictated a harsh, austere postwar reality.

In the North there was elation. The cheering began at midday on Monday, April 3, the instant word clicked over the telegraph lines that Richmond, at long last, had fallen. Church bells rang out, and crowds gathered to celebrate in the streets throughout the North. "In New York," spat embittered Richmond editor Edward Pollard, "twenty thousand persons in the open air [had] sung the doxology."[9] The occupation of no other southern city came close in importance. After the city fell but before Appomattox, Mary Lee, the general's crippled wife, bravely told her friends to keep the faith: "Richmond is not the Confederacy."[10] She would not have convinced people in the North.

The contrast in mood was not just between North and South. For all those southerners of African descent, more than a third of the population, this was a celebration far more profound than any white northerner or southern Unionist could know. The Jubilee, freedom from bondage, had come at last, and it had come in their lifetime. It was no less a joy to southern free blacks living at the margins of slave society.

Their jubilation was short-lived. The day after Lee arrived, Federal cannon boomed out warnings. These were not celebratory salutes as they had been after Appomattox: Abraham Lincoln had been shot. Now it was the turn of the whole nation to reel in shock. In cold fury, General Grant cabled orders to arrest every paroled Confederate officer in town who had not taken the oath of allegiance. They did not arrest Lee.

For Richmond, the death of Lincoln added one more trauma to a dizzying fortnight of disasters. When she heard the news out in a country town west of the capital, Alice Payne sensed that the blame would fall on the defeated South and could only lament to her diary in choked, laconic syllables, "Poor Virginia gone gone forever."[11]

The first half of April 1865 brought apocalypse to the Confederate people of Richmond and deliverance to those who favored the other side. Their mixed experiences of terror and elation, bitterness and joy, punctuated the end of an era, and it was not just for Richmond. It was for the whole reconnected but not yet reunited nation. With a caustic pen, Constance Cary, twenty-two years old that spring and a hot-blooded southern patriot, rhapsodized sarcastically about "the fruit trees a mass of blossoms—the grass vividly green, the air nectar" on the second day of the hated Union occupation.[12] For her, for her Confederate neighbors, for the whites who did not support the cause, and for the black people of Richmond, both free and enslaved, April 1865 turned their world upside down. It overshadowed everything that had come before in their city. It influenced everything that followed. And it signified nothing less than the re-creation of the United States of America.

CHAPTER 1

CITADEL

Winter into Spring, 1865

Virginians . . . exult in the beauty of their unconquered city
& say Oh but you should see it in the summer!
—Thomas Conolly[1]

The place the Confederacy chose for its capital lay on the north bank of the James River, eighty miles inland from the Chesapeake Bay. There, at the river's head of navigation, a long, rocky cataract that was audible for miles around marked the border between rolling Piedmont hills and coastal plain. This geological fault line made Richmond a natural entrepôt long before it acquired political significance. Indians first camped at the spot where they had to portage their canoes around the rapids. White men erected a wooden cross there barely a month after the Jamestown settlers reached the New World. According to tradition, William Byrd II gave the place its English name when he looked back down King James's river, at the bend it makes below the falls, and thought it reminded him of Richmond-upon-Thames. True or not, the story made a fitting creation myth for a city that steeped itself in Anglophilia.

When Patrick Henry demanded liberty or death in St. John's Church, Richmond was a rude collection of unpainted clapboard dwellings that hugged the flood-prone waterfront called Shockoe Bot-

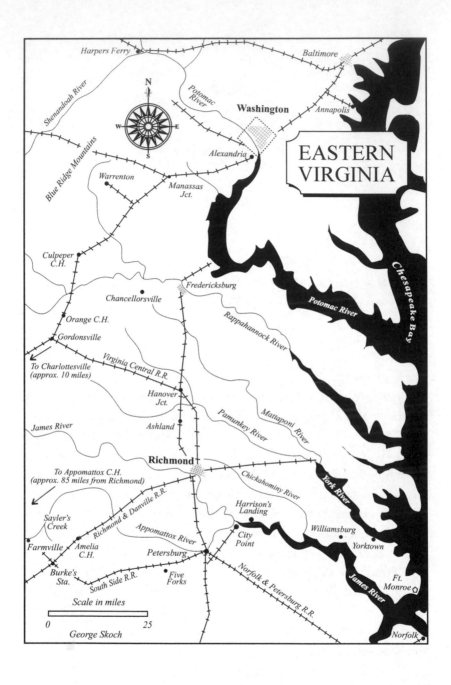

EASTERN VIRGINIA

Harpers Ferry

Baltimore

Shenandoah River

Potomac River

Washington

Annapolis

Blue Ridge Mountains

Warrenton

Manassas Jct.

Alexandria

Culpeper C.H.

Fredericksburg

Chancellorsville

Rappahannock River

Potomac River

Chesapeake Bay

Orange C.H.

Gordonsville

To Charlottesville (approx. 10 miles)

Virginia Central R.R.

Hanover Jct.

Mattaponi River

Pamunkey River

James River

Ashland

Richmond

To Appomattox C.H. (approx. 85 miles from Richmond)

Chickahominy River

York River

Sayler's Creek

Richmond & Danville R.R.

Harrison's Landing

Williamsburg

Yorktown

Farmville

Amelia C.H.

Appomattox River

Petersburg

City Point

James River

Ft. Monroe

Burke's Sta.

South Side R.R.

Five Forks

Norfolk & Petersburg R.R.

Scale in miles

0   25

Norfolk

George Skoch

tom. After the Revolution, tobacco and slave trading gave the town the twin pillars of its antebellum prosperity. Then a spurt of industrial growth at midcentury financed a city of fine public buildings, churches, and stylish mansions on the hills that by 1861 looked down on a bustling commercial district.

That the Confederacy enticed Virginia to join it—with Richmond as its national capital—was a doubtful outcome right up to the moment it happened. Before the war, with each passing day Virginia looked less like its neighbors farther south. Its farms raised not just tobacco but corn and wheat, garden crops and livestock. Economic change was transforming the state capital at a breakneck pace. The clangor and smoke of iron foundries proclaimed the gospel of industry. Trade in manufactured goods forged powerful ties of commerce and friendship with Baltimore, Philadelphia, and New York.

Entrepreneurs adapted their distinctive system of labor to these new ways of making money. And that creative adaptation gave Richmond's version of slavery a quality increasingly unlike the plantation variety in the rural South. Hired-out surplus slaves, many of them handling their own arrangements for room and board, moved easily among the large free black population. Together, enslaved and free blacks constituted nearly four-tenths of the city's population.

Ties to that other South, however, remained strong. Hotheads in the Democratic Party, looking to the past when they imagined the future, endorsed the schemes of Deep South extremists and dreamed of a slave republic free of northern interference.[2] Radicals lusted for disunion and were outraged when more cautious men dominated Virginia's secession convention in 1861. For months, the conservatives thwarted any attempt to join the new Confederate States of America, formed by the seven seceded states of the Deep South. They abhorred the idea of leaving the Union. A sentimental attachment to their Revolutionary heritage and the Virginia distaste for change governed their attitude. Above all, they distrusted the allure of southern independence and feared it would wreck their growing commercial ties to the North.

Left to their own devices, Virginians might have avoided civic suicide. Instead, external events emboldened the radicals and cowed the conservative Unionist majority. Abraham Lincoln forced the issue when he called on loyal states to help stamp out the fires of rebellion ignited at Fort Sumter in Charleston harbor. The middle ground was cut away. Virginia and the other slave states of the upper South had to choose. When the call for troops came from Washington in April 1861, conservative Unionists in Richmond hesitated. They had held the line against secession for a time, but at the end of the day, they reckoned that they could not stomach war against other southerners. They chose disunion and got war with the North instead.

The war to break or preserve the Union began over constitutional issues triggered by slavery. Did the Federal government threaten the right of states to sanction property in human beings? Was secession a right or treason? But for average white Virginians, the greatest perceived threat was to hearth and home, and they fought longer and harder than might have been expected. For most of them, the later arguments among historians about whether the true cause was states' rights or slavery would have made no sense. The southern way of life they defended included slavery because they could not imagine any other way to order relations among the races.[3]

Once Virginia sided with the Confederacy and Richmond became home to the new southern national government, the city attracted fortune-seekers and refugees from across the South. Full of hope, congressmen came not just from the total of eleven states that ultimately seceded but from Kentucky and Missouri as well, with representatives also from the territory of Arizona and from the Cherokee, Choctaw, Creek, and Seminole nations. Now the city boasted three levels of competing bureaucracies—those of the local, state, and national governments. The newly minted Congress of the Confederate States shared the Capitol with Virginia's legislators.

At first, war brought an economic boom, with government contracts mushrooming on all sides. Before the advent of inflation, supply bottlenecks, and military reverses, happy prospects for gain flooded the city with strangers and civil servants. The dual task of the government—to prosecute the war and to build a new nation-state—created a swelling tide of business. A sign of the times was publication of a special directory for the benefit not just of newcomers but of native Richmonders as well, overwhelmed as they were in their own city by the influx of outsiders and the growth of new government offices.[4]

JUST AS IN the antebellum era, for Confederate Richmond it was Capitol Square that defined the psychic as well as the civic center of town. The Capitol dominated not only the square but the whole skyline as well, and its portico of Ionic columns, two rows deep, cast a shadow far beyond the city. The building was designed by Thomas Jefferson when, as minister to France, he was besotted by the architecture of antiquity and sent home plans inspired by a Roman temple in Provence. This first American neoclassical building set an example for civic architecture everywhere in the country, at the time and for a century after.

It was the first president, though, not Jefferson, whose image pervaded the space. Jean-Antoine Houdon's austere, classical marble statue of George Washington, said by some to be the finest sculpture in all of America, stood in the rotunda of the Capitol. Thomas Crawford's more grandiose equestrian Washington, mounted on a high stone base, dominated the north corner of the square, a beacon for public meetings and an icon honoring the Father of the Union. The statues and even the iron fencing and fountain on the square were symbols of republican virtue that elite Virginians revered in this central green space in their principal city. Those symbols took on new meaning with civil war and would do so at the war's conclusion and in a fashion few could have imagined in the first flush of secession.

Mid-Victorian Richmond was a churchgoing town at a time when Americans increasingly associated piety with urban respectability. In the capital of the Confederacy, ministers played a distinctly civic as well as religious role. Except for St. John's Church to the east, the most prominent houses of worship clustered within a few blocks of Capitol Square. Second Presbyterian, near Fifth and Main, filled its pulpit with one of the city's most eloquent preachers. The ruddy complexion, muttonchop whiskers, and stern gaze of Moses Drury Hoge

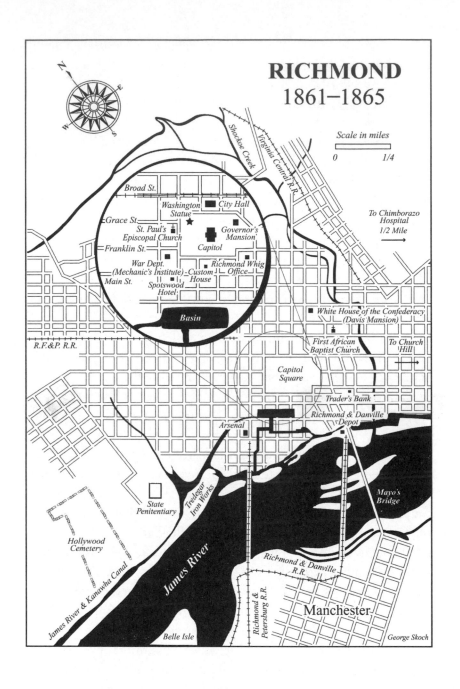

RICHMOND
1861–1865

Scale in miles
0   1/4

To Chimborazo
Hospital
1/2 Mile

Broad St.
Washington   City Hall
Statue
Grace St.
St. Paul's   Governor's
Episcopal Church   Mansion
Franklin St.   Capitol
War Dept.   Richmond Whig
(Mechanic's Institute) Office
Main St.   Custom
Spotswood   House
Hotel
Basin

R.F.&P. R.R.

Shockoe Creek
Virginia Central R.R.

White House of the Confederacy
(Davis Mansion)

First African
Baptist Church

To Church
Hill

Capitol
Square

Trader's Bank

Arsenal

Richmond & Danville
Depot

Mayo's
Bridge

State
Penitentiary

Tredegar
Iron Works

Hollywood
Cemetery

James River

James River & Kanawha Canal

Richmond &
Petersburg R.R.

Richmond & Danville
R.R.

Manchester

Belle Isle

George Skoch

were well known in the capital. His sermons and the example he and his wife, Susan, set for their neighbors gave hope to the faithful even in 1865 that the cause would prevail.

At the northwest edge of the square stood the most prominent Episcopal house of worship, St. Paul's. Its portico of Corinthian columns echoed the classical motif of the Capitol, and its needlelike spire greeted travelers approaching the city from afar. Every Sunday the German-born rector, Charles Minnigerode, looked out from the pulpit through his professorial wire-rimmed glasses on a congregation sprinkled with notables of the Confederate hierarchy, including his frequent dinner guest and confidant President Jefferson Davis. The South's most famous diarist, the acerbic Mary Chesnut, once repeated a report of seeing fourteen generals at St. Paul's with the waspish conclusion that "less piety and more drilling of commands would suit the times better."[5]

A few blocks to the northeast, Robert Ryland served as pastor of the largest church in the city, First African Baptist. It and three other churches enrolled about a third of the city's black residents.[6] By law, they had to have white ministers. But their deacons composed a formidable leadership whose lengthy public prayers—they were not allowed officially to preach sermons from the pulpit—expressed the aspirations of the congregation. No doubt their private petitions for divine deliverance anticipated a different earthly salvation from the kind sought by their white neighbors.

Close by, the houses of the wealthy perched on the hilltops, architectural testimony that white Richmond constituted one of the most prosperous communities in America. One of the most prominent local men, Lewis Crenshaw, a rich flour manufacturer, remodeled a neoclassical house into a three-story Italianate mansion fitted up with the latest French Rococo Revival furnishings. When war came, he sold it to the city—furniture, gas-lit chandeliers, and all. In turn, the city leased it as the southern executive mansion, the White House of the Confederacy.

Domestic slaves lived cheek by jowl with their owners, usually in garrets and crannies of the grand houses or in outbuildings behind.

Crenshaw, whose diversified businesses included one that specialized in weaving coarse woolen clothing for slaves, kept fifteen bondspeople for his own use. Most households included far fewer. Free black domestics usually insisted as a matter of pride on boarding out, but fully half of the city's households contained both black and white members.[7]

Few merchants approached Crenshaw's level of success, and most lived modestly in rooms over their shops. Artisans and industrial workers, both white and free black, lived farther from Capitol Square. They congregated in low-lying areas along the Rocketts wharf, in unfashionable neighborhoods directly across the river from the city, and in places with unappealing names like Screamersville and Penitentiary Bottom.

Three blocks east of the square, the traffic in human beings thrived in such auction houses and holding pens as Robert Lumpkin's jail. A handsome four-story brick building sandwiched between livery stables and brothels, it had barred windows to prevent its inmates from escaping. From Lumpkin's and like establishments, Virginia sold thousands of its native sons and daughters to provide the muscle that cleared new land in Alabama, Mississippi, and other expanding slave states farther south and west.

At the lower edge of the square, the new fireproof Custom House became offices for the Confederate president and most of his cabinet secretaries. The commercial center of town spread out below this ad hoc Confederate government quarter, in the district that sloped down to the river, where ships tied up and the canal carried narrow packet boats westward to still water above the rapids. On the edge of the James, some of the largest mills in America converted grain into flour and flour into fortunes for the owners. Their business networks were international, and some concerns developed a lucrative trade with South America, exchanging flour for coffee.

More than forty tobacco manufactories crowded the city and spilled over into the less fashionable suburb of Manchester on the south bank of the river. They filled the air with a rich, golden, mellow aroma, a distinctive Richmond scent that before the war sometimes even overpowered the predominant town smells of bituminous coal and woodsmoke and horse manure.

The city's commerce, though, consisted of more than processing tobacco and wheat or selling the labor that grew them. Brick kilns, lumberyards, textile mills, box and nail factories—in all, more than three hundred manufactories—fueled the engine of wealth that gave Richmond its antebellum prosperity.[8] This critical mass spawned an abundance of commission merchants, bankers, and lawyers, whose offices clustered nearby. Upriver at the western edge of the city, the sprawling complex of the Tredegar ironworks forged the metal that industrial society needed for railroads, for steamships, and for more and more machines. Switching to artillery and armor plate, Tredegar became the workshop of the Confederate war effort.

As a destination for business travelers, Richmond boasted fine hotels, the finest among them being the new Spotswood, an attractive five-story brick building with an elaborate iron facade, located just below Capitol Square. The hotel welcomed nearly every prominent Confederate visitor and was, sneered a northerner, "as thoroughly identified with Rebellion as the inn at Bethlehem with the gospel."[9] The Exchange Hotel and the Ballard House, connected by an iron bridge across the street that separated them, gave the Spotswood its stiffest competition. Smaller hotels and dozens of boardinghouses catered to the needs of less well heeled travelers.

Before the war the city enjoyed a reputation for the quality of its publications. In cultural matters, the *Southern Literary Messenger* spoke with authority, but it was newspapers that gave Richmond journalism its incendiary sparkle and, with the coming of war, gave voice to southern independence. The major dailies were the *Whig*, the *Enquirer*, the *Dispatch*, and the *Examiner*. The *Examiner*'s editor and proprietor, John Moncure Daniel, a former diplomat, led the field for violent, acidulous invective. He counted nine duels to his credit and egged on the radicals who demanded secession in 1861. Earlier he had declined a challenge from Edgar Allan Poe, whose work he afterward rated highly. "The only records of a wild, hard life" shone "with the diamond hues of eternity," said Daniel of Poe's words, inadvertently describing some of his own.[10]

Daniel cultivated a reputation for misanthropy and wore expensive clothes that accentuated his long raven hair, thin lips, and gleaming dark eyes. When the conflict that he helped bring on finally erupted, the highly strung journalist tortured Jefferson Davis with fine editorial cruelty. Daniel surrounded himself with a coterie of editors known for their brilliance and sarcasm. John Mitchel, an Irish nationalist who had escaped a British jail, quixotically embraced the Confederacy and found a congenial home with the *Examiner*. Edward Pollard, an equally fierce secessionist, had traveled abroad and affected a more cosmopolitan air than most Virginians. Pollard's turbulent character, "marred by episodes of sex and violence," fit right in with the circle of clever, angry young men that Daniel employed.[11] Pollard contributed less than Mitchel to the *Examiner*, but he would leave a powerful mark in another way when the war was over.

BEING THE ADMINISTRATIVE center of the struggle for southern independence put a premium on space and drove up rents on even the meanest living quarters. Landlords put off repairs and made room for more tenants. Tent cities covered the fairgrounds and parks. On the outskirts, army camps and hospitals sprouted over the landscape. Incongruously named for a mountain in Ecuador, Chimborazo occupied the heights above the river east of town. With more than a hundred buildings and nearly as many conical Sibley tents, it became a self-sustaining city unto itself. For a time Chimborazo was the largest military hospital in the world.

The toll of sick and wounded prompted public-spirited women of means to open a series of small private hospitals that usually ran more efficiently than the large ones maintained by the army. But the army closed down the smaller establishments because of the competition for resources. Women of middling means found work in government offices. For those of humbler status, opportunities mushroomed with the army's manpower needs. The demand for uniforms and tents employed hundreds in the needle trades. The munitions laboratory on Brown's Island near Tredegar gave others a more dangerous income. In 1863 a teenaged worker carelessly tapped a cartridge too hard and set off an explosion that shattered the building and killed her and scores of other women. In the capital's burgeoning population, there were plenty to fill their places.

Richmond's prewar size of about forty thousand souls more than doubled, perhaps even tripled, from the influx of bureaucrats, soldiers, opportunists, and refugees. Thousands of prisoners crowded in, too. There were jailed civilian Unionists, Yankee officers warehoused in Libby Prison, and enlisted men sent to shiver on Belle Isle in the middle of the James or in vacant tobacco warehouses before being shipped south to Andersonville. Irish and German accents vied with the native southern drawl, for Richmond, like urban centers of the North, had attracted large numbers of immigrants before secession. Indeed, census takers noted a foreign place of birth for at least a fifth of the white population before the war.

Martial law decreed wide-ranging powers for the provost marshal to unmask traitors and ferret out deserters trying to hide in this bloated population drawn from every state in the Confederacy and beyond. Despite popular concern about spies, the gruff provost marshal at the end of the war, Isaac Carrington, spent most of his time in the less glamorous pursuits of enforcing conscription and signing passes. The latter annoyance inadvertently blurred an important distinction in southern society. As a Confederate senator complained with unselfconscious frankness, having to show passes circumscribed the liberty of white men and put them on the level of marginalized free blacks.[12]

A few Richmond Unionists stood their ground and paid the price. John Minor Botts, a barrel-chested former U.S. congressman famous for his aggressive, pompous rhetoric, headed the list. He and fellow Unionist Franklin Stearns, a distiller from Vermont, ran afoul of the authorities for their outspoken opinions. It happened not long after Jefferson Davis's 1862 inauguration as head of the "permanent" Confederate government. Standing beside Crawford's statue of Washington, Davis had invoked the spirit of the first president and denounced Lincoln for trampling civil liberties in the North. Within two weeks, though, he declared martial law and arrested Stearns and Botts.

More notorious was the eccentric, wealthy abolitionist Elizabeth Van Lew, whose advice Botts sought and whose clandestine orders Stearns obeyed. She offended Richmond society by taking food to Yankee prisoners of war. Among her confidants was the chief aide to the Confederate provost marshal. It was said that she placed one of her free black servants as an agent in Jefferson Davis's household.[13] Some people even credited her with prompting the Union army's cavalry raid of March 1864. Her role as instigator of the raid is open to question, but it is certain that she played a bizarre part in its aftermath. After striking fear into the hearts of Confederate Richmond, the leader of the raid, Col. Ulric Dahlgren, fell to a southern bullet. Outraged by papers found on his body proposing to assassinate Jefferson Davis, the Confederates buried Dahlgren's remains in secret. But Van Lew and her fellow spies learned the location of the grave and just as secretly disinterred and reburied their fallen hero. Of no military value, their action nevertheless resonated ominously with Confederate Richmonders. And it suggests the confidence and the reach of the Unionist underground.[14]

If the military authorities were unable to crack that Unionist underground, the city fathers were no more successful dealing with most of their own problems. Bureaucratic spats with both state and national governments marred the efforts of the city council to deal with wartime exigencies. Disagreements arose over exemptions from conscription, the effect of martial law on residents, preparation for local defense, whether to connect railroad lines inside the city's limits, even over the burial of dead soldiers. Their one success was in providing a measure of relief for the city's poor and families of soldiers.[15]

Military construction and its manpower requirements disrupted the local economy and wrought dramatic changes in the lives of all Richmonders. The effect was especially marked for black men and women. Slaves performed most of the noncombatant tasks: building earthworks and providing labor for the commissary, railroads, military hospitals, and manufacturing. At first the system of hiring out surplus slaves worked well, but the demand for labor and the selfishness of owners led to increasingly stringent impressment laws. These statutes drew both slaves and free blacks into the maw of Confederate war work.[16]

The war impoverished some businesses and enriched others. Tobacco production plummeted, but government contracts smiled on the city's ironworks and their proprietors. By 1865, though, that prosperity was past. Even Tredegar languished for lack of raw materials. A hard winter, the hardest in local memory, reinforced the shabby appearance of most buildings. The Capitol showed signs of abuse, its whitewashed brick columns and stucco walls dingy with neglect. By then, as well, though the wartime peak of population had passed, the city still suffered from overcrowding and showed it. "Everyone lives in filthy conditions here in Richmond," complained a temporary resident. "I have never been so filthy in all my life."[17]

WHILE RICHMONDERS STRUGGLED to face the day-to-day challenges of a wartime capital, for four years commanders and armchair strategists on both sides pored over their maps, North and South, concentrating on the city at the falls of the James. In the summer of 1862, the Union's savior seemed to be George B. McClellan. He built and drilled an impressive army on the outskirts of Washington, D.C., and when he was ready, he deployed it in the greatest amphibious campaign the world had known. His plan was to attack Richmond from the southeast, decapitate the Confederacy, and bring the rebellion to a speedy conclusion. When his lead regiments marched to within sight of the capital's church spires, McClellan lost his nerve. Sensing that failure of will, the new Confederate commander, Robert E. Lee, counterattacked in a rapid-fire succession of battles, the Seven Days. At a terrible cost in southern casualties, Lee threw back the northern army.

His success spared Richmond from fighting on its doorsteps for two years. During that time the Confederacy lost the war in the West, failed in two attempts to take the fight to northern soil, and suffered gradual constriction from the blockade of southern ports. Those years of conflict placed the state, if not yet its capital, squarely in the cockpit of war: Fredericksburg, Chancellorsville, Spotsylvania, the Wilderness. These and dozens of other once-unnoted Virginia place-names lost their obscurity when they became infamous and bloody battlegrounds.

Then, with ever-growing resources and a dogged resolve, the Union's greatest commander, Ulysses S. Grant, inexorably brought the war back to the southern capital. Unlike the Union generals who preceded him, Grant targeted the Confederacy's armies rather than its capital. But because those armies chose to defend Richmond, it still amounted to the same thing. After the middle of 1864, Virginia's principal city once more became both objective and symbol of the war.

The war carried Virginia on a runaway train ride of alternating hope and despair toward some terrifying unknown. A thousand contingencies could have led to outright southern victory, to northern fatigue, or to some other unimagined denouement. The one certainty was that war did what no hellfire preaching by secessionist radicals ever could—the crucible of armed conflict fused Virginia to the Confederacy with bonds of iron. And the strength of those bonds would make postwar divisions, political and racial, all the more acrimonious and long-lasting. By 1865, few parts of the South identified more strongly or more fervently with the cause than Richmond. For residents of the Virginia capital, though, that allegiance had sorely eroded by spring, when it was about to be put to one final, brutal test.

Since the previous summer, the contest between the armies of Grant and Lee, which earlier had spilled blood on dozens of fields across Virginia and beyond, concentrated on a much smaller stage. They now maneuvered for advantage in central Virginia in the narrower confines of opposing networks of trenches and forts. To any visitor in the early months of 1865, the physical stamp of war was everywhere. A triple ring of fortifications protected the capital region, most strongly on the eastern side. They described a forty-mile arc that slashed the earth from northeast of Richmond down to Petersburg twenty miles below and on to the southwest. Massive earthworks stripped bare hundreds of acres and consumed entire forests of pine and hardwood.

Once the conflict closed in around the city, residents became accustomed to seeing a grizzled, prematurely old general riding around town on a white horse as decrepit as its rider. A Virginian and a West Pointer of average ability, Richard Stoddert Ewell was, in the words of a fellow officer, "a queer character, very eccentric, but upright, brave and devoted."[18] He lost a leg to amputation at Second Manassas, but a wooden replacement let him return to the army. Discredited by erratic performance and injured falling from his horse, he had to give up field command and was placed in charge of the capital's defenses. The Department of Richmond gave him a force of regular troops with an effective total of 4,529 men by late March 1865, about half the nominal total.[19] To these could be added inexperienced and poorly disciplined reserves and an assortment of local defense troops.

Among the latter were a scratch force of government clerks, convalescent soldiers from the teeming military hospitals, and mechanics from the munitions factories whose work exempted them from conscription but required them to bear arms if the enemy threatened the city. The abrasive Ewell frequently sparred with bureaucrats over the use of these men. It irritated him that they resented his requests, as though desk work was more important than preventing the Yankees from taking Richmond. In his opinion, only northern timidity prevented a disaster. For the moment, fortune favored the defenders, safe behind their massive earthworks and artillery emplacements, and not their enemy, the hard-luck, inexpertly led, but much larger Army of the James. Of that enemy, Ewell said with asperity, "We cannot trust always to his want of enterprise."[20]

One of Ewell's officers was James Kemper, a lawyer and former state legislator who had led the drive to take Virginia out of the Union. Gravely wounded at Gettysburg, he spent three months in Federal prison camp. After his exchange, with his wounds not completely healed, he took over the Richmond reserves, under no illusion as to how feeble his troop strength really was. For the four battalions sent to the lines outside the city, the attrition rate from death and disease, but mainly from desertion, reached 80 percent after three months. Even under the best officers, Kemper lamented, these discontented, even mutinous men melted away like frost in the sunlight.[21] Desertion, the fatal metronome ticking out the cadence of southern defeat, quickened its beat.

War-weariness, even among staunch Confederates, was apparent when the city postal clerks met at the end of March 1865 to wish the postmaster, John Steger, a happy retirement as he stepped down. At the same gathering, they took the opportunity to denounce the army for interfering with their work by calling them out for local defense duty. The next day a large shipment of mail arrived from the south, but the clerks could not sort the letters, for Ewell once more ordered them out for guard duty all night. "If this is not trifling with the people," fumed the *Whig*, "we don't know what is."[22]

CHAPTER 2

DAILY BREAD

Late March

If ever people had need to know the plain truth, and to look it steadily in the face, we, in our present position, are that people.

—*Richmond Daily Examiner*[1]

The war for southern independence had come down to the fate of a single city, or so it seemed to Richmonders. As spring approached in 1865, unlike as in years past, they could see no hope anywhere on the horizon. Stories of last-minute European diplomatic recognition, long a staple of the rumor mills, found few believers. Union armies ranged at will across the lower South. The Federal navy finally closed Wilmington, North Carolina, the last Atlantic port of consequence for blockade runners. Civilian morale plummeted. The government was reduced to running pitiful notices in the newspapers asking for donations. "There is neither dishonor nor danger in making this frank avowal to an intelligent and patriotic people," pleaded the ailing Confederate treasury secretary, George Trenholm.[2]

In late March, if the armies of the Union did not completely surround Richmond, they threatened to do so. The city's only reliable remaining rail link with the outside was the Richmond & Danville line, running to the southwest. Increasing Federal cavalry raids disrupted communications with the Confederate hinterlands to the west of the capital. And to the east, along the line of trenches that snaked up from Petersburg, the defenders looked out at the daunting growth in the armies under Grant. The largest concentrations of troops faced one another at Petersburg. These consisted of the bulk of Lee's Army of Northern Virginia opposing Grant's Army of the Potomac. Closer to Richmond, the smaller of the Union armies, the Army of the James, threatened the capital.

DESPITE THE DIRE military circumstances, the threadbare shops of Richmond offered an array of goods and services for those with money to buy them. Residents may have doubted whether Powhatan Weisiger's new shipment of "fine French hats" in late March really had been run through the blockade from Paris. But it was clear that the genuine coffee and tea for sale at a steep price in other shops had indeed been smuggled past Union picket ships. For those with both money and leisure time, $400 was enough to charter the small side-wheel steamer *Bonita*. Capt. T. M. Southgate invited parties of ladies and gentlemen to go with him down from the Rocketts landing to the best spots for fishing, though presumably not as far downstream as the domain of the Federal gunboats only seven miles or so below the city.[3]

The experience of a wealthy foreign visitor suggests the opportunities for entertaining even this late in the war. Thomas Conolly was an extravagant member of Parliament with vast estates in Ireland and a taste for adventure and louche women. By the time he signed the register at the Spotswood in March, the management had cut up its carpets for army blankets and was serving dinner on cracked and broken crockery. Conolly was nevertheless thrilled to see Richmond—"its Spires & white pillared capitol shining above the haze & Roofs in the setting sun."[4]

He waltzed his way through town, dispensing gold sovereigns and consuming oysters and champagne as though there were no privation. Hard currency could still winkle the most astonishing luxury goods out from their hiding places. To supply his hospitality, he relied on Tom Griffin, a free man of color who owned two eateries and catered private dinner parties for wealthy patrons of the city's hotels. Griffin provided Conolly with elegant meals for his new Virginia friends, complete with mint juleps. "Very swell, despite the blockade. Must have cost him a pretty sum," wrote Malvina Gist, a sociable young widow and one of Conolly's guests.[5]

Given the austerity of a city threatened by a hostile army, however, more mundane goods dominated local trade. It was a sign of the times that one of the most popular products owed its existence to the miseries the soldiers endured in the trenches nearby. Every day newspapers trumpeted the virtues of specialty unguents. Purcell, Ladd & Co. boasted of the efficacy of an ointment that was "a certain cure for itch and destroyer of Camp Vermin." Colesberry's establishment on Governor Street hawked a competing remedy.[6] These cheerful promises of cures seemed to mock the suffering of the lice-ridden men shivering and aching in the muddy earthen forts surrounding the city.

The lengthening days heralded spring planting time, even in the midst of a military stalemate that dug up the countryside for miles around. Farmers who had saved a few workhorses or mules from the grasp of the impressment officers began to think about putting in a new crop. In town, merchants advertised seed and fertilizer in the hope of sales. E. H. Chesterman announced he had on hand ample supplies of phosphate of lime and white guano, touted as the best fertilizer for corn.[7]

If Chesterman was advertising his Mexican bird droppings to farmers, it meant that politicking was about to begin, for municipal elections, set for April 5, coincided with spring planting. Candidates took out notices in the papers to thank the voters who had, through the same medium, urged them to run for city council. More plentiful notices filled the "Lost, Strayed and Stolen" columns, however, and it is likely these attracted more attention than the political advertisements.

William Backer offered a liberal reward for the return of his small black terrier lost on Broad Street. The Rev. Dr. Minnigerode announced that he had lost his gold watch chain somewhere between his church and his house at Third and Main. Richard Hollern declared that he had found a large white sow on Main Street and would give it to the person who could prove ownership and pay for the food the pig had eaten in his care. Mrs. W. R. Smoot was in no doubt about what had happened to her property. She offered $100 Confederate (pennies in U.S. currency) for a large blanket shawl that a thief had taken from her back porch.[8]

The papers also earned a steady revenue in debased Confederate dollars from the purchasers of notices seeking and offering employment. A householder on Broad Street hoped to find a white girl to clean, wash, and iron. A discharged soldier, formerly a music teacher at a young ladies' seminary, announced his availability to prospective employers. He assured them that he was no longer liable to be called back into the army.

Lt. William Harwar Parker, superintendent of the Confederate naval academy, had gone to sea at fourteen and had taken part in the first clash of ironclad ships in 1862. He hoped the notice he placed in a Saturday-morning paper would accomplish a more humble mission. His advertisement expressed his desire to find "several Waiter Boys" to serve at table on the *Patrick Henry*, the academy's school ship.[9] Parker did not specify whether he preferred these "boys" to be free blacks or slaves.

They could have been the latter, because the practice of hiring out slaves helped keep the peculiar institution viable. William Gray, a wealthy merchant, was one of the most prominent slave-hiring agents in the city. Plantation owners in the surrounding counties depended on him to find work for their surplus hands. Some of the thirteen men, women, and children who occupied Gray's household at the beginning of the war were part of this mobile labor force. For Gray and his wife and their five children, and indeed for the enslaved people in their midst, this arrangement was a part of the natural order of things. And so it continued into 1865, when Gray placed a familiar notice in the paper offering "For hire, a Negro Woman, who is a good washer and ironer and house-cleaner, and a good seamstress."[10]

The old problems of unfree labor remained, however, as the decision made in March by two slaves attested. Because fourteen-year-old Billy, no last name given, chose to run away, his owner offered a reward for information on the young man's whereabouts. The youth had left the farm where he worked to visit his mother in town but had not returned. He "has a pleasant countenance, and generally smiles when spoken to; had on a military cap, grey roundabout or coat, grey pants, and a dilapidated pair of shoes, one of his toes being out." George Gary was similarly inconvenienced when Colin ran away. Gary sought help in apprehending the thirteen-year-old slave, who was "about four feet ten inches high; dark brown color, and has a small scar under the left jaw, caused by scrofula."[11]

The thing uppermost on the mind of the average person, black or white, free or enslaved, was food, for the shops and markets were bare of much that was affordable. The city bakers sold loaves in three sizes at $1, $2, and $3 apiece. These were ridiculed as being so slight that, according to one cynic, the middle loaf almost required a microscope to see and the smallest certainly did.[12] Every family that could afford to do so had its stock of provisions for an emergency—usually rice, dried apples, peas, potatoes, lard, and in lucky households, hams.

The *Examiner* claimed there were fewer beggars seeking sustenance in 1865 than before. Earlier in the war, the poor took to the streets to protest the lack of food. But by the fifth spring of the conflict, ordinary Richmonders were too obsessed with earning the next meal to think about public protest. A soldier's wife was close to the mark when she wrote her husband that "the one topic of conversation everywhere and on all occasions is 'eating,' even the ministers in the pulpit unconsciously preach of it."[13]

The scarcity and expense of food led to a rash of theft. Early one morning in late March, gunfire interrupted the sleep of residents on Grace Street. Two burglars broke into the house of John Steger, the recently retired postmaster, and stole a small barrel of flour. Policemen chased them into an alley. Just as they were about to overtake the fleeing men, the police fired at them, but both burglars escaped. Steger recovered his flour. Not even charities were safe. Crooks broke into the

Soup House at Metropolitan Hall and stole bacon intended for the poor.[14]

As a result, the courts overflowed with cases of petty and serious crime. Some of it could be laid to the war, if only the desperation that drove people like the Steger burglars to steal food. Or sometimes to steal people. Thomas, a slave, came before the city's aldermen in their official judicial capacity accused of feloniously abetting seven other slaves in running away. Thomas pleaded not guilty, but the court unanimously said it did not believe him. The aldermen ordered that he receive thirty-nine lashes, "to be well laid on by the Sergeant of this City at the public whipping post," and that he be sold out of state. They inflicted punishment in the jail yard where the city whipping post stood, a tall octagonal pole with iron clasps fastened at shoulder height for securing the victim's wrists.[15]

Martial law continued to fill prisons like Castle Thunder, a converted warehouse, with its military and political victims. As March came to an end, William Moncure was booked as a spy, while William Bruce was sent from the army as a "suspicious character." Cpl. N. W. Maddox of the Nelson Light Artillery was thrown into prison and charged with desertion and seriously wounding the officer sent to arrest him.[16]

Those convicted of serious crime did time at the state penitentiary located on the western edge of town on a bluff near Hollywood Cemetery overlooking the Tredegar ironworks. Sometimes they became the main event at the free entertainment provided by the penitentiary— public execution. The increase in crime, the constriction of civil liberties imposed by martial law, and the ominous booming of distant artillery all combined to give Richmond residents a sense of unease and foreboding. The capital no longer felt like a safe place to be, and the thin gruel of Confederate patriotism ladled out by John Moncure Daniel's *Examiner* did nothing to fill empty stomachs.

Educated southerners knew from history the harsh fate of failed rebellions. They did not have to look far into the past to find draconian examples. Only two years before, at the same time Lincoln declared all slaves in the Confederate States to be free, the tsar freed Russia's serfs and then brutally crushed a nationalist revolt in Poland. The rising ended with the execution of rebel leaders on the walls of the citadel of Warsaw. Would the North dictate a similar ending in Richmond?

Before spring 1865 it would have been wrong to speak of an inevitable outcome. But by then, the weight of loss and repeated battlefield reverses for the South meant that only one military outcome seemed possible. And yet, in what shape that outcome would manifest itself was still unknown. As long as uncertainty lasted, hope stayed alive for many Confederates in Richmond, despite the dangerous state of their city.

THE UNION'S Army of the James, facing Richmond from the east and southeast, had a new commander that spring, Maj. Gen. Godfrey Weitzel. An earnest Teuton with a great black beard, he had honed his engineering skills at West Point and learned soldiering in the regular army, but he was too cautious, not at all a bold field commander. And he was about to learn a lesson in political generalship that nothing in the army had taught him. His force consisted of parts of the white XXIV Corps and the black XXV Corps after his superior, Maj. Gen. Edward O. C. Ord, led a portion of the Army of the James south to reinforce Grant in front of Petersburg.

Weitzel suspected the main action would take place farther south between Lee and Grant. But he worried that it might fall to him to launch his own attack against the network of trenches, minefields, and emplacements for large-caliber artillery that guarded the eastern approaches to Richmond. He also could not rule out a spoiling attack from the Confederates against his own lines. It irritated him that the military telegraph enabled Ord to continue to meddle at a distance. One cable warned him of the hazard of mines, something he knew about quite well. "Don't let your columns take the roads," the impetuous Ord scolded, "keep them in the woods and bypaths. Send cattle and old horses up the roads first."[17]

In late March a spy entered Weitzel's lines with a novel piece of intelligence. According to the agent's report, in the southern capital "a parade has been made of the negro soldiers raised, and they were put in line with some white soldiers."[18] It was true. After months of acrimony in Congress, where legislators denounced the step as a betrayal of first principles, the Confederacy was raising companies of black men to fight for the South.

Here was the bitterest of ironies, one that many Confederate patriots could not contemplate without pain. Did this mean that slavery, the distinguishing trait of southern society and the proximate cause that precipitated the war for southern independence, was to be discarded now? Some Confederates thought they could have it both ways: use black soldiers to win and thus preserve slavery for most of those still in bondage. Others saw the inherent contradiction of this radical change. Perhaps events would push the South to jettison the peculiar institution. Certainly events had compelled many white southerners to view secession differently than they had before the war. Before 1861 they had dismissed secessionist firebrands as idiots and scorned their dream of a separate nation as an illusion. Now they had learned through the trauma of civil strife to seek that grail— southern independence—and value it above all their earthly possessions. Even above slavery.

Curious citizens gathered in the afternoons to watch as black soldiers, recruited by two majors attached to General Ewell's staff, marched and drilled on Capitol Square. Even the *Examiner*, accustomed to dispensing John Daniel's contempt for the idea of arming slaves, was impressed: "The knowledge of the military art they already exhibit was something remarkable. They moved with evident pride and satisfaction to themselves."[19]

Was this a fair account, though? The truth probably lay somewhere between the newspaper's gushing report and that of the Union spy who believed only "the lowest class of negroes" signed up. White observers, whether Confederate or Union, seemed not to consider that black men might volunteer for their own purposes. In the trenches east of Richmond, the only African American reporter with the Union army had his own opinion about these novel recruits to the southern cause. He thought they were joining to increase their chances of escaping to Union lines. They might fight for the South at first and even inflict casualties on their true friends, but it would only be a tactical maneuver to put them in a position to turn their guns on their white officers and switch sides.[20]

Even supporters could not bring themselves to view these men as individuals. Virginians, wrote a journalist after viewing the drill, were convinced "that Sambo can be taught to handle a Southern musket quite as well as the negroes in the Yankee army." Doubters like William Owen, commander of a southern artillery battery, disparaged the fighting ability of the former slaves he saw on parade. "The darkies are very jubilant," he sneered, "and think it great fun. The music attracts them like flies around a molasses barrel."[21]

The appearance before the mayor's court of two black men named Ned and Robert underscored the difficulty of recruiting African Americans. Charged with being runaway slaves, the two men proved they were in fact soldiers in one of the new black units. The mayor remanded them to the provost marshal for return to their company. Even more telling was the experience of Oliver and George, slaves convicted of burglarizing Dr. Minnigerode's house and sentenced to hang for it. When the governor commuted their death sentences to serving in the army, the *Examiner* denounced him for "slimy benevolism."[22] The recruiting officers objected to criminals being foisted onto their unit. Though the reprieve saved Oliver and George from the noose, their good fortune cannot have boosted the prestige of the black units.

Despite widespread opposition, when the idol of the South publicly supported the measure, he carried the day. General Lee requested the aid of every African American male, slave and free, from eighteen to forty-five. He was desperate. These men, he pleaded, "are now necessary to enable us to oppose the enemy." He even favored compulsory enlistment rather than first trying to recruit volunteers. Jefferson Davis, brought by the Confederacy's peril to advocate emancipation for any black man who bore arms for southern independence, supported the measure. It had come to the point, the president wrote to a friend, where "we are reduced to choosing whether the negroes shall fight for us or against us." He reached that decision when it was far too late, but reach it he did. Privately Lee warned that enemies of the system would do everything in their power to thwart it.[23]

The black Confederates drilled every day at their rendezvous point at the corner of Cary and Twenty-first streets. Recruiting notices encouraged owners to outfit their slaves who wished to join up with a gray jacket and pants, a good pair of shoes, and a cap and blanket. About a third of the first batch of recruits were free, the rest slaves who had volunteered with the permission of their owners. Other patriotic Virginians offered money to purchase slaves willing to go into the army.[24]

Maj. Thomas Pratt Turner was an especially enthusiastic recruiter. He may have seen it as a chance for personal advancement beyond his job as jailer of Libby Prison, where the cookhouse prepared rations for the African American recruits as well as Union prisoners. "Go to work and work, work, work," he telegraphed a friend. If people only knew Lee's opinion, he argued, they would support the innovation. But the Libby jailer feared that Virginians would sooner lose their wives and daughters than give up their slaves. Lee would not have been pleased to hear that his own daughter, Agnes, who watched the black companies drill, was one of the scoffers.[25]

Plainspoken Sgt. Marion Fitzpatrick probably echoed the feelings of the average Confederate soldier. As he prepared to return from a Richmond hospital to his hard-pressed regiment in the muddy Petersburg trenches, he, like Lee, was willing to take help from whatever the source. "The negro troops have been called out," wrote the simple Georgia farmer to his wife, Amanda. "I have seen two companies. I hope it will work well."[26]

CHAPTER 3

WAITING

Late March

They pant for our extermination.
—*Richmond Daily Dispatch*[1]

At the War Department, a brick building at Ninth and Franklin, across the street from Capitol Square, clerks continued to churn out memoranda, requisitions, orders, and copies of letters sent and received. In paper orders, if in little else, the Confederacy was richly endowed. At his office there, in the former lecture rooms of the Mechanic's Institute, Robert Kean ruminated about the decay of the government and the atrophy of its armies. "The end seems to be surely and swiftly approaching," he confided to his diary.[2] The scholarly and introspective Kean, whose droopy mustache gave him a pensive look, had been a passionate advocate of states' rights and secession before the war. Now the consequences of his radical opinions were all too apparent to him.

Kean worked for Assistant Secretary of War John Archibald Campbell, a former justice of the U.S. Supreme Court, whom the Davis inner circle viewed with suspicion. For months Campbell had vainly urged the government to seek terms from the North, however meager they might be. Kean and Campbell deplored Davis's shortcomings as a leader, and each confessed to the other that he could see no cause for hope. When Campbell asked his opinion on the state of affairs, wrote Kean in midwinter, "I told him by the end of March I thought we would all be fugitives."[3]

For weeks their fellow bureaucrats had quietly made plans and taken tentative steps to evacuate the capital. They shipped papers and equipment south by rail, but without enough vigor to alarm the citizenry or to accomplish the desired end. The thought of evacuation made Confederates who still wanted desperately to believe in the cause rage at doubters. "Wherever three or four are gathered together," seethed the Pennsylvania-born chief of ordnance, Josiah Gorgas, "there are ominous whispers & dubious shakings of the head." Persuaded to join the Confederacy by disappointments in the prewar army and the sentiments of his Alabama wife, the combative, energetic Gorgas performed logistical miracles to bring weapons and ammunition through the blockade. He had nothing but scorn for waverers. "The Senate it is now Said are ready for any terms—the cowards," he fumed. "Pity a few could not be taken out & hung or shot."[4]

They adjourned in mid-March, in Robert Kean's words "full of wrath" and devoid of hope.[5] Many of the Confederate legislators left town tacitly acknowledging what was to come, arguing among themselves about petty issues as their world collapsed around them. The Virginia legislature stayed in session a little longer. A few members gathered every day in the Senate and House of Delegates, but without a quorum, neither chamber could conduct meaningful business. The few House delegates who remained made the impotent gesture of threatening absent colleagues with rebuke by the sergeant at arms.

Since the Yankees closed in on Richmond nearly a year before, people had boasted that despite the odds, Lee would defeat Grant, if only the armies would come out of their trenches and fight another great campaign of maneuver. Thoughtful observers knew those entrenchments were all that stood between Lee's shrinking Army of Northern Virginia and Grant's superior forces. The moonscape of barren earth, denuded of trees cut down to create fields of fire and build obstructions to entangle an attacking foe, was the very tool of war that magnified Confederate manpower and enabled the South to resist a more numerous enemy. Lee wrote Secretary of War John Cabell Breckinridge that the situation was no worse than they had expected from the beginning because of the enemy's greater resources: "Indeed, the legitimate military consequences of that superiority have been postponed longer than we had reason to anticipate."[6]

Desertion increased with the approach of spring planting time. No other immediate factor threatened southern prospects more. Officers exhorted their men to turn in comrades suspected of plotting to leave the army. Gen. James Longstreet praised three Alabama privates for apprehending a deserter before he could make good his escape. They convicted the man and sentenced him to be shot on the last day of March to encourage his brothers in arms. Executing a few deserters to deter others was a miserable calculus, and the officers knew it. The threat of punishment did not stop hundreds from taking the risk and slipping away. In a pessimistic report at the end of March, Lee enumerated the bald truth of the matter. In nine days he lost 1,061 soldiers to desertion. He had only about 50,000 in all. Such attrition gave him a sense of foreboding, and he conceded, "I do not know what can be done to put a stop to it."[7]

CIVILIANS IN THE capital could sense what Kean and Campbell and Gorgas knew from inside information. They could guess at the hemorrhage of desertion that troubled Lee. But many of them chose to ignore the signs. It would be up to others to determine the outcome, anyway.

And so they waited. In the city and around it they watched the wild geese fly north and the buds begin to swell on the trees. "The croakers croak about Richmond being evacuated, but I can't and won't believe it," wrote Judith McGuire, a clergyman's wife who had fled occupation of her home in northern Virginia and taken a job in the Commissary Department. William Brown, no less ardent in his southern sympathies, feared the worst. He wrote on March 27 that everyone thought the government would soon have to leave the capital to keep the army fed. "I would not be supprised if the evacuation should take place in a very few days.—I hope not but every thing looks that way now."[8] He resolved to remain in the city even if it fell to the enemy and face imprisonment rather than take the oath of allegiance to the United States.

John Beauchamp Jones should have been in a better position to speculate on the future because of his work in the War Department. A writer and editor before the war, he suffered from poor health but not enough to keep him from scribbling his fears and ruminations in his diary. A querulous, dyspeptic man, he wondered like everyone else about the heavy cannon fire they could hear on most days from the direction of Petersburg. But because the sound had become as much a part of the ambient noise as the rush of water through the falls of the James, it did not distract Jones from planning to visit friends west of town in the first week of April.[9]

Sarah Cooper knew the dangers of living in Richmond, but she planned to return from the plantation she had been visiting to the west. Her husband, Samuel, though New Jersey–born, was Confederate adjutant general by virtue of being the highest-ranking general from the prewar army to side with the South. People accused him of being subservient to red tape, and his fidgeting manner did not inspire confidence. He pleaded with his wife in unequivocal words not to come back to Richmond. Conditions were grim and could only worsen. Because privation was rampant and the Yankees were likely to succeed, the aging Confederate general implored his wife, "Let me beg and urge you *not* to come here."[10]

At the army medical complex on the plateau east of the city, high above the river the wounded, the sick, and the malingerers waited in their wards. The chief surgeon, Dr. James McCaw, whose administrative talent had created the vast facility, organized the Chimborazo Hospital Battalion, five companies of fifty men each. These convalescents might soon be called to help defend the capital. In the meantime, they waited, as did a young widow named Phoebe Yates Pember, who carved out a unique niche for herself as matron of a wing of the vast Chimborazo facility. The pragmatic, sharp-featured South Carolinian cared for the sick and wounded but gave no quarter to the shirkers who congregated at the hospital.

William Lohmann, thirty-nine, a Prussian-born grocer and restaurateur, waited as an unwelcome guest of the Confederate government. For a third time, he was confined to Castle Thunder with others suspected of disloyalty. His lawyer failed to secure his release. The authorities were right to keep Lohmann locked up, and not just because he dabbled in the black market in food. They did not know it, but he was one of Elizabeth Van Lew's agents. The previous spring he had provided the coffin used in the Unionists' dramatic theft of the remains of the Federal cavalry raider, Col. Ulric Dahlgren.[11]

Though he was not in jail like Lohmann, Henri Garidel felt like a prisoner. A Louisiana Creole whose grandparents had emigrated from France, Garidel worked as a minor bureaucrat in Richmond. The "cheap, greasy leavings" served up at his boardinghouse did not help his hemorrhoids or a long-running intestinal complaint, all of which aggravated his naturally sour temperament. Despondent, he began to project onto fellow Confederates his resentments over separation from his family back in occupied New Orleans. This compulsive, pessimistic, pipe-smoking worrier poured out his sorrows in the journal that he kept throughout his two years in the Confederate capital. His common refrain, repeated often, expressed his longing for his wife and children: "I live and breathe only for you, to see you again."[12]

Frances Taylor Dickinson had an entirely different temperament from that of the gloomy Garidel. The wife and daughter of Baptist ministers, Fannie Dickinson lived with her husband and children in her parents' house on the corner of Franklin and Shafer streets, a block beyond the military camp on the western edge of town. Her husband, Alfred Elijah Dickinson, a large, robust young man, warmhearted and gregarious, was a born raconteur who had already made a name in Baptist circles. Throughout the war he had preached and ministered to soldiers, shared their privations, given them encouragement. Fannie, like Alfred, was an optimist, and neither husband nor wife guessed at the evacuation to come.

Another Fannie waited in the slave quarters on James Wickham's plantation north of town. In the last week of March, she went into labor. Even in the pangs of childbirth, she was working for her master. The son she bore was destined to be the last African American born into bondage on the Wickham plantation. A week after her baby drew his first breath, there would be no need and no sanction for the account book listing mother and child for their monetary value.[13]

WILLIAM PARKER WAITED at the Confederate naval academy, his floating anomaly bottled up at Richmond on the steamer *Patrick Henry*, far from open salt water. For months Parker's sixty midshipmen studied navigation and trigonometry to the sound of artillery fire. On occasion, their mobile classroom went down the James to help if an attack by the Federal navy threatened. In late March the academy moved the *Patrick Henry*, with its foul-smelling bilges, up to the Rocketts landing at the eastern edge of town. Parker's superiors decided that the rickety school ship, a side-wheel steamer that had been one of the first vessels pressed into Confederate service at the beginning of the war, would serve the South better being sunk to block the river channel. Parker dutifully moved his midshipmen to a warehouse across the street from Elizabeth Van Lew's property, installed the mahogany table and silver service of their wardroom, and waited.[14]

They waited in the diminutive fleet that guarded the river approach to the city. These ships were all that remained of the Confederate navy, save for a few commerce raiders and blockade runners still on the high seas. Adm. Raphael Semmes commanded three ironclads, the *Virginia II*, *Richmond*, and *Fredericksburg*, and a handful of wooden gunboats anchored below Drewry's Bluff, about seven miles downstream from the capital. Discouraging letters from home, dismal rations, and confinement on board ship induced the men to slip away when they could grab the chance. Even though sailors had dry hammocks to sleep in, unlike the miserable infantrymen in the trenches, demoralization cut into the navy's readiness. Semmes recalled that sometimes when a party rowed ashore, "an entire boat's crew would run off, leaving the officer to find his way on board the best he might."[15]

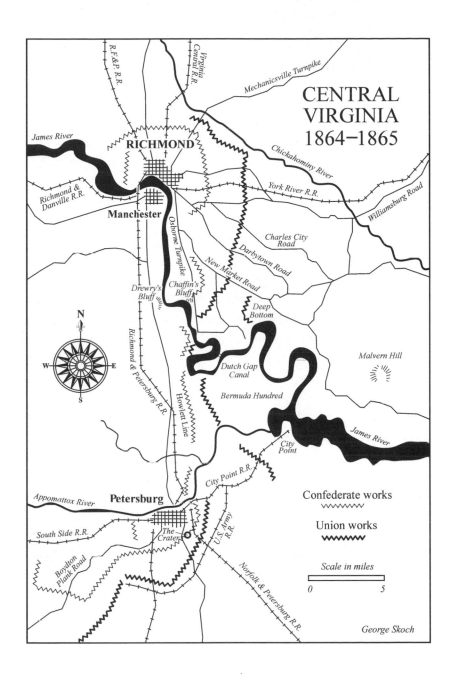

CENTRAL
VIRGINIA
1864–1865

James River

RICHMOND

Manchester

R.F&P. R.R.

Virginia Central R.R.

Mechanicsville Turnpike

Chickahominy River

York River R.R.

Williamsburg Road

Richmond & Danville R.R.

Osborne Turnpike

Charles City Road

Darbytown Road

New Market Road

Drewry's Bluff

Chaffin's Bluff

Deep Bottom

Malvern Hill

Richmond & Petersburg R.R.

Howlett Line

Dutch Gap Canal

Bermuda Hundred

James River

City Point

City Point R.R.

Appomattox River

Petersburg

U.S. Army R.R.

South Side R.R.

The Crater

Boydton Plank Road

Norfolk & Petersburg R.R.

Confederate works

Union works

Scale in miles

0   5

George Skoch

N
W   E
S

Yet he and his men—most of them, at least—continued their watchful waiting in case Federal gunboats tried to force their way past. In his makeshift office on a barge tied up beside the *Virginia II*, the admiral dipped his pen into his inkwell and scratched out a plaintive letter to an English friend. He said the fate of Richmond would be decided long before the friend broke the wax seal on the letter. He vowed not to abandon the city without a fight and still hoped against the evidence that the South would prevail.[16]

They waited in the forts and earthworks around Richmond. Edward Porter Alexander, a handsome, jaunty artillery general not yet thirty years old, applied his energy to refining the eastern defenses. A natural tinkerer, earlier in the war he had worked on signal systems and the only southern observation balloon. Most recently he had applied his ingenuity to a maze of land and marine mines. "I dont see how the Yankees can fight us on this side of the river," he wrote his wife in the last week of March, "for it would only be fun for us & murder to them." But as he willed himself to disbelieve rumors of evacuation, he revealed the homesickness that afflicted even this most optimistic Confederate officer. "Oh Dearest Bessie," he lamented, "you dont know how I long to sit by that bed & hold your hand & bathe your face & comb your hair."[17]

Southeast of Richmond, in the trenches near Chaffin's Bluff overlooking the river from the north, William Basinger waited. A major in the 18th Georgia Regiment, he cursed the mud, longed for the warmth of the lower South, and toyed with the notion of raising a black regiment. He considered emigrating if the Confederacy lost but did not believe it would come to that. Basinger kept the faith and wrote his mother in occupied Savannah to do the same. By a friend, he sent her a photograph taken of him in Richmond and enjoined her never to stop hating the enemy. "After what has passed," he affirmed, "undying hostility to the Yankee is the only sentiment . . . undying hostility, in peace as well as war, in defeat as well as in success."[18]

Elsewhere in the eastern defenses, Lt. Moses Purnell Handy gossiped with his friends about the coming campaign. The son of a Presbyterian minister from Portsmouth, Virginia, Handy was only seventeen, full of himself and youthful optimism, not yet cynical from seeing friends die around him before their time. As a courier for the head engineer of the Confederate army, in the course of his duties he frequented the various headquarters offices and befriended the military telegraph operators. They retailed the latest rumors gleaned from the terse dispatches that clacked out in monotonous taps from the telegraph keys. In late March the keys chattered about raids and troop movements and possible evacuation. Most couriers thought the decisive campaign was about to begin.

South of Handy's part of the line, they waited in the trenches facing east from Petersburg. Marion Fitzpatrick, the soldier who hoped recruiting black men would "work well," had joined Company K of the 45th Georgia Regiment at the age of twenty-two. An earnest, religious farmer with a high forehead and a mop of thick, dark hair that could not hide his large ears, he fought in every major battle in the East, was wounded at Glendale and Fredericksburg, and gained promotion to sergeant major. A bout with fever landed him in a Richmond army hospital, where he thought about his young wife at home. "I long to hear from you all again," he wrote Amanda. Happily for him, three of her letters arrived while he recuperated. He wrote back that "the war news is highly encouraging, and our troops are in the best of spirits." When he rejoined his unit, however, he discovered that in his absence a small action had devastated the regiment in a few minutes. It lost six killed, two wounded, and 118 captured. When he learned this news, Fitzpatrick thanked God for causing him to miss the skirmish, "or else I might now have been captured or killed."[19]

THE UNION ARMY built three precarious wooden observation towers more than a hundred feet tall that, on a clear day, afforded signalmen with good field glasses a view into Richmond. One tower stood outside the headquarters of General Weitzel, the new commander of the Army of the James. The observers sent a stream of reports about troop movements and trains coming and going. As early as February, Union commanders outside the city began hearing stories from deserters coming into their lines that the Confederates were planning to evacuate. One report said they had made arrangements to concentrate their stores of tobacco and cotton for easy burning.[20] Was this true? And if so, how should they take advantage of such reports? As with much military intelligence, interpreting the information was more difficult than collecting it.

The pickets of the opposing armies were close enough to talk to one another—and to see clearly the deadly obstacles that awaited whichever side chose to attack. When the occasional fraternizing between pickets became too frequent, commanders ordered up artillery barrages to discourage them. Luman Rumrill, a soldier with the 9th Vermont Regiment, had no head for spelling but kept his sense of fun during the monotonous and dangerous hours on picket. He teased his family in a letter home: "We are doing picket duty in about half a mile of the joneys. . . . Come down hear and see the joley reb We can see them every day just as plain as we can see the stares in the night."[21]

It was not just Weitzel's threadbare enemies who had to contend with desertion. The virus infected even well-provisioned Union regiments. The 10th Connecticut suffered so many desertions that the angry corps commander stuck the unit up front on the picket line, where, he swore, it would be "very difficult for them to get away." On the last Sunday of March, the 1st Brigade of the XXIV Corps finally had some excitement to break the monotony. The officers called out the whole brigade to witness punishment meted out to one of their number, Pvt. Frederick Brandt, Company E, 81st New York, charged with desertion. The war ended for Brandt on that cold and windy day—in the presence of his comrades but at the wrong end of a firing squad.[22]

Thomas Morris Chester waited with the men of the United States Colored Troops, the USCTs, who were the special interest of this reporter for the *Philadelphia Press*. A tall, muscular man with a stern brow and full beard, Chester had seen more of the world than the average thirty-year-old. He had sailed back and forth across the Atlantic to Liberia, but with the war he gave up on colonization and became the only African American journalist to report from the front for a major paper. A sarcastic writer, he lampooned his enemies and heaped scorn on their cause. But he wrote with great empathy for the USCTs. He shivered in the trenches with them and recorded the tedium of their ordeal and their apprehensions about assaulting the imposing, interlocking system of Confederate trenches and forts. They had not forgotten their horrific losses at the battle of New Market Heights the previous year when fourteen of their men won the Medal of Honor but scores died in an assault on the southern lines.

The soldiers gossiped like soldiers everywhere and were puzzled by maneuvers within their own army that they could not decipher. The signs pointed toward movement, but when and where they could not tell. Chester heard that the Confederates were drilling companies of black soldiers, and knew that the white officers of the USCTs were anxious to learn whether slaves would fight for the South. He was confident they would not, at least not for long: "They will, without doubt, turn right side up."[23]

Like Chester, Garland White had something to prove. Born into slavery, he escaped, fled north, and became pastor of an African Methodist Episcopal church in Ontario. On the outbreak of war, he offered to recruit fellow refugees in Canada for the Union. His offer was premature, but when the North finally put black men in uniform in early 1863, White helped raise the 28th USCT in Indiana and hoped to become its chaplain. Before knowing whether he would receive a chaplain's commission, he joined as a private, "to be with my boys."[24]

He did eventually become a chaplain, one of only fourteen African Americans to earn that distinction among the 133 men commissioned as spiritual advisers to black regiments.[25] He suffered hardships with his men and preached the gospel and Union victory to them nearly every day. He was an unlettered parson himself—"I never went to School a day in my life. I learnd what little I know by the hardest." But completely illiterate privates often asked him to write their families if they should die in battle.[26] When he stood on the parapet and looked west toward the Confederate capital, dressed in his black frock coat, with a silver "U.S." badge pinned to his black felt hat, Chaplain White was looking home. He had been born in Richmond, and now he wanted to return.

Reinforcements streamed up the James River to swell Grant's army. One of the newest arrivals, Daniel Nelson, a young doctor fresh from his Boston internship, had just taken a commission as acting assistant surgeon. Cocky, optimistic, even exuberant about his assignment, he began a diary. Despite the mud and rain, everything he saw fascinated him in this "Delightful country, full of Peach blossoms, & the desolation of War." Impressed with the buildup of matériel and men being orchestrated from headquarters at City Point on the James, Nelson felt certain that something must happen soon, surely before the terrible heat and enervating humidity of Virginia summer arrived. He was eager to be part of what he envisioned as the great final battle. But he reassured his wife, Sarah, back in Holliston, Massachusetts: "Don't you *worry* one bit about me. . . . We are far in the rear of our fortifications and as safe as in Holliston."[27]

At his headquarters, Ulysses Grant waited, too. With a turn in the weather, he would be ready to set the campaign in motion. He had endured repeated criticism of his strategy and his record, but he retained Lincoln's faith in him, and he repaid that faith with battlefield success. By dint of doggedness, will, and moral courage, he had led the Union army to the brink of victory and he meant to secure it there on Virginia soil. This would be his moment.[28]

It was true that he had more than twice as many men as Lee, but the attacker needed more than double the number of the defender, especially when the attack must be against an entrenched position. Grant did not deny that the resourceful Confederates had built some of the most powerful defensive works in the world and would contest them fiercely.

In the midst of the constant attention to the needs of his army, he took a moment at the beginning of March to write his father. "I am anxious," he confided, "to have Lee hold on where he is a short time longer so that I can get him in a position where he must loose a great portion of his Army. The rebellion has lost its vitality."[29] Despite this confident assertion, reinforced by continuing reports of Confederate desertion, Grant still worried, even with the immense assets at his disposal. He thought it likely that Lee and Joseph E. Johnston, moving up from the south, would try to combine their armies. What could he do to thwart such a move, and if he failed, what could the Confederates accomplish?

Grant could sense the effect of desertion as well as Lee. He did not depend on Confederate weakness to lay his plans, though. He would advance when he was ready, regardless of the condition of his enemy's army. He had not forgotten the lesson he learned early in the war as colonel of an Illinois regiment when he realized that the enemy "had been as much afraid of me as I had been of him."[30] He dictated cable after cable to his commanders to prepare for the day when the rains would stop and the mud roads dry up enough to move their regiments in what he hoped would be the last campaign.

THEY WAITED IN Washington. Secretary of War Edwin Stanton had begun his career as a brusque, irritable courtroom lawyer. An anti-slavery Democrat, he developed a warm friendship for Lincoln as they prosecuted the war together. With the president away from the capital visiting Grant, the tireless Stanton kept an especially close eye on the military situation. Neither he nor his assistant secretary, former newspaper editor Charles Dana, fully trusted the Union's generals. War was indeed too important a task to be left entirely in the hands of men in uniform. Dana suspected that if Grant achieved a break-through that spring, Stanton would send his assistant secretary south to gather firsthand reports, as he had done in the past.

They waited across the Potomac, too, where the loyalist governor of Virginia had established himself. A shrewd railroad attorney and businessman, Francis Pierpont owed his Unionist sentiments more to hatred of the slaveholding gentry of Tidewater than to love of their human chattels. After the Richmond government seceded in 1861, he led the movement to create West Virginia from Unionist counties in the western part of the state. Then he headed the "restored," or loyal-ist, government that represented portions of seceded Virginia that had been occupied by the Federal army. He set up his minuscule headquar-ters in Alexandria just across the river from the District of Columbia and safely behind Union lines. A nuisance to be tolerated in the eyes of the local Federal commanders and an object of derision to Confederate Virginians, Pierpont and his exiguous regime had almost become an embarrassment to the Lincoln administration.

Like the other watchers, Pierpont eagerly awaited the beginning of the spring campaign. He hoped that before summer he would enter Richmond as governor of the whole commonwealth, once more loyal to the United States of America. He wrote Grant of his desire to occupy the governor's mansion and officiously added that he would gladly welcome the general into the parlor there when he arrived. On that subject, he requested that Grant's soldiers allow no harm to come to state records or, especially, to Jefferson's Capitol. "In the rotunda," he lectured the general, "is the finest statue of Washington extant."[31] It would be a great shame if Houdon's likeness of the Father of the Country suffered any damage when the city changed hands.

CHAPTER 4

A DAY FOR FOOLS

Saturday, April 1

We are in a tight box now.
—Lt. Col. William Owen, CSA artillery[1]

In the early hours of the last Saturday in March, the Confederates launched an audacious attack on Fort Stedman, a salient in the Union fortifications east of Petersburg. Lee, the wizard of strategy, was making his move to break the encircling enemy, to act before Grant did. Of late, he had been a sour and aloof commander, grumpy, saturnine, and more curt than ever. His aide Walter Taylor described him as "unreasonable and provoking at times."[2] He had justification: the military situation could scarcely be more dire. But if his stroke against Fort Stedman succeeded, it would force Grant to make a significant adjustment to his lines. While he did, the Army of Northern Virginia would have a few days' grace in which to slip away to join Joseph E. Johnston's smaller Confederate force in North Carolina. If he could combine with Johnston, Lee had a chance to defeat William T. Sherman's army, marching up from the south, and then turn and meet Grant with a larger force than he commanded at Petersburg. It was only a chance, but he knew it was better than waiting for attrition to defeat him in the trenches.

After a brilliant beginning in the predawn darkness that combined stealth, guile, and heroic effort, the attack on Fort Stedman faltered and then failed utterly. The southerners fought with desperate courage, but after they had torn a hole in the Union line, their enemy counterattacked with overwhelming force. A killing crossfire engulfed the southerners and forced them back. When it was over, they ended up where they had begun at the cost of thousands of casualties they could ill afford.

Grant believed he had just witnessed their last offensive gasp, heartbreaking for them and full of promise for him. In a few days, probably by the beginning of April, if the roads would dry out from the heavy spring rains, he would marshal his forces and try to crush the Confederate lines, now even more highly attenuated than before. Now Lee feared that, in the wake of his failure at Fort Stedman, he would not be able to disengage from his fortifications at a time and in a manner of his own choosing.

It has been argued that the end for Richmond began with the failure at Fort Stedman. Perhaps, but in a symbolic sense, it began on the following Thursday, the wet and miserable next-to-last day of March, during the lull before Grant acted. While former slaves learned to shoulder arms on Capitol Square and their white officers tried to ignore the scoffers, one block to the north a principal enemy of the scheme lay dying. At ten o'clock that morning, John Moncure Daniel's doctor poured a glass of brandy for his consumptive patient. When he turned to administer the dose, he found that the editor of the *Examiner* had quietly died. The vitriolic pen that had derided Lincoln's "imbecility, buffoonery and vulgar malignity"—and denounced Jefferson Davis in even more hateful terms—would write no more. Because of the latest rumor, brought to his deathbed by solicitous friends, the editor died with whispers in his ear of a great victory by Lee at Petersburg.[3]

Even journalistic rivals called his death a public calamity. In the obituary, Daniel's editorial colleague John Mitchel described him as a passionate man, "of warm attachments and bitter hatreds; above all things Southern and intensely, almost fanatically Virginian."[4] He was not yet forty. At Second Presbyterian, Moses Hoge preached an inspiring funeral sermon, and then friends of the deceased followed the coffin out of the church to burial at Hollywood Cemetery overlooking the falls of the James. Those in the funeral party who knew that President Davis was sending his family south that same day may have wondered whose obsequies were being read—Daniel's or the Confederacy's.

THE ILLUSION THAT Daniel took to his grave persisted a little longer in the minds of many Richmonders. The next morning, the sun finally came out after days of soaking rain and gave the hopeful another tenuous reason to buttress their optimism. The turn in the weather matched perfectly the occasion announced by a couple in the Saturday-morning *Dispatch*. They invited all of their friends to celebrate their wedding, not at a house or a church, but at the base of the great statue of Washington on horseback in Capitol Square. Following the ceremony, Hidalgo Cortes and Felicia Alvarez said they would mount their horses and ride slowly around the statue to the congratulation of their friends and leave by a path strewn with flowers.[5] By this point, the reader of the happy couple's announcement should have realized it was a hoax. Even as the city faced the threat of military conquest, someone on the editorial staff still had enough humor to concoct this elaborate April Fools' joke.

Though Cortes and Alvarez were fictive lovers, others showed that hope still endured amid the depressions of war. While Hoge, Minnigerode, and their clerical brethren were kept busy reading services for the dead, they also performed joyful ceremonies of marriage. Right up to the end, couples exchanged their vows before the clergymen and their friends and family. Soldiers on temporary leave and brides who knew they were sending their grooms off to combat rather than sharing a wedding trip affirmed their faith in their individual futures even as they wondered about that of the Confederate States.

The same morning as the fictitious wedding, Mayor Joseph Mayo convened his court at the stately City Hall at the upper end of Capitol Square. He showed no inclination toward whimsy, even if it was a day

for fools. Seventy years old and a great-grandson of the man who surveyed the original town of Richmond, Mayo had held public office for
more than forty years, twelve of them as mayor. Balding and clean-
shaven in an era of ubiquitous facial hair, he favored the high starched
collar, cravat, and brass-buttoned waistcoat of a former time. They fit
his authoritarian manner, especially his stern treatment of free blacks,
which constantly let them know they occupied the lowest rung of society, outside slavery.

On that Saturday he demonstrated once more why black people
disliked him intensely. Barbara Clora, who said she was a free citizen
of Caroline County, came up before the court "for being at large."
Mayo ordered her whipped and returned to her home. Thomas, the
property of Julian Handsford, faced a charge of theft. Despite the lack
of proof, Mayo ordered him whipped anyway.[6]

The city council as well as the courts met on Saturday. The councilmen appropriated money for the Richmond Soup Association and for
the Male Orphan Society. They heard a dispute over the alleged failure of the keeper of Shockoe Hill Cemetery to clothe his black
gravediggers in an appropriate fashion. They dealt with numbingly
complex details of tax financing for the city gasworks. And they heard
a plea to pull down an unsafe building owned by the proprietor of the
Whig, because the brick wall threatened to fall on pedestrians.[7]

Henri Garidel had had a bad Friday night. The noisy insomnia of a
tubercular tenant in the adjoining room of his boardinghouse had
kept him awake. After he dressed and cleaned his boots, the dour Creole went downstairs to read the newspaper before breakfast. He discounted the upbeat tenor of the latest reports from the front and
concluded that a great battle was coming, one that would be disastrous
for the Confederacy. When he made a second trek to the post office,
however, his diligence was rewarded with a letter that arrived on the
flag-of-truce boat. Because his wife numbered her letters, he could tell
that twelve earlier ones had gone astray. But the one that got through
made him happy, and that was enough for Garidel. He even noticed
the sunshine.[8]

The rate at which people tried to convert their possessions into cash on Saturday provided another index to the city's prospects. Auction-eers competed for advertising space in the papers to announce their sales, and red flags sprouted from windows to show where hopeful sellers offered their wares. In the next week, the contents of entire houses were slated to go under the hammer. Robert Dabney promised to sell an assortment of furniture and groceries, and threw into the mix ten dozen bottles of five-year-old brandy and a gold watch and chain. James Taylor, surely the most optimistic of real estate develop-ers, planned to sell forty unimproved lots on the east side of town.[9]

Well-read refugees from the surrounding countryside had brought their libraries with their other possessions into town since the begin-ning of the war, making Richmond a book buyer's paradise. Now the rarest editions could be had very cheaply indeed. Books, condemned military horses and mules, bolts of cloth, silverware, carpenter's tools—everything imaginable was being hawked by the auctioneers.

One seller, the popular actress Ida Vernon, had run the blockade from abroad to give benefit performances. Now, on doctor's advice, she announced she was leaving for Europe to restore her health and of-fered her entire theatrical wardrobe for sale. The records do not say what offers she received, if any, for her "Feathers, Silk Tights, Wigs, Shoes, Gaiters, Swords, Lace Flounces," and a hundred other impracti-cal items.

The last sale of a particular kind took place that Saturday at the Odd Fellows' Hall on the corner of Franklin and Mayo streets. There, S. N. Davis promised, "I will sell at auction, This Morning, Twenty Likely Negroes."[10]

The gravediggers of Richmond got no relief on Saturday, except for the blessing of a warm sun to dry up the soil, thoroughly sodden from the week's rain. It put the same strain on their backs to shovel out the viscous red Virginia clay for a private soldier's last resting place as it did for grander corpses, like that of John Moncure Daniel. One of the interments that day was for the remains of Pvt. Samuel Lovett, 45th North Carolina Regiment. A farmer who enlisted at twenty-one, Lovett had been captured at the battle of Spotsylvania Court House almost a year before. He spent the brutal winter of 1864–65 in the stockade at Elmira, New York, where the mortality rate rivaled that of Andersonville. At the end of February, they paroled Lovett and sent him to the prisoner exchange on the James River supervised by Robert Ould for the Confederacy and John Mulford for the Union. Upon release, Lovett was too sick to leave his cot in an army hospital. He gradually declined and died the first of April. That same day, the Hollywood gravediggers shoveled still-damp soil over his remains, in section W, number 698, on the last quiet day in Confederate Richmond.[11]

The proprietors of Buckley & Budd's Opera House expected a full house Saturday. For $4 Confederate the rowdies could enjoy singing, dancing, minstrel bands, and blackface burlesques. For April Fools' evening, they promised to deliver an appropriate farce, a performance on the eve of defeat that suggested the hostility of many to the plan to attract black Virginians to the southern cause. They called the farce "Recruiting Unbleached Citizens of Virginia for the Confederate States Army."[12]

WHILE RICHMONDERS WENT about their Saturday routines, in the afternoon at a rural crossroads named Five Forks southwest of Petersburg the consequences of Lee's failed attack on Fort Stedman the previous week at last became manifest. By a generous estimate, the Confederates had roughly enough men to stand and link hands— should they have chosen to do so—along the entire forty-plus miles of trenches that arced from northeast of Richmond and then down beyond Petersburg.[13] But by the 1st of April, even that symbolic gesture would no longer have been possible. In the days since Fort Stedman, Grant had aggressively continued to move his regiments to the southwest. In response, the Confederates had to thin their ranks as they tried to cover the lengthening defensive perimeter.

To counter the Union flanking threat, Lee sent several brigades under George Pickett. Beset by uncertainty and anxiety ever since Gettysburg, and repeatedly blaming others for his own mistakes, Pickett saw a chance to redeem his reputation in battle. In the rain on Friday afternoon, March 31, beyond the far end of the Confederate defenses, the southerners pushed back the Federal attempt to outflank them. By sunset, Pickett's men had forced their opponent on the defensive, but the hesitant Confederate general ordered a halt as night fell. When the sun came out on Saturday morning, the Union regiments were gone from the Confederate front. In the deceptive quiet, Pickett left the field. Feckless to the end, he and some other Confederate generals left their posts for a fish fry. In their absence, a Union attack fatally pierced the southern defenses, undid their gains of the previous day, and, worse, gave the Federal army the chance it had looked for.[14]

Lee feared he could not stitch his lines back together and might have to disengage, not just from that one sector but from Petersburg and from Richmond as well. He had wanted to make that disengagement on his terms, but that was not to be. For years to come, Confederate veterans would argue the culpability of the commanders absent from Five Forks. As in the past, the unreliable Pickett tried to blame others for the disaster and would not recognize Lee's order relieving him of command. (A few days later at Appomattox, Lee spotted Pickett and spat out his opinion with the contemptuous rhetorical question "Is that man still with this army?")[15]

Whether Pickett and the others had been irresponsible was beside the point. On Saturday a brisk wind was drying up the roads very fast, and that meant a major Union advance would soon be feasible. Grant's men would have crushed the overextended Confederates sooner or later. If it had not been that April Fools' afternoon when Pickett and his friends drank whiskey and picked the bones from grilled shad, it would have been soon enough thereafter. The thin Confederate defenses had finally stretched beyond the limit, beyond the skill of their commander to mend.

When he heard news of the disaster, New Orleans artillerist William Owen, who had earlier scorned the recruiting of black Confederate soldiers, recorded his worries in his diary that evening: "We are in a tight box now, and only wondering where and when our lines will be broken."[16] He had scarcely put his apprehensions down on paper before Grant answered his question.

———

As the Richmond provost marshal, Maj. Isaac Carrington reported to General Ewell. Weeks before, the general had instructed him to prepare to destroy all of the government-owned cotton, tobacco, and military stores in the city. The order came from the commanding general, Robert E. Lee, and represented the agreed-upon Confederate policy not to leave anything of value to the enemy. Carrington made a survey and discovered that there was little cotton but considerable tobacco. In the days leading up to the evacuation, he and Ewell conferred often about their efforts to concentrate it in a few warehouses for easy burning. Their discussion on April Fools' Day was no longer a hypothetical one, for the fatal ramifications of Five Forks began to become obvious to them by the time the sun set. They knew there was a better than even chance Lee would order the evacuation within twenty-four hours. If so, they could not take with them even a fraction of the military supplies remaining in Richmond.

In the finger pointing that erupted after the evacuation, Ewell stoutly defended his actions. He and his supporters argued that he was obeying orders from General Lee, and Lee was carrying out Confederate government policy. That dispute was later. But a fierce and confusing debate began even before the first torch was lit. Ewell insisted that he would carry out his orders to burn the tobacco warehouses. The chief ordnance officer, Josiah Gorgas, objected. He said they could just as easily ruin the large bundles of cured leaves by pouring turpentine over them at no danger to the surrounding buildings. Mayor Mayo also protested Ewell's orders. For his part, Breckinridge doubted Ewell's assurance that burning the tobacco posed no danger to the city. But though he could have countermanded Ewell, he did not. The chief engineer, Jeremy Gilmer, vehemently objected to Breckinridge and Ewell's intention to burn the railroad bridges. Gorgas agreed and argued in vain that such an act would also risk igniting the arsenal.[17]

At seven-thirty on Saturday evening, Ewell received an order to call out the local brigades to replace regular troops being taken from the trenches and sent south to reinforce Lee. Ewell sent word to another general, who was preparing to leave for Petersburg, that he could scrape together fifteen hundred men in the locals to put into the trenches. "Do you think," he asked with words that reflected the extremity of Confederate fortunes, "that any of the Engineers employees (colored) would be willing to take up arms for this occasion, or expedient that they should?"[18]

Sgt. H. E. Wood, 18th Virginia Infantry, had gone to bed Saturday night at the Chimborazo Hospital, where he was convalescing. A messenger woke him with orders to assemble his unit, one of the five hospital companies, and report to Ewell on Capitol Square. When he arrived, he could see flashes on the horizon, like sheet lightning, "painting hell on the sky" down toward Petersburg. He found Ewell huddled with his staff and city officials near the statue of Henry Clay at the lower end of the square. Wood went up to Ewell and touched his sleeve to get his attention. The general turned and gruffly told the sergeant to be quick about it. When Wood explained his presence, Ewell detailed a guide to show him where his men should fill the gap in the lines east of town after the regulars departed.[19]

Ewell now had fewer regulars to help the locals defend ten miles of fortifications east and southeast of town. The one-legged general could count on a cavalry brigade under Martin Gary, one veteran division holding the center under Joseph Kershaw, and Custis Lee's division near the river.[20] But he would only have them for a night and a day.

Capt. McHenry Howard turned in late Saturday night at Chaffin's Bluff, downstream from town and on the north side of the river. He recalled that as he drifted off, "a faint red glare illuminated the tent, followed by a low muttering like distant thunder." In other circumstances, he might have thought a storm was brewing, but he knew better. "Flash after flash shone through the canvas, and the muttering presently became almost continuous, although very little louder."[21]

It did not matter that Lee was stripping the Richmond defenses to shore up his position to the south. It would not be enough. Grant ordered an attack all along the Petersburg lines for the early hours of Sunday. When it succeeded, Lee knew he could no longer delay retreat. Five Forks had marked the inevitable result of too few men defending too many miles of terrain. Now here were the consequences. There would be no breathing space to move his army quietly from its entrenchments to attempt a union with Johnston. Now he would have to conduct a fighting retreat toward the southwest.

Still, with luck, he might pull it off. After sending orders by telegraph and courier all up and down his lines, Lee cabled Breckinridge. This was the moment they had feared and expected: the Confederate army was abandoning its capital to the enemy. But Lee said he had taken every measure to give this grand maneuver disengaging from more than forty miles of trenches a chance to succeed. Furthermore, to follow the southern army, Grant's men would have to march increasingly farther from their base of supply at City Point. The Army of Northern Virginia might still escape and regroup. He even allowed himself a comment that, in other circumstances, might be considered sanguine but in retrospect was delusional: "It will be a difficult operation, but I hope not impracticable."[22]

DESPITE THE SUNSHINE on Saturday morning that began to dry the earth, the James River began to show the effects of so much rainfall earlier in the week. Upstream and to the west, the runoff gradually raised the water level, increasing as it did the roar produced by the seven-mile stretch of falls and cataracts that funneled the James toward the downtown waterfront, "brawling over broken rocks," as Charles Dickens had described it on a visit years before.[23] Serious flooding seemed likely, so much so that the newspapers began to predict a greater inundation than had occurred in years. Already, basements in the oldest part of town, where Shockoe Creek emptied into the river, had started to fill up. Prudent merchants began to move their goods to drier ground.[24]

The threat of flooding and the clanging of the fire bell early Sunday morning might have reminded pious residents of a popular sermon topic as they prepared for church. Yahweh promised Noah after the Flood never to destroy the earth by water again, but ministers warned that one day it would be swept away not by water but by fire. The *Ex-*

aminer, now no longer with John Daniel at the helm, reassured readers. For the time being, the paper suggested, flooding and not burning
was the more important threat on Sunday. The alarm was false, the
paper said, "and proceeded from the burning out of a chimney on
Twenty-first street, between Main and Cary. No damage done."[25]

CHAPTER 5

SABBATH REST

Sunday, April 2, Morning

A day never to be forgotten. Poor old Richmond given up to the Yankees!!

—Margaret Brown Wight[1]

Despite troop movements on Saturday evening and the call-up of local defense forces to fill gaps in the line, the next morning most civilians still did not suspect immediate evacuation. Or if they did, they did not act on their suspicions. They chose to ignore the week-long shipment of government boxes and crates from the Richmond & Danville terminal. They did not yet know about Five Forks or its significance. Word of Lee's greater defeat at Petersburg early that morning would soon burst upon them, but that awful intelligence still lay a few merciful minutes of ignorance in the future.

Afterward, when it was all over, they remembered their last Confederate Sunday morning as one of clear, crystal-blue skies, of warmth that heralded new growth, of pristine, irenic beauty completely at odds with the tumult that soon overtook the city. Mary Fontaine called it an exceptionally lovely day "when delicate silks that look too fine at other times, seem just to suit; when invalids and convalescents venture out in the sunshine." Edward Pollard remembered the distant fields across the river glistening in the morning light of a cloudless sky as the peal of church bells called the devout to services.[2]

One of the worshipers was George Washington Camp, a banker and former vice mayor of Norfolk, Virginia, who had been a member of the delegation that surrendered that city to the Union army. When he took a long walk before church, even the neglect of four years of war could not keep him from thinking Richmond was the most pleasant spot on earth. All along the streets, trees were just beginning to come into leaf. A lime-yellow haze covered the wooded slopes along the river as the buds began to open, and, Camp mused, "we could but say it was indeed God's day & God's City, the place of his peculiar favor."[3]

Union soldiers made similar remarks. George Bruce, a captain in the 13th New Hampshire Regiment with Weitzel's Army of the James southeast of the city, remembered long afterward the first flush of spring that Sunday. And, he wrote, "through the hushed air I heard distinctly for the first time the church bells of Richmond . . . and at the same time, though less distinctly, the subdued murmur and roar of the battle fifteen miles to the south."[4]

AT MOST PROTESTANT houses of worship, the first Sunday of the month was communion Sunday. At St. Paul's, the bright sunlight of late morning streamed through the tall eastern windows and filled the nave with light. The congregation was mainly female, many of them in mourning dress, which the lengthening toll of casualties had made standard attire. Besides President Davis and other high government officials, there were some convalescent soldiers in uniform and a few old men in civilian suits. Like communicants at other Episcopal churches, they followed along in their prayer books or from memory as they prepared to celebrate the Eucharist. Accounts of the service have left conflicting stories about the text of the lessons for the day, but one of them had Dr. Minnigerode reading a passage from Psalm 46 that could not have been more appropriate: "He maketh wars to cease unto the end of the earth; he breaketh the bow, and cutteth the spear in sunder; he burneth the chariot in the fire."[5]

Just before communion began, a messenger from the War Department entered the back of the church. He handed a note to the sexton, a pompous man who gloried in the petty perquisites of his office. He took the note and walked down the center aisle to Jefferson Davis, alone in his accustomed pew. Not yet sixty, the Confederate president looked far older. Gray, wrinkled, and old was the way observers uniformly described him in 1865. A nervous stomach, racking pain in his face, and the disfigurement of blindness in one eye made the burdens of office heavier. And yet he carried himself erect and bore those burdens with stoic resolve. "I never saw quiet determination more strikingly manifest in any person," wrote the visiting Irish parliamentarian Thomas Conolly.[6]

As Confederate military fortunes withered, at times Davis seemed resigned to defeat, at other times oblivious to that outcome. Contentious, aloof, increasingly autocratic, and never easy in his relations with those around him, he nevertheless devoted himself totally to the cause. He couched the South's prospects starkly as a choice between independence or extermination and was willing to grasp whatever expedient would secure his goal. Eventually, he concluded that that goal, independence, trumped the preservation of slavery, the institution that had divided the United States and created the Confederacy in the first instance. In the waning days of 1864 he made the momentous but stillborn proposal to accept gradual emancipation in return for recognition of the Confederacy by Britain and France. Two months later, the South's extremity impelled him to embrace arming slaves. By then it was too late. By then, though he may have been refusing to admit to himself the likely outcome of the war, his spirit of fatalistic determination kept him going. And the outward manifestation of that spirit was what was on display that morning in St. Paul's.[7]

The sexton touched Davis on the shoulder to get his attention. The president was used to such intrusions, and it was not the first time duty required him to leave church unexpectedly. Some parishioners thought they caught a look of alarm in his good eye as he strode out of the church. Others said he looked ashen. Another, more honest about her inability to discern the president's thoughts, said Davis's face was impassive and she could read nothing in it.[8]

False alarms had scared them before, but this time the news from the battlefield was different, a later chronicler wrote, and it "fell upon them like a thunder-clap from clear skies, and smote the ear of the community as a knell of death."[9] A navy clerk who was there, searching for a metaphor that could capture the shock of the moment, chose similarly apocalyptic words: "Had an unseen hand written the coming doom on the wall in letters of fire, the effect could not have been more appalling or more instantaneous."[10]

What the sexton brought Davis was a copy of a telegram the War Department had received from Lee. His lines were broken, the general reported. There was no hope of repairing the damage. He must retreat at once to save his army. They must evacuate Richmond that night.

It was not the first time Davis received bad news from Lee that morning. He had heard an earlier ominous report on his way to church but decided to continue on his walk to St. Paul's in hopes that Lee's next message would be less dire. It was not. The president did not share the contents of the message with anyone, and the service continued after he left. Only in recollections written later did it end abruptly with this epiphany of disaster borne by the hands of the sexton.

After the president left, Minnigerode continued the service, placing the paten and chalice containing the bread and wine on the table. Worshipers listened as he intoned the familiar words from the Book of Common Prayer asking divine guidance for the Confederate president and all Christian rulers that they might dispense justice impartially and punish vice and wickedness. As the sexton came back to ask other officials to leave, however, ripples of concern washed over the congregation and disrupted their attention to higher things. By the time the service had ended, many people feared the worst. Kate Mason Rowland spoke for them all later that day when she described "this sad, last, communion, perhaps, in our free city!"[11]

At First African Baptist, Dr. Ryland, the white pastor, preached his last sermon to a congregation part free and part enslaved. Though a slave owner himself, Ryland condemned the separation of families and laws forbidding slaves to read the Bible.[12] In the afternoon, J. B. Jones, the War Department clerk, wrote, "The negroes stand about mostly silent, as if wondering what will be their fate. They make no demonstrations of joy." Because Jones expected them to be exuberant over the prospect of Union victory, he interpreted their demeanor as subdued when it was in fact prudent anticipation of the coming change. They would make their sentiments known soon enough, but for the last Sunday under Confederate rule, the African Americans of Richmond knew it was more important than ever to hide their feelings. Another observer remembered how heartily the black employees of the government—teamsters, messengers, and assorted departmental workers—threw themselves into the frantic effort to pack up for evacuation. He wondered if their energy was the result of "sympathy for the predicament of their employers, or an eagerness to be rid of them."[13]

LIKE THE CIVILIANS in Richmond, soldiers at Grant's City Point headquarters along the James could only wait for news and speculate how decisions made elsewhere would affect them. At the chapel of the Christian Commission, a private charity that provided food and spiritual nourishment for soldiers, they could hear the cannons booming away toward Petersburg. A visiting clergyman from Massachusetts who spoke that morning heard them too but did not mention these portentous sounds in his sermon.

When the service was almost over, however, the army's provost marshal, Gen. Marsena Patrick, stepped up to the pulpit to read the latest telegrams from Grant at the front. No one cheered despite the encouraging news. Patrick thought they should give special prayers for the success of their army, and he led them himself. It was a convincing performance. The devout Patrick looked the part of an Old Testament patriarch, with a wild, white beard he had let grow to biblical proportions. "You could almost have heard a pin drop," reported a soldier in the congregation. The general "took it for granted that the Almighty regarded the cause of Jeff Davis and that of Satan in the same light, and he prayed for the complete overthrow of the rebel army, and their utter annihilation." Reflecting on the service later that evening, Patrick said, "It was a time of His own presence, I verily believe— Then we Sang America & separated."[14]

At 10:45 A.M., just as the pews began to fill up in Richmond churches and the Union troops at City Point prepared to offer their prayers, in the quiet sector southeast of the city Godfrey Weitzel received word from Grant: the victorious Army of the Potomac had breached the Confederate trenches in front of Petersburg. The end was at hand. "Keep in a condition," he admonished Weitzel, "to assault when ordered or when you may [feel] the right time has come."[15]

WILLIAM PARKER, the superintendent of the Confederate naval academy, had stayed in town Saturday night but returned to the school ship *Patrick Henry* in time for Sunday-morning muster. As the midshipmen were piped down from inspection, he saw a company of local troops going downriver and wondered what it meant. Shortly after, about noon, a curt message from Navy Secretary Stephen Mallory ordered him to assemble the whole corps of students at the Danville depot by six o'clock that evening.

Parker told the cooks to prepare three days' rations of salt pork and cornmeal and ordered a subordinate to lead the midshipmen to the station. In the meantime, he walked to the Navy Department to learn the reason firsthand. On the way, he passed a large body of Union prisoners being sent down the river to be exchanged. The Confederates customarily marched prisoners to exchange at dawn, never in the middle of the day. At that instant, Parker knew the evacuation had come. When he reached headquarters, he learned that he and his students were to guard the treasury on its flight by train. Now the sixty midshipmen would face their greatest challenge, and on dry land far from the tang of salt air.[16]

Moses Handy, the courier lieutenant with the engineers, was up at five o'clock Sunday morning, but not to go into town to church as he had hoped. His colonel ordered him to take charge of loading wagons with material to strengthen the trenches facing the northern army. None of Handy's messmates stirred when he was awakened, and so he cooked his own cornmeal ashcakes on the fire and fried a slice of bacon in solitude. Just as he finished, the wagons arrived, thirty of them. Handy mounted his horse and rode out to supervise loading a new batch of abatis, tops of pine trees shorn of foliage and with branches sharpened to a point. When piled in front of breastworks, this mass of pointed sticks helped deter an attacking enemy. With the thinning of Confederate ranks, every enhancement the engineers could give to the trenches helped.

Another courier rode up at a quick trot and interrupted Handy and the black teamsters in the middle of their work. He told them to dump their loads right where they were and return to camp as fast as they could. Their general needed the wagons back at headquarters. Handy dismissed the teamsters and rode back ahead of them. When he arrived, he saw a group of officers talking in low voices in an attempt to conceal what their long faces gave away. There was no confirmation yet that Richmond would be evacuated, but all the signs pointed to it.

One of Handy's friends confirmed the unhappy tone of the dispatches. The courier laughed it off and, already with the wisdom of a veteran despite his seventeen years, turned in to his bunk and took a nap. If he could not get leave to go to church in town, he would at least catch up on his sleep. When he awoke, about the time church services ended, a courier just in from the south verified everything: "The *Blue-bellies* are crowding into Petersburgh, and Richmond's a goner!"[17]

Frank Potts, a twenty-six-year-old quartermaster stationed north of the James, wondered Saturday night if orders to move troops from the Richmond defenses down to Petersburg meant evacuation was at hand. On Sunday, Potts nevertheless rode into town after breakfast to attend church. On the way he ruminated, like Handy, about the meaning of all the troop movements. He accepted that evacuation seemed likely but would not consider the possibility of defeat.

When he reached town, he found the usual rumormongers loitering about the hotels and offices. He dismissed their tales of disaster, found a friend at the Spotswood, and went with him to the office of the adjutant general. Samuel Cooper would tell them the truth. But General Cooper, who had just written his wife warning her not to return to the capital, could give the young soldiers no hope. From him they learned that the worst rumors were true. As church bells called the faithful to worship and Potts tried to assimilate the news, Thomas Conolly, the British visitor, accosted him. Conolly, ignorant of what Potts now knew, asked the quartermaster to join him for a dinner party that night, but Potts begged off.[18]

Henri Garidel was up at six. After dressing for church, he went downstairs and sat in the sun on the back porch of the boardinghouse, smoking his pipe in the cool of the morning. A devout Catholic, Garidel attended high mass at St. Peter's. Though the church was diagonally across Grace Street from St. Paul's, Garidel did not notice anything amiss until he went to his office. Then he learned about the plans for evacuating the city. "I think that things are about to explode," he scratched in his journal.[19]

One of the absent state legislators, John Coles Rutherfoord, a lawyer and planter from Goochland, the second county to the west, came to Richmond that morning. Out of step with his colleagues, as was often his habit, the morose, depressed Rutherfoord made his way back to the capital for a private reason, not a public one: he was to be a pallbearer at a funeral. He accompanied the remains of the deceased on one of the narrow, slow packet boats that crept in from the west on the James River and Kanawha Canal. After discharging his duty at the last funeral in Confederate Richmond, he learned of the scene at St. Paul's. By the time he made his way to the Capitol for an emergency joint meeting of the legislature, he knew the worst.[20]

In similar scenes repeated throughout town, at different times from midday into early afternoon, the news of impending calamity spread ripples of disaster across the surface of a quiet pond. Gottfried Lange, a German-born saloon keeper and shoemaker, first heard when he was idly smoking his pipe at the corner of Fourth and Broad streets. It was about noon when a one-armed captain in charge of the guard at the president's house told Lange the news. He recalled the same sense of shock as other Richmonders, but unlike native-born Virginians, he was reminded of his childhood, when he witnessed the fall of Erfurt at the end of the Napoleonic Wars. The fire and the plundering by Russian and Prussian troops were still vivid memories. Lange went home and told his wife to pack their most valuable possessions in a metal trunk. All that afternoon he sweated in his basement as he dug a hole in the floor to hide the trunk and then covered it with an iron sheet, a layer of sand, and the original bricks from the floor.[21]

At the governor's mansion, Elizabeth Smith, wife of the incumbent, coolly contemplated her situation. After forty-four years of marriage to William Smith, she had seen her share of exhilaration and tragedy. Enduring eleven pregnancies, she had buried three infants and later grieved over the loss of three grown sons. In the midst of her husband's frantic meetings that day, she approached him and said, "Smith, I may feel like a woman, but I *can* act like a man." She told him to attend to public matters. She would arrange to move their household in the morning from the mansion on the northeast corner of Capitol Square.[22]

Fannie Dickinson went to church as usual, but she did not understand until later what the minister meant when he hinted at the end of his sermon that he might soon be prevented from speaking to the congregation again. She went home in ignorance and ate her Sunday dinner at the large house on the westernmost stretch of Franklin Street. Her husband, Alfred, had gone to preach to the soldiers down along the river and would not return until evening. After the midday meal, her sister came in breathless and announced that Richmond would be evacuated. Fannie broke down and cried but not before she had run out of the room to avoid alarming her children. When their Sunday guests hurriedly left, Fannie, her mother, and her sister began hiding valuables. Concealing bacon ranked high on their pragmatic list.[23]

For years Virginians of African descent en route to new owners farther south had waited in the slave pens enclosed by high brick walls near Capitol Square. Although at least one auction had taken place just the day before, most traders had already sent their property south and west to Lynchburg and other places still in Confederate hands. As a result, on Sunday the slave pens, normally filled to capacity, held few inmates. About fifty people, however, remained at the largest of them, Lumpkin's jail. When their owner learned of the evacuation, he planned to take them on one of the last trains south. Robert Lumpkin would be disappointed in that plan, and so it would be in the capital of the southern republic that his slaves would welcome their deliverance from bondage and greet the Jubilee.

CHAPTER 6

A FUGITIVE GOVERNMENT

Sunday, April 2, Afternoon

*Now all is chaos & confusion. Was there ever a country in
such a condition[?]*

—Margaret Brown Wight[1]

When he left St. Paul's, Jefferson Davis turned right to hurry the
one steep block downhill to the War Department. As he
turned, before him loomed Crawford's equestrian statue of Washington, bronze hand outstretched, as though pointing to the danger that
had overtaken the Confederacy to the south. At the foot of that statue,
in a pouring rain on Washington's birthday three years before, Davis
had invoked the spirit of '76 when he took the oath of office as president of the "permanent" Confederate government. He told his eager
listeners, huddled under a sea of umbrellas, to emulate that spirit and
embrace adversity as "the crucible in which their patriotism was refined."[2] Now the young republic he led was fast melting away.

At the War Department he spoke briefly to John Breckinridge
about the slip of paper the secretary of war had sent. At forty-four, the
attractive Kentuckian with the long polished mustache was the
youngest member of Davis's cabinet and the one whom the president
most respected. Vice president of the United States under James
Buchanan and a successful Confederate general, Breckinridge had

been war minister only since February. In little more than a month, his efficiency in collecting supplies for the army caused others to wish Davis had appointed him sooner, before it was too late.

In the telegram that prompted Breckinridge's note, Lee had said, "I see no prospect of doing more than holding our position here till night. I am not certain that I can do that. . . . I advise that all preparation be made for leaving Richmond to-night."[3] In his reply, Davis complained about the disruption that sudden evacuation would entail. Indeed, a few days before, Lee had led him to believe he could count on several days' advance warning, certainly more than the few hours he now received. The president acquiesced, but in words that suggested his loathing to do so: "Arrangements are progressing, and unless you otherwise advise the start will be made."[4] This less-than-energetic reply angered Lee, and he vented his frustration to his staff. Davis was still denying what was apparent to everyone in Richmond by then, but he had reason to resent Lee for that earlier, misleading promise of more time.

The president called an immediate cabinet meeting at the executive offices in the former Custom House at the foot of Capitol Square. In addition to his cabinet, he sent word inviting Governor Smith and Mayor Mayo. Davis read the bleak news from Lee and ordered every cabinet member to prepare to leave that night. He delegated to Breckinridge the task of providing transport to Danville, a tobacco town on the Virginia–North Carolina border, though he still did not give up hope that happier news might click over the telegraph lines from the army. If there was any doubt of the finality of Lee's warning, however, another message from the commanding general dissolved it. "I am," Lee telegraphed at three o'clock, "in the presence of the enemy."[5]

Since the night before, General Ewell had faced the daunting task of defending the capital with an anemic force, while at the same time planning for the greater likelihood that he would have to abandon the city altogether and march his small command southwest to join Lee. He had perhaps five thousand soldiers to defend ten miles of formidable earthworks and interlocking artillery positions. On the left of Ewell's lines, looking east from Richmond, were the cavalry under

Martin Gary, a thin, balding South Carolinian with a violent temper. He would be the last to leave. In the center, seasoned men under Joseph Kershaw looked out toward the advanced pickets of Weitzel's XXIV and XXV Corps of the Army of the James. On the right, down near Chaffin's Bluff on the river, Custis Lee commanded a division. The assorted local defense forces, reserves, cadets of the Virginia Military Institute, and the walking wounded hospital companies added at most two thousand more men of dubious reliability.

By midmorning Ewell knew his task was no longer defense of a static position. He rode back into the city and found orders instructing him to pull out of Richmond, but not until after dark and if possible after the moon had set. Although twilight would come by 7 p.m., the moon would not disappear until 1:26 a.m. the following morning. In the meantime, he had plenty to do to set his command in motion. After issuing orders, he took a train the twenty miles down to Petersburg for a last face-to-face conference with Lee. When they had finished their desperate plans, the commanding general made a gesture that touched Ewell. Knowing his subordinate's fondness for sweet potatoes, Lee insisted that he take two of them for his dinner on the train back to Richmond.[6]

FOR THE PAST week the Treasury Department had been ordering wooden boxes for shipping its papers. Mann Quarles, the youngest teller in the department, had stayed at his office at night helping perform a sort of triage on the documents, some to save, some to abandon, some to burn. On Sunday afternoon Quarles and a few others began the task of boxing the coin and bullion. When he noticed that in their haste they were not making an account of what was in each box, he devised a system on the spot. He folded several sheets of brown paper into a makeshift booklet and on each of the pages wrote a description of the contents of each box and of the markings on the outside of the box. When the box was full, he sealed it and kept the seal in his pants pocket.

As they cleaned out the contents of the office's half-dozen safes,

Quarles locked each strongbox and put its keys in the single safe that had a combination lock. All during the packing, he remembered, they kept the furnace in the basement going, "red hot with Confederate Notes, Bonds, papers &c. until all were destroyed." One of the department's last disbursements, Treasury warrant number 3504, paid out $1,500 in gold to Secretary of State Judah P. Benjamin the day before. All properly signed and countersigned, it was charged to the "Secret Service" account, a mysterious payment that, in light of later events, would elicit wild speculation about its purpose.[7]

The sickly War Department clerk, John Jones, ran into Assistant Secretary John Campbell hurrying down Ninth Street. Jones was delighted to learn that his department required only a few employees to accompany the government to Danville. It advised every clerk with a family, like him, to remain in town. Fannie Miller, a copying clerk at the department, also ran into her supervisor on the street. Robert Kean was burdened down with as much baggage as he could carry when she met him and asked if she should go, too. With tears in his eyes, he bid her farewell, saying he could not in good conscience advise "a lady to follow a fugitive government."[8]

Kean's colleagues had shipped a prodigious number of boxes west to Lynchburg, Virginia, in the past few weeks. On Sunday they packed nearly eighty more, enough to fill two carloads, and sent them toward Charlotte, North Carolina. As industrious as they were, like their colleagues at the Treasury, they could not send everything. They heaped less important documents into mounds in the street outside and set them afire.[9] As night came on, the flames illuminated the facades of the surrounding buildings with a flickering light that foretold greater burning to come.

DESPITE THE DECLINING fortunes of the Confederate cause, sporadic little victories in skirmishes in North Carolina and Virginia continued to generate a trickle of Yankee prisoners sent to Richmond by rail. They presented a pitiful sight, "human *fungi*," in the scornful words of the press: "Dirty, begrimed, ragged, scores of them barefooted and bareheaded, with stolen toweling bandaged about their feet and heads, limping, hobbling and cursing, they appeared the scabs, scavengers and scum of all creation."[10]

Because of this influx, Robert Ould, the Confederate agent of exchange, was a harried man. Stocky, energetic, and handsome, with a neat, close-cropped beard and high forehead, the eloquent Ould had risen from humble beginnings in the District of Columbia to a prosperous career in the law. His impiety and penchant for gambling added a touch of danger to his personality. None of this kept Ould from winning the respect of his superiors, because his efficiency in bringing prisoners home provided the largest source of new Confederate manpower. On Sunday, though, General Grant ordered all prisoner exchanges halted while the fighting raged. Ould managed to take about two thousand of his charges down the river in hopes of returning with a like number of southern men before his Union counterpart, John Mulford, could stop the process.[11]

In the afternoon, long files of prisoners passed through the streets in an incongruous parade, literally marching under guard past offices where Confederate clerks were hurriedly packing up before they abandoned the city. Most of the prisoners were men captured on Saturday in the Petersburg lines and sent north to Richmond by train. They spent only a few hours at Libby Prison before shuffling out to board one of the two remaining Confederate flag-of-truce steamers. The *William Allison*, the larger of the two craft, carried most of the men. On the passage downriver, nothing seemed out of the ordinary as they maneuvered around the three ironclads that guarded the water approach to the capital. But the prisoners knew something was amiss from the activity they witnessed in town and repeatedly asked the crew why no one had required them to sign paroles not to bear arms until properly exchanged.

When the *Allison* reached the exchange landing, they hove to, and Mulford came on board. In the captain's cabin, he and Ould spoke at some length, as they had done dozens of times before. They had developed a professionally if not personally cordial relationship, and each respected the efforts of the other to secure the best conditions and early release of his prisoners. When Ould and Mulford parted, the southern commissioner knew it would be their last meeting as equals.

While the two commissioners talked, the guards marched their charges ashore. By then the day was waning, and the released Union soldiers took with them their brief impressions of Richmond and vivid accounts of the preliminaries to evacuation. "The streets," they reported, "were alive with people of all classes conditions and ages, manifesting intense excitement."[12]

A Navy Department messenger arrived just in time to interrupt Admiral Semmes as he sat down to Sunday dinner on board his flagship, the *Virginia II*, one of the Confederate ironclads that Ould's flag-of-truce steamer passed. Proud to the point of prickliness, Semmes chafed at being reduced to nothing more than commander of a floating artillery battery. He was a stern man, and his dark, pointed mustache, twirled and waxed to an alarming width, enhanced the impression he was not to be trifled with. Annoyed, Semmes pulled an order from Navy Secretary Mallory out of the sealed package and read the electrifying words "Upon you is devolved the duty of destroying your ships this night."[13] That accomplished, he was to convert his sailors into soldiers and join Lee.

It came as a shock because Semmes had not expected the end to come so soon. When the rich Anglo-Irish parliamentarian Thomas Conolly visited him the week before, Semmes had put on the required brave face and showed the British tourist around the *Virginia II*. Back in the wardroom, in front of his officers Semmes bluffly told Conolly he was sure the South would ultimately win.[14] That had been bravado for the foreigner, but Semmes still could not believe the end had come so quickly in the mundane shape of this slim, sealed order brought in by a courier who had the bad manners to interrupt his dinner. It irritated Semmes that Mallory had not given him more warning. For the South's second-highest-ranking and most successful sailor, though, orders were orders.

Semmes knew he could not do much before the sun set, or he would raise the enemy's suspicions. It seemed incongruous to him to contemplate the destruction of his fleet. "The afternoon was calm, and nature was just beginning to put on her spring attire," he remembered. "The fields were green with early grass, the birds were beginning to twitter, and the ploughman had already broken up his fields for planting his corn."[15] It made him sick at heart to know that when the *Allison* steamed back past him, the cheers of the returned prisoners at the sight of the Confederate flag flying from his halyard—and they always cheered—would soon turn to tears.

The admiral sent an officer ashore to the closest signal station for more news from the Navy Department, but no clarification came over the telegraph line to guide him. At first Semmes decided that once night fell he would run the ships the short distance back up to Drewry's Bluff, blow up the ironclads, and then steam up to Richmond in the wooden gunboats. But being enjoined to stealth, he decided instead to scuttle the iron ships quietly rather than set explosive charges.

On its way back upriver, Ould's flag-of-truce ship came upon the three Confederate ironclads. Since the *Allison* passed downstream earlier, the ships had raised steam and cut away the outriggers designed to thwart drifting mines. The current was swift from the runoff after the previous week's rains. With their undersized engines, the ironclads encountered heavy going as they struggled upstream. The *Allison* gave one of them, the *Fredericksburg*, a tow. After casting off the line to the ironclad at Drewry's Bluff, the *Allison* continued on to the capital. With no regulation running lights, it relied on the captain's knowledge of the river and a first-quarter moon to guide it safely past the mines to Richmond.[16]

AT MAYOR MAYO'S request, the city council gathered at four o'clock in a dingy room in the upper story of the Capitol. Nearly three years before, in the spring of 1862, a Union army had approached within sight of the city's church spires. Mayo had vowed eternal defiance then. He would never surrender. But now he told his colleagues that the government would evacuate the capital that night and take the army with it.

While they continued to deliberate, confusion was growing. Mayo was his own courier, hurrying back and forth between the council meeting and Confederate officials for the latest word. "Excited, incoherent, chewing tobacco defiantly," recalled a sympathetic witness, he was "yet full of pluck, having the mettle of the true Virginia gentleman."[17] He left the meeting in search of Breckinridge but returned empty-handed. The council then agreed that when it finally adjourned for the evening, it would reassemble at nine o'clock Monday morning, a pledge the members doubted they could keep.

First they reached an important decision: they must destroy the liquor supply before civic order completely collapsed. David Burr, a wealthy investor in tobacco, shipping, and insurance, made the motion. Uppermost in his and his colleagues' minds was the prospect of their city being sacked by its own drunken residents within a few hours. The council appointed twenty-five men in each of the three wards to act on behalf of the city. Their mission was to destroy all the liquor they could find and give the owners dubious receipts pledging the city's credit for repayment.

After taking this bold step, some councilmen drew back from the destruction of private property. Nathanael Hill moved that they not destroy any liquor until they received explicit orders for the evacuation. His resolution lost in favor of tobacco merchant James Scott's compromise: they would immediately begin to gather the liquor to a central warehouse and destroy it when it became necessary. They soon realized that there was hardly time to locate the liquor and destroy it where it was stored, much less move it to another location.

Some members still refused to face the most important task before them. Particularly vocal were Hill and Richard Walker, business manager of the *Examiner* and, since Thursday, the paper's owner upon the death of his friend John Daniel. But the majority knew their duty. Allen Stokes, a commission merchant, took the lead. He proposed—and the council agreed—that they appoint a delegation "to meet the Federal authorities to make such arrangements for the surrender of the City as may best protect the interests of the citizens."[18]

WHILE HIS CABINET secretaries saw to their departments, the president remained in his office. The chief clerk, Micajah Clark, supervised the removal of the executive office's archives. In the meantime, Davis's aides took other papers to pack in a trunk back at the presidential mansion. Davis did not leave his office until five o'clock, by which time he learned two small pieces of intelligence that would guide his course. Breckinridge had heard from Lee, who said he thought the Danville railroad would be safe until the morning. The competent secretary of war also told his chief he had arranged for a presidential train to leave from the Danville station about seven. In the event of a break in the line, they would take horses in one of the cars to give them another option for escape.

As Davis walked home from the office, nervous citizens accosted him on the streets and asked if the rumors were true. Years later Davis would claim that when he admitted the truth they replied, "If the success of the cause requires you to give up Richmond, we are content."[19]

The house Davis was leaving was filled with private memories as well as official Confederate ones. His had been a tempestuous marriage. He had tried to dominate headstrong Varina Howell in Mississippi before they were married and afterward, in Washington, when he was a senator and cabinet officer. Nearly two decades his junior, she had resisted. The stress of war, however, had brought them closer together.

On Friday, Jefferson and Varina had made a tearful parting at the Danville station, as the two children clung to their father and begged to stay with him. She argued with him, but in this instance he was the more insistent: she must leave the capital because evacuation was imminent. Before she left, he ordered a small Colt pistol and fifty rounds of ammunition from the ordnance depot and showed her how to use them. Rather than submit to capture, he told her, she must "force your assailants to kill you."[20]

At least in this matter he showed a forlorn realism, even if he still did not entirely accept the necessity for evacuation. He sent her away with the children, her sister, a black coachman and maid, and the children of a cabinet member. Davis gave her their remaining money and kept for himself a single $5 gold piece. Before they left, she had sold much of what furnishings belonged to them. This did not amount to much because the presidential family had occupied the Crenshaws' completely furnished mansion. All that was left for the president to do Sunday evening was pack a few clothes and toiletries in a carpetbag.

Edward Pollard, writing after the fact, unfairly blamed Davis for Confederate failure. But the editor was not far off the mark when he described the president's refusal to acknowledge impending defeat, "in the last moment . . . issuing edicts, playing with the baubles of authority."[21] Even then, Davis would not admit the likelihood of failure, but he was not the only one. That same afternoon, Lee dictated a long letter to the president discussing in hopeful details the Confederacy's plans for recruiting black men to the colors. That he diverted precious minutes from directing his army's withdrawal suggests a certain lack of realism on the part of the general, too.[22]

At the presidential mansion, they acted out the unraveling of Confederate authority in miniature. From midafternoon on, three loyal aides sorted and packed papers. When Davis arrived, he found them still at work, but there were also some hangers-on getting drunk. He had sent his secretary, Burton Harrison, on the train with his wife on Friday, but Harrison had left a trunk with confidential dispatches from Lee. Davis directed the aides to put the other papers in the trunk. He suggested to his housekeeper that she pack up the furniture and left a note commending her to Mayor Mayo's care. The president did not completely trust the woman, though, because she might fail to do his bidding out of fear the Federal occupiers would punish her.[23]

Davis remained calm throughout. Once he had packed his few personal belongings, he "sat on a divan in his study, sad, but calm and dignified."[24] At length, the carriage arrived to take him to the Richmond & Danville depot. As he stepped up into the seat, he lit one of his ubiquitous cigars and took his leave of the White House of the Confederacy.

THE SHOCKING NEWS from Petersburg left many civilians uncertain about what to do. One of them sought out the one man in the government she trusted for good sense, Assistant Secretary of War Campbell. He told her to stay in town. She would be perfectly safe. John

Jones, the editor-clerk who worked under Campbell in the War Department, ran into him that afternoon hurrying down the street, law books under his arm, talking to himself.[25] That image of an absent-minded legal scholar could not have been more misleading. Campbell was no more eccentric than that other conspicuous Richmond resident erroneously thought to be scatterbrained, Union spy Elizabeth Van Lew.

A strict constructionist from Alabama, Campbell, when he sat on the U.S. Supreme Court, had voted with the majority in the Dred Scott case that held that blacks were not citizens. He had emancipated his own bondsmen, however, at the time of his appointment to the Court. "A cold man, hard, and with an air of great superiority" was how the French consul in Richmond described him. Partly bald, Campbell had a high forehead and bushy eyebrows that gave him a severe, intelligent appearance. Serious to the point of haughtiness, he lived for work. If he lacked the vocal presence of a political orator, his thin voice nevertheless conveyed a quiet authority. "His personal majesty overcame you—it was almost oppressive, even when he was most friendly."[26]

As assistant Confederate secretary of war, he administered the distasteful conscription law and made his share of enemies issuing and withholding passports for civilians wishing to go through southern lines to the North. By early 1865, he was convinced the cause was hopeless. In March, Campbell wrote his boss, Secretary of War Breckinridge. "The South may succumb," he said, "but it is not necessary that she should be destroyed."[27] He now bent his efforts to that end.

Davis was no good for the South in this moment of ultimate crisis, Campbell later recalled. He was "unfitted to manage a revolution or to conduct an administration. Slow, procrastinating, obstructive, filled with petty scruples and doubts . . . an incubus and a mischief."[28] Campbell resolved to remain in Richmond while the rest of the Confederate government fled. He held no brief, had no commission from that government to treat with the Union forces. But the fifty-four-year-old jurist had one more thing to do for Virginia, though he was not a Virginian, one more effort to make for the whole Confederate South. And his actions would resonate far beyond the city on the James. Indeed, they would attempt to alter the outcome of the whole war and give a different result to the four years of internecine bloodshed.

CHAPTER 7

FLITTING SHADOWS

Sunday, April 2, Evening

Everything seemed to go to pieces at once.
—George Cary Eggleston[1]

Sometime late on Sunday, compositors at the *Examiner* set the type for the last commentary that would ever appear in that fiery advocate of southern independence. Dated "Monday Morning, April 3, 1865," and probably written by the Irish editor, John Mitchel, it was destined to be read by very few Richmonders—and by none under the Confederate flag. "We are now in the very crisis and agony of the campaign," the writer admitted. "Yesterday may have been the decisive day of protracted fighting before Petersburg. Any hour may decide the fate of Richmond, if that fate be not already determined."[2]

ALL SUNDAY AFTERNOON and into the night, Clement Sulivane toiled at a disheartening task. He was a twenty-six-year-old Confederate army captain from Maryland, a border slave state that remained with the Union but divided bitterly and sent thousands of soldiers to both sides. Sulivane was supposed to form up a local brigade of soldiers who were on detached duty as government clerks and mechanics in the munitions factories. He knew the brigade's military value existed largely in the fantasies of his superiors, but orders were orders. As if building sand castles at the shore, he would assemble a company, only to have it melt away. It did not help matters that senior officials repeatedly stole his men to pack up archives and supplies that they wanted to take with them.

Provost Marshal Isaac Carrington had a bigger headache. Two weeks before, he had joked to a friend that a new pair of boots put him "in such good marching trim . . . if the Yankees come." It was no longer a joking matter. A coarse man, rough to the point of brusqueness, he had just the temperament for the job of keeping public order during the evacuation. In the meantime, he also had the responsibility of providing directions for Ewell's force after it abandoned the capital. There were three possible lines of march, one southwest along the railroad, another along the north bank of the James River, and a third in between. Carrington tried to find experienced guides to lead the way. Down the rail line at Bacon Quarter Branch, the unhelpful assistant quartermaster replied to his hurried request with a disconcerting cable: "I have no one here who knows anything about the road to Danville."[3]

Carrington's most important duty concerned the demolition that officials had argued about for days. General Ewell stuck grimly to his orders, despite the arguments, and told the provost marshal to be ready on short notice to burn the government tobacco warehouses. Carrington assigned three officers to the warehouses in question— Shockoe, Van Gronin's, and a third one near the Petersburg depot. He notified the fire department and warned it to have its engines standing by in case any of the flames spread.

Ewell also gave Clement Sulivane another task besides forming up the fugitive local forces. With a nervous tic, the curt older man ordered him to take his tiny command and protect Mayo's toll bridge until the army's rear guard under South Carolina general Martin Gary passed over to the south side. By that point, Carrington's men should have fired the tobacco warehouses and the railroad bridges. It would be up to Sulivane to perform the final act of demolition and burn Mayo's bridge, the last intact span across the river.

A bridge of that name had crossed the James since 1788, when a grandson of the man who surveyed the original site of Richmond built the first one. Toll income made the Mayos rich and emboldened them to rebuild each time ice or floods destroyed their livelihood. Like its predecessors, the bridge in 1865 passed from the little community of Manchester on the south side of the James, over an island in the middle of the stream where the tollbooth stood, and then on into the heart of the capital's business district at Fourteenth Street. Since Sunday afternoon, civilian traffic clogged the bridge and threatened to delay the army's withdrawal. Sulivane feared conditions would be much worse by dawn when he would have to carry out his orders.

The driver of one private conveyance, an army wagon carrying the body of Gen. A. P. Hill and the general's widow and children, had already discovered the difficulty of crossing against the flood of traffic that poured southward over the bridge. A Union soldier had shot the general through the heart earlier on Sunday near Petersburg, and his family wanted to bury him at Hollywood Cemetery on the north bank of the James. Dolly, the widow, sat beside her husband's body as the wagon creaked over the rutted highway. A cape covered the general's face but not his left hand, mangled by the same bullet that pierced his heart. The image that stuck in Dolly's mind from the journey was of the wedding band, still on that wounded hand, glinting in the light.

When the wagon reached the south end of the bridge in the afternoon, it had to wait until after midnight for the torrent of refugees to abate. The widow and children left the wagon while the two Hill nephews accompanying the body pressed on. They took the remains to a building on Capitol Square, while they looked for a coffin. No one answered their calls at Belvin's furniture store, so they went in anyway, took a pine coffin, and placed the corpse in it with some difficulty because the box was slightly too small for the body.

Burial at Hollywood was now out of the question. With the city descending into anarchy and the Federal army expected at any time, the nephews decided instead to opt for a temporary grave at the family home. That meant recrossing the bridge to the south, but it also meant the traffic would be in their favor. As the impromptu hearse rejoined the congestion, wagons and carriages and pedestrians from all parts of the city converged on Mayo's bridge.[4]

A few blocks downstream from the bridge, a northern officer prisoner had supervised a vital distribution for his fellow inmates during the past few months. The Union army had collected parcels of shoes and clothing from individual families and private charities and sent them up the river by flag-of-truce boat. On Sunday morning the officer was engaged in this work as usual, but in the afternoon word came to put all the men on the steamer for exchange. Before long, Libby Prison was empty of Union soldiers. Major Turner, the prison official so lately inspired by raising black troops for the Confederacy, came to the Union officer that night and said, "Well, Captain, I am going to leave you Libby; we have concluded to evacuate the city."[5]

Turner himself received new orders to create a mobile prison administration. He was to gather a small guard and enough surgeons and prison officials to handle the expected influx of POWs generated by the campaign as Lee's army moved to the west.[6] It was unclear whether the adjutant who conveyed these orders really thought the major could patch together such an organization on the fly. But he had his own orders and so passed along the one for Turner. A more pressing challenge for the Confederates than creating a mobile Libby Prison would be to avoid capture themselves.

FIVE RAIL LINES fed into the city at the beginning of the war, but only one link offered any hope of salvation to the Confederate government that Sunday. The Richmond & Danville line originated from its depot on the north side of the river, at the foot of Fourteenth Street next to the north end of Mayo's toll bridge. Like the rest of the South's rail network, the Danville line lacked the steel rails, gravel-ballasted roadbeds, and coal-fired engines found in the North. All the rails in Virginia were iron, not steel. The ties, cut from oak and other hardwoods along the route, were laid directly in the dirt rather than in a gravel roadbed. And all of the engines were wood burners, a circumstance that required frequent stops for both fuel and water. The Tredegar foundry had not produced a single new rail since the beginning of the war, leaving the South's railroads to cannibalize themselves. Abused by overwork and deferred maintenance along the line, trains leaving from the Danville station could not hope to travel faster than about ten miles an hour.

Peter Helms Mayo had had little food or sleep since Friday. Employed by the Department of Railroad Transportation, young Mayo was responsible for moving soldiers between Richmond and Petersburg. There was much to do, as observers in the Union watchtowers east of the capital could see that weekend. Shortly after noon on Sunday, Mayo received different orders: to prepare a train especially for the president and cabinet and another to bear the archives and treasure of the Confederacy to Danville. Because it was Sunday, railroad workers were scattered throughout the city. Mayo used the steam whistle on an old shifting engine to give the signal for them to assemble at the depot. By early evening, he was ready for his special passengers and freight.[7]

THE CONFEDERATE FORCE defending Richmond north of the James prepared as stealthily as possible to disengage from its trench works, cross the river, and strike out to the southwest to join Lee. At some points of the line, in an arc sweeping from northeast of the city to the river on the southeast, only a few hundred feet separated the opposing armies. Their respective pickets were even closer. Until nightfall, about seven o'clock, the Confederates tried to maintain the usual appearance of Sunday rest in their camps. Then, almost until the moon set, early the next morning, regimental bands filled the air with patriotic tunes.

Neither night nor military music, however, could conceal the noise of a giant string of camps in the process of moving. The creak of wagons, braying of mules, and shouts of soldiers ordering and cursing one another should have alerted the Union men nearby, but they did not. Sometimes, by accident or through the stupidity of a soldier, a hut or pile of brush would catch fire. Even that did not alert their enemies. Try as they might, officers could not prevent the commotion or stifle the shouts. Before the main body of Confederate infantry passed through the city, long mule-drawn supply trains rumbled over the cobbles, converging on the toll bridge. "The wheels of the great army wagons," wrote Susan Hoge, "were deafening all night."[8]

Moses Handy, the young Confederate courier, returned to camp at eleven o'clock, his underfed horse cantering at a measured gait. A fire still smoldered in the hearth of his own cabin, but he could find no sign of life in any of the others, only a pet dog and her puppies that followed him through the bivouac. At his office, the maps, stationery, and drawings were scattered about. Piles of documents wrapped in official red tape smoldered in the fire. He returned to his cabin for one last look, patted the dog on the head, and headed for the Osborne Turnpike for the ride into town.

At a telegraph office he learned that his general and staff were already at engineer headquarters in town. The operator gave him another dispatch for the colonel in charge of the intermediate line of fortifications that he would pass on his way into the city. "Lest you should lose it," the telegraph man said, "I will give you its substance: 'Spike your guns . . . and scatter your ammunition, before evacuating your post."[9] Some artillery batteries followed orders by chopping their wheel spokes with axes and pounding rat-tailed files into the touchholes of their cannon. But many, perhaps most, of the guns they left behind remained in working order.

Soldiers, provost guards, wagons, caissons, and the inevitable stragglers clogged the main road into town. To Handy, they even seemed to be in good humor. Some of them were singing, and others chaffed him for the lean condition of his horse. By about midnight he reached the intermediate line of fortification, where he attempted to deliver the order given him by the telegraph operator. The colonel in charge had already abandoned his post but had failed to spike his guns or destroy his ammunition. Handy found the guard tent empty, too, so he threw the message on the hearth fire.

After he left, he fell in with Gen. Porter Alexander and a colonel of engineers. The colonel was gloomy and Alexander, the perennial optimist, tried to jolly him up as they rode. Handy secured leave for an

hour to visit relatives and then made his way to the engineers' headquarters to see what role the evacuation would have for him.

As the army gradually disengaged from its fortifications east of the
city, many soldiers left their units. Some, like the young courier,
wanted a chance to say farewell to relatives in town. Some never intended to return. Porter Alexander completed arrangements for his
batteries to cross the river and, with two or three hours to spare, rode
off to the house of his sister-in-law, Lucy Webb, matron of a nearby
officers' hospital. The house was full of men in uniform, and her
kitchen "was cooking a steady stream of biscuits & meat in shape to
take in one's hands & eat, or to pack in one's pockets & haversack, &
every man was both eating & packing all he could carry."[10]

The hospital provided the rations, but Alexander feared Webb
would have nothing left for herself before the night was over. It was
well after midnight when he left for his post at Mayo's bridge to give
orders to each battery as it passed. "The city was a sad sight," he wrote
the next day, "every house was alight & open & the women & children generally crying on the steps or standing silent on the corners of
the streets." Josiah Gorgas's family was among them. The ordnance
chief made arrangements for a wagon to move his belongings sometime before daylight, but he could not remain. His wife, Amelia, resolved to stay in the city. "About midnight I left her," he wrote, "still
standing like a brave woman over the remnants of her household
goods."[11]

At the Crenshaw household, one of Richmond's wealthiest, they
passed out food to the men marching by—hoe cakes, ham, biscuits,
whatever was at hand. Betty Saunders, a plain, square-jawed young
woman who was living with the Crenshaws, helped distribute the
food. She was expecting a particular soldier. Walter Herron Taylor, one
of Lee's adjutants at his headquarters, had telegraphed in the afternoon to alert Saunders. By prearrangement, they were to be married
that night. In her wedding dress of black muslin and gray linen, she
waited. Shortly after midnight Taylor arrived. Dr. Minnigerode performed the ceremony in the upstairs sitting room so the crippled lady
of the house could also attend. During the brief ritual, intermittent

sobbing by the few guests accompanied the exchange of vows. Min-nigerode wept with them.[12] After a wedding meal, the newlyweds parted, and Taylor rode away to rejoin the army.

It was a romantic interlude in a hellish night for Confederate Richmond. Romantic or not, Taylor had acted irresponsibly. Lee agreed to his surprising request for a few hours' leave to run up to town to be married, even though he needed every possible hand at his under-staffed headquarters to help orchestrate the withdrawal. Taylor com-mandeered the engine of the last hospital train to Richmond in order to overtake another train up ahead.[13] He succeeded but in his personal quest did not stop to think that appropriating a train for his own use might jeopardize the men in the hospital cars.

At Chimborazo, hospital matron Phoebe Pember said good-bye to soldiers fit enough to leave. Her male nurses left to follow Lee's army, and her black cooks disappeared. Many patients were recently ex-changed prisoners. Their experience in Federal detention camps spurred some of them, still recovering from illness, to hobble off to avoid recapture. "The miracles of the New Testament had been re-enacted," the cynical Pember recalled later, inured by long practice to suspect every patient of malingering, "the lame, the halt, and the blind had been cured." From her perspective on the plateau east of town, she had a distant view of the turmoil that enveloped Richmond households that afternoon and evening. As night fell, she wrapped herself in a shawl-blanket and sat watching the frantic preparations down below.[14]

At the governor's mansion, Elizabeth Smith supervised the packing of her family's personal belongings. The superintendent of public buildings helped her box up the cutlery and silverware that belonged to the Commonwealth of Virginia, save only a few serving pieces for the family to use. With the governor's concurrence, the superinten-dent put this chest for safekeeping in the vault of the Exchange Bank.[15]

JOHN HALE, the Treasury Department's chief clerk, had been busy that afternoon sending his last dispatches. These were mainly telegraphic arrangements for safeguarding the bullion on the journey south. On the authority of Treasury Secretary Trenholm, Hale requested transportation for seven of his clerks and insisted that they ride with the boxes of gold and silver. He asked for passage as far as Charlotte, North Carolina. In his haste he added—whether consciously or not—that the clerks' tickets take them to Charlotte "and return."[16]

When midshipmen from the naval academy arrived at the Danville depot early in the evening, they formed up outside the building and listened as their officers told them they were entrusted with guarding the government's archives and its treasure. Then they marched into the depot while the train was still being loaded, fixed bayonets, and cleared the building. When Superintendent Parker arrived later, he found his students guarding the train as they had been ordered.

The treasure consisted of an undetermined amount, variously estimated afterward to be anywhere from a quarter to a half million in bullion and specie: Mexican silver dollars, Maria Theresa dollars, double-eagle gold pieces, ingots in squat, square boxes, and bags and small kegs of assorted coins of silver and baser metals. A little less than half belonged to the Confederate government, and the rest was the property of the Richmond banks. Or so the senior bank teller told Parker. The sailor never saw any of it, only the boxes and barrels that contained it. That was enough for him; he knew his duty.[17]

With his officers and sailors added to the midshipmen, Parker commanded a force about a hundred strong. Because of the crush of people trying to finagle a seat on one of the last trains, he told guards at the station doors to refuse entry to anyone. There were plenty of faint-hearted patriots trying to requisition seats. Passengers crowded both presidential and treasure trains, on every flat surface, including the tops of the cars. Parker, a third-generation sailor, had been at the evacuation of Norfolk, Virginia, three years earlier. He had seen it before—the increasing timidity of guards to assert order, the gradual descent into chaos, the drunken looters. The anxious scenes around the depot, where his midshipmen still maintained a semblance of authority, were harbingers of the anarchy to come after the last train departed.[18]

Among those seeking a place was slave trader Robert Lumpkin. He did not come alone but brought with him the last coffle of slaves in the Confederate capital, about fifty men, women, and children bound together in chains. They would be worth nothing to him in the morning. His only hope of preserving his investment was to move them south with the government to the shrinking part of America that still recognized slavery. Parker's midshipmen turned them away at the depot door. Dejected, Lumpkin had no choice but to march them all back to his brick slave jail near Capitol Square for their last night in bondage.[19]

While he waited at the depot—for hours, as it turned out—Parker had a chance to observe the Confederate leaders. He thought Davis maintained a "calm and dignified manner" while all around him was chaos. Besides Davis, only Breckinridge won his admiration.[20] One figure stood out conspicuously among the cabinet secretaries and aides-de-camp. Anna Trenholm had sent her daughters on ahead on the special train with Varina Davis on Friday. As the only female passenger on the president's train, she cared for her sick husband, Treasury Secretary George Trenholm. He boarded the carriage well provisioned for the trip with a hamper of peach brandy—"supplies for the inner man," in the words of a colleague. It did him little good, as self-medication with alcohol and morphine made Trenholm a very sick man indeed.[21]

The delay stretched on into the night. Some passengers thought Breckinridge and the president were hoping for a last-minute stay of execution from Lee. Davis may have hoped for such word, but Breckinridge did not, and none came. They talked at length with the railroad president in his office at the Danville station. When Davis returned to his seat on the train, it was about eleven o'clock. The secretary of war mounted his horse and spoke to the president through the open window for a few moments longer. He intended to stay in town until Ewell's force left.

It was nearly midnight when the overburdened train inched out of the station and out onto the trestle across the James. The treasury train left even later, with midshipmen stationed in each car, armed with two revolvers each. At the beginning of the journey, as soon as each train left the depot, passengers on the left side were only a few yards from the nearby toll bridge. Through the gloom they would have been able to see, slipping slowly past their windows, the unhappy sight of army engineers piling up pine knots and barrels of tar and turpentine for the last act of demolition. Secretary of the Navy Mallory remembered the view of the city: "As the fugitives receded from the flickering lights, many and sad were the commentaries they made upon the Confederate cause." Perhaps their commentaries were silent reflections, for another passenger recalled, "I never knew so little conversation indulged by so large a number of acquaintances together."[22]

Lt. John S. Wise, the nineteen-year-old son of a former governor, vividly remembered the incongruous cargoes of these trains, constituting a veritable "government on wheels." The passage of time and postwar alienation from other guardians of the Confederate legacy encouraged Wise to embellish his recollections of this momentous night. For he wrote with extravagance and little sympathy of "trains bearing indiscriminate cargoes of men and things. In one car was a cage with an African parrot, and a box of tame squirrels, and a hunchback!"[23]

OUTSIDE THE CITY, in the countryside to the north and west still in Confederate hands, knowledge of what was happening in the capital spread erratically. To the north, the minister of Emmanuel Church at Brook Hill went about his usual Sunday duties. Cornelius Walker discounted rumors of evacuation. After he conducted an afternoon service for the black members of his church, however, he was troubled to learn that a neighbor had gone into Richmond because he feared bad news. Walker himself made his way on foot to the quarters of the Virginia Military Institute at the former almshouse on the northern edge of town to see his son, one of the cadets. The minister heard progressively more ominous reports confirming evacuation. Despite these portents, he was still able to write that evening, "Beautiful moon light night, & as I passed through the outskirts heard distant church bells, wh[ich] seemed to reassure me."[24]

Josiah Gorgas was reassured, too. When he walked down to the

Danville depot a little after midnight, stillness and order prevailed in the streets. Before leaving Richmond, he wanted to check at his complex of arsenal buildings near the entrance to the Tredegar ironworks. When he had satisfied himself and walked back out through the arsenal gates, the sentry was still on duty. Everything seemed in place for an orderly evacuation when he left on one of the last trains about one in the morning. He had failed to persuade his superiors not to burn the warehouses and bridges, but he gave special, explicit orders that nothing under his direct command should be destroyed, "lest fires might be general, & the innocent inhabitants suffer."[25]

Even as Gorgas took heart from his inspection of the arsenal, however, cracks in the veneer of law and order were radiating out from the center of town. They almost trapped the few state legislators still in the capital. On Sunday afternoon, a rump of both houses of the legislature met at the Capitol. Governor Smith shuffled back and forth between their deliberations and conferences with Davis and Breckinridge. At nine o'clock, with the bleak news from Lee confirmed, the legislators decided to leave by packet boat in two hours. The James River and Kanawha Canal would take them westward toward Lynchburg more than a hundred miles away.

At eleven, they gathered at the canal turning basin, four blocks below Capitol Square. By then disorder was spreading. "Scene of confusion. No one in authority," noted state legislator John Coles Rutherfoord as he waited.[26] To their consternation, the legislators discovered that cadets of the Virginia Military Institute had commandeered one of the boats meant for them. The VMI colonel and a state senator got into a heated argument that threatened to become a brawl. One of the cadets' guns accidentally discharged and killed a man.

David Stewart and another legislator left the basin to get orders to sort out the tangle from Governor Smith, still at his office at the mansion. Sixty-seven years old and full of bluff southern patriotism, "Extra Billy" Smith had earned his nickname long before for tacking additional fees onto his contracts for delivering mail. After a term as governor depleted his personal finances, the shrewd and pugnacious Smith revived his fortunes in San Francisco at the height of the Gold

Rush. He returned to Virginia and served first as a Confederate brigadier and then as governor again. He was not as spry as the day when he had led a charge at First Manassas, dressed in a business suit because he had no uniform and carrying a vivid blue umbrella to ward off the hot July sun, if not Yankee bullets. He had demonstrated great physical courage on that day, and circumstances seemed about to require more of the same before the sun came up again.

Smith decreed that a boat be set aside for the legislators and authorized the captain of the guard "if necessary to clear the Boat of all others."[27] A clerk dashed off the order, the last Confederate directive issued on the gubernatorial stationery. The frantic circumstances are apparent in the blobs of ink and slashing pen strokes of the clerk. The palsied signature of the governor contrasted with Smith's bold decisions and his determination to carry on. In a few hours, men of a different allegiance would be scribbling out orders on the same letterhead.

When Stewart and his colleague raced back to the basin with the order in hand, they compelled the boat that had pushed off from the wharf to return. Most of the remaining legislators boarded the narrow wooden vessel, as overloaded according to its own limits as the railcars of Davis's train. Stewart's colleague jumped aboard, and just as he took the last piece of luggage from Stewart, the boat shoved off again. The hapless Stewart and four other legislators were left with the second boat weighted down by state-owned weapons. Luckily for them, they found the last team of mules in the stables and a driver to hitch them to the boat. It was after one o'clock when the mules strained at their harnesses and pulled the boat, now so low in the water that it often scraped bottom. It inched westward with maddening slowness.[28]

The governor put the state's second auditor, H. W. Thomas of Fairfax, in charge of the Capitol and other public buildings with instructions to make the best arrangements possible with the enemy. Thomas had his hands full already. All night long he carted out papers from his office—contractors' accounts, claims filed by survivors of soldiers killed in action, the mundane evidence of Confederate administration.

They were not important enough to evacuate and went only as far as the impromptu bonfires in the street outside Thomas's office. There they lit up the darkness as they curled and dissolved in the flames.[29]

Because he hoped to reestablish the state government in Lynchburg, Governor Smith declined Davis's offer of a seat on the presidential train headed for Danville. Giving the last orders to the auditor, he took leave of Elizabeth and his daughter, Mary Amelia. A few minutes after the last canal boat left, so did Smith. With his son and George, a slave, he set off in the dark up the towpath on horseback.[30]

John Campbell, the assistant secretary of war, remained at his department until all the public buildings were empty and the trains and packet boats had gone, leaving him the highest-ranking Confederate official in Richmond. The only sounds he heard were the rumble of army wagons and the tramp of soldiers' shoes as the defenders of the capital marched south across Mayo's bridge to join Lee. His son, a nephew, and two sons-in-law left with them. By then, a southern memoirist would later write, "all the flitting shadows of a Lost Cause had passed away under a heaven studded by bright stars."[31]

CHAPTER 8

MAD REVELRY
OF CONFUSION

Monday, April 3, Darkness to First Light

Hell is empty, and all the devils are here.
—*The Tempest,* act 1, scene 2

The first sign of chaos sprang from the city council's efforts to prevent it. About midnight—not long after Davis's train left—the ward committeemen designated to destroy the city's liquor began their work. They easily identified the major legal supplies and soon had whiskey barrels by the dozen rolling out of warehouses and into the streets. A sharp stroke with the blunt end of an ax was enough to send the contents cascading into the gutter. They threw bottles of brandy and wine out the windows to smash on the cobblestones below.

Following orders, they handed out receipts pledging the city would make good on the loss at a later date. Government commissaries undertook the same task at the Confederate storage building at Cary and Pearl streets, a former wholesale grocery store where they kept huge quantities of medicinal whiskey and brandy.

With the last government trains departed, no more steam whistles pierced the night air with their shrill cries. In their place, the more ominous sounds of thumping axes and shattering glass attracted attention, and enough unbroken whiskey casks remained to cause mischief. As if by magic, the actions of the committeemen conjured up a crowd intent on plunder, lured by the alcoholic scent that presaged the collapse of law and order. Soon intoxicated men, women, and, it was later said, even children crouched down on their knees to scoop up the liquid from the gutters in their hats and hands.

The city council had inadvertently encouraged the very thing it had hoped to avoid. Stragglers who slipped away from their regiments as they marched through town added to the disorder. If the committeemen had had a few more hours to complete their task, or could have done it during daylight, under guard, the provost marshal might have cowed the mob. In the dead of night, with the army in retreat, it was a task at once hopeless, thankless, and demoralizing. What followed, lamented a Confederate chronicler, was "a mad revelry of confusion."[1]

WHEN HE WALKED to engineer headquarters at Nineteenth and Franklin streets, the courier Moses Handy was surprised to find the streets full of people. At headquarters, officers were sitting around a coal fire to ward off the night chill. Even though it was April, it was a cold evening. Couriers fiddled their time away, awaiting orders. The engineers' black teamsters slept on their wagons or slipped away to take part in the plunder that was spreading through the business district. The few guards in evidence made a feeble attempt to assert authority by periodically halting and questioning black people and soldiers on the street. But the islands of order, like the engineers' office, were gradually sinking beneath the rising tide of anarchy.

When Handy learned that his command would not abandon the city until dawn, he asked permission to leave the quiet of the office and investigate the wild scenes outside. At Antoni's confectionery store, the proprietor offered to give the mob all of his wares if they would not wreck the shop. Guards arrived just as he gave away the last stick of peppermint. Broken glassware, candies, jellies, cakes, and children's toys were trampled underfoot. Handy stuffed a pound of cream candy into his pockets, a present from a looter, and an acknowledgment that he was now one, too.

The courier then fell in with a dozen men, most of them soldiers, at the sign of a large gilded hat, the trademark of Dooley's factory. He entered the storeroom and saw men ransacking the furnishings, with hats of all kinds strewn about, civilian and military, straw, beaver, and silk. Handy chose artillery and navy caps and a parson's beaver. He meant to replace his own worn hat with the artillery cap, give the navy one to a friend, and sell the beaver for profit. But by the time he regained the street, he had lost the two caps. He threw away the beaver hat with an oath and turned away in disgust. He did not deign to refuse the gift of two more hats from another looter, however. "It is every man for himself," said the thief, "and the devil for us all, to-night." As the hours of darkness waned, deserters, hungry civilians, and slaves anticipating their coming freedom filled the streets. They shoved their way into storefronts, breaking windows and pillaging as they went. George Camp, the banker who had mused the day before on how beautiful the city was, watched them, appalled. "Thousands of low whites & negroes held the streets & staggered under the loads of goods they had stolen."[2] He had never in his life seen so many drunken people.

RAPHAEL SEMMES LATER claimed that the glow in the sky from fires in town changed his mind about how to scuttle his fleet. His memory was faulty, because there were no large fires until closer to dawn. For whatever reason, instead of silently sinking his flotilla, he reverted to his original plan for a more dramatic finale. After his sailors packed up their personal belongings, they armed themselves from their ships' stores and improvised haversacks and canteens for the march once they reached shore. No later than three o'clock in the morning, the last of the ironclad crews transferred to the wooden gunboats for the run up to Richmond. As they did, demolition squads set charges aboard the three large armored vessels sentenced to die there at their moorings.

Their work was not as secretive as they hoped. The Union picket ship that night was the *Commodore Perry*, a wooden side-wheel steamer. The sailors on watch no longer had a clear view of the closest Confederate ironclads, as they normally did, because Semmes had run all of his ships upstream to Drewry's Bluff after dark. Though they could no longer see their adversaries, shortly after three o'clock the Yankee tars spotted a dark object drifting downriver toward them. They snagged it with grappling hooks and identified it as the raft that Confederate sailors moored alongside their ships to make repairs. Because all of the tools were still on board the raft, the northern sailors guessed what their enemies were up to—and it was a sure sign that the Confederates were about to evacuate Richmond.[3]

An hour and a half later, the *Virginia II* exploded with a shock of earthquake proportions. Semmes had not steamed far upstream when the spectacular eruption occurred. Though it marked the death of his flagship, he later admitted it was a grand sight: "The fuses were of different lengths, and as the shells exploded by twos and threes, and by the dozen, the pyrotechnic effect was very fine."[4]

Participants and later commentators understandably disputed the timing of events during the evacuation, given the confusion of the day, as well as the tricks of memory. But two reports from the Union side give a benchmark for fixing the time of the destruction of Semmes's flagship, with its indisputable, deafening end. Both confirm that the first explosion, that of the *Virginia II*, took place at about an hour and a half before sunrise, which occurred at 5:52 a.m. on April 3.

The first report came from a journalist with the Union army, who recorded the moment in a telegram marked 5:00 a.m. and sent shortly thereafter: "Just a half an hour since a most terrific explosion . . . took place in the Upper James, followed by a second one just at this moment, that leaves no doubt in the military mind here that the rebel rams [ironclads] have been blown up."[5]

The second account came from the log of the Union steamer *Malvern*, riding at anchor ten miles downstream from Semmes's fleet. This report noted the detonation with even greater precision: "At 4:35 a heavy explosion in W.N.W. direction."[6] These stupendous punctuations, first the *Virginia II* and then another, sent shock waves rolling over Richmond. Mirrors and windowpanes rattled for miles around. The explosions signaled to both sides that great events were in train.

For the Confederate sailors, a frustratingly calm interlude followed. At one of the military bridges across the river, still downstream from the city but tantalizingly within sight of it, the drawbridge was down to allow soldiers to cross from the north bank to the south. It took an hour before the retreating army let the wooden gunboats pass. By then the first streaks of dawn appeared. Up ahead, Semmes could see that in Richmond the east-facing windows caught the rays of the sun, "mimicking the real fires that were already breaking out in various parts of the city."[7]

Down in the commercial center of town, Ewell's men took all they could from the commissary depot and loaded it on wagons sent to rendezvous with Lee's army. When they had filled as many vehicles as they could find horses and mules to pull, they flung open the doors. Hundreds of people of all ages had already gathered with buckets and bags and tubs to fill with plunder. They jostled one another as they waited impatiently for the soldiers, who represented the last semblance of order, to let them in. When the moment came, they surged through the gates. They brawled and scrapped for whatever the quartermasters had left—slabs of bacon, cured hams, barrels of flour and sugar, even sacks of coffee beans smuggled through the blockade.

Some officers sent surplus provisions to the houses of their friends. The minister's wife, Susan Hoge, was grateful that General Ewell sent her a barrel of potatoes and flour. She made arrangements to order additional supplies from the commissary but could not find a horse to pull her wagon. A friend carried bags to fill for her, but the mob prevented him from returning.[8]

Taking surplus food that the army could not carry off with it was one thing, but respectable opinion on all sides denounced the looters. However, Thomas Chester, the black reporter with the Army of the James, defended the people who ransacked and stole. He identified the leader of part of the mob as an African American who carried an iron crowbar on his shoulder and wore a bright red cloth tied around his waist. The looters, white as well as black, followed him from store to store as he smashed doors and windows with the crowbar. Chester did not see any of this in person but interviewed eyewitnesses the next day when he arrived with the Union army. "It was," he pronounced, "retributive justice upon the aiders and abettors of treason to see their property fired by the rebel chiefs and plundered by the people whom they meant to forever enslave."[9]

Fannie Dickinson heard about the wild disorder when her minister husband, Alfred, came in with a colleague at one in the morning. They had spent the day preaching to the soldiers entrenched east of Richmond and brought with them tales of the anarchy developing downtown, "bonfires burning, whiskey poured out on the street, cannons and wagons in motion." Optimistic and energetic Alfred was unwontedly mute after what he had seen. "Perfectly stunned," in Fannie's words. "I think he hardly knew what he said or did."[10]

When Confederate soldiers marched in from the eastern defenses and saw the looting, some joined in. Most stayed with their units and seethed at the sight of civilians stealing the food that had been gathered for the army but was now thrown to the winds. The anger of the soldiers rose as some of the mob taunted them about welcoming the Yankees. Men who had lived in muddy trenches on stale cornmeal and a bit of rancid bacon watched in disgust as immense quantities of the army's coffee, sugar, and ham disappeared into the gloom on the backs of looters. These were Richmonders who apparently had no interest in the well-being of the scruffy soldiers in gray homespun uniforms who defended their city. Repelled by the sight, Porter Alexander blamed the disorder on "ludicrous irish & dutch & negroes, men women & children," as though he could not bear to admit that there might be native-born white people among the despoilers, even those who had supported the Confederacy.[11]

The Virginia state penitentiary stood on a hill to the west of the city and, like neighboring Hollywood Cemetery, commanded a view of the river. The building, designed by Benjamin Henry Latrobe in the heady days of rehabilitative penal philosophy, now confined about 350 men who did not share the architect's optimism. In the first hour of Monday, just before riding west, Governor Smith had ordered the superintendent and a portion of his officers to leave the prison for other duty. A smaller number of guards than usual remained.

When the inmates heard rumors that the Union army would soon arrive, they began to shout and bang on their cell doors. They managed to break out of their cells in small groups and gathered in the prison courtyard. There they threatened the guards and cowed them into giving them the keys to the outer doors. A clerk later admitted he and his colleagues gave in to the inmates because they feared for their lives. After pillaging storerooms, the enraged prisoners dispersed throughout the city but mostly to the business district to take part in the looting. Before they all had left, however, some of them thought to set the penitentiary on fire.[12]

A similar scene took place at the city jail but with a different outcome. In the face of the clamoring and screaming of their charges, the guards fled before any prisoners broke out. Only the resolute turnkey stood at his post. As a result, no prisoners escaped, and when it arrived, the Federal army stationed a guard to keep them locked up.[13]

At Tredegar, owner Joseph Reid Anderson sought assurances from the government that his foundry would not be burned. Mallory, the navy secretary, thought it should be part of the demolition plan. Gorgas argued against it, and Breckinridge sided with the chief of ordnance. Anderson took no chances. He called on the Tredegar battalion, recruited from his workers, to stand guard all night with loaded guns. The looters had no stomach for taking on armed mechanics when there were so many unguarded buildings to sack. When ammunition stored nearby began to explode later that morning, powerful shock waves blew out most of the windows at Tredegar. They damaged some of the roofs, but the munitions factory of the Confederacy, with its rolling mills, foundries, and machine and boiler shops, came through largely intact.[14]

In the widespread disorder, punctuated by explosions and fires and pillaging mobs, surprisingly few people were injured or killed. Adding up all accounts, including some clearly exaggerated ones, the total number of dead that day came to about two dozen. At a shop on Main Street, the proprietor fired his shotgun at a man breaking into the showroom glass. The thief, a Confederate straggler, was said to die from the load of buckshot in his stomach. Another man engaged in sacking a government-owned clothing store fell through a hatchway and broke his neck. At the same building a soldier, frustrated at not getting the clothes he wanted, stabbed another in the stomach and left him with the bayonet sticking in his bowels. Before the guards withdrew from their posts in front of the storehouses, some of them fired on the mob threatening to break in. In some instances, the looters shot back, and an undetermined number of people died in the crossfire.[15]

The largest confirmed number of casualties came with the destruction of the city powder magazine, a small brick building on the slope of a hill near the city poorhouse. When the superintendent of the poorhouse learned that Confederate forces intended to destroy the magazine, he moved his charges, still in their nightclothes, a safe distance away from the building. After waiting longer than they expected, some of the inmates returned to fetch warmer clothes just when the explosion occurred. Because the magazine was located in a ravine, much of the blast expended itself against the hillsides. As it was, the nearby city hospital and the poorhouse lost most of their windows. Eleven paupers died outright from concussion and flying bricks. A piece of masonry crashed through the roof of a house nearby and killed a man in his bed. "Nothing but a long narrow trench in the ground, looking like the grave of a resurrected giant, marks the spot where the magazine stood."[16]

KNOWING THE GRAVITY of his duty, Provost Marshal Isaac Carrington conferred with both Breckinridge and Ewell repeatedly before sunrise. The secretary of war reiterated the orders Ewell had given Carrington: it was necessary to set fire to the tobacco warehouses. And the bridges. About dawn, Ewell left Carrington at the corner of Fourteenth and Cary streets, where he told the provost marshal they could no longer put off the deed. Carrington then told the men assigned to burn the three warehouses to do their duty. At two of them, Shockoe and Van Gronin's warehouses, they immediately applied the torch. The railroad bridges came next.

Charles Ellis, president of the Richmond & Petersburg Railroad, had stayed all night at his depot. It was uncomfortably near the third warehouse slated for burning, and Ellis hoped to prevent Carrington's men from harming his property. When, toward morning, he thought he had succeeded, he went home, exhausted, to lie down for a nap. As soon as Ellis left, the soldiers set fire to his bridge. Though they spared the tobacco warehouse because a trainload of wounded soldiers remained in Ellis's nearby depot, it caught fire from the bridge anyway and nearly burned the patients alive. At the last minute, army doctors organized a party to shift them to safety. The flames spread so rapidly to the depot that the superintendent only barely managed to move his sick wife out of the building on a litter.[17]

Up to this point the night was calm, without any wind at all. At first when Carrington's men set the fires, the smoke rose straight up into the still air. Then a breeze began to blow. For Richmond it was an ill wind from the south that grew in strength as the sun rose, red and angry.

By DAWN President Davis's train had traveled only half the distance to Danville. There were frequent stops for wood and water and longer delays because of bad tracks. It would be afternoon before the train arrived in the tobacco town on the North Carolina–Virginia border. On the way, it passed another train filled with civilian refugees from Petersburg. They hoped to reach safety in the capital but were thrown into panic on meeting the fugitive presidential entourage and its news of Richmond's fall. Later on, Davis's train came upon a wreck. A hospital train had gone off the tracks and killed five wounded Alabama soldiers. Their mangled corpses lay alongside a long hole that two slaves were digging to receive them, yet another portent of doom.[18]

Rumors about what had happened in the capital rode into Danville on the presidential train. Richmond had been plundered by "a mob of the lower classes of the city, composed, it is said, mostly of the foreign element." So opined the Danville newspaper. "A number of its people [were] insulted, outraged, robbed and massacred," continued the paper's fanciful account. It concluded that the extent of the disaster proved there had been many and powerful "secret enemies" within.[19]

Several more trains made it from Richmond to Danville after Davis's. Each brought new rumors to contradict the last: "Lee was giving Grant a fearful castigation; so enfeebled were the Yankees, that, although Richmond was open to them, they did not enter it—Richmond was in ashes—Richmond was filled with nigger soldiers—Richmond was not disturbed—Richmond has ceased to be."[20]

The canal boats filled with state legislators made much less progress than the presidential train. Despite the slowness, the delegate from Goochland County, John Rutherfoord, remarked on the buoyant, defiant, even cheerful tone of the VMI cadets on board.[21] The boys were too young to despair like their elders at the loss of their capital. Governor Smith had fared slightly better in his ride through the darkness and up the canal towpath westward. High water from heavy spring rains had breeched the canal banks in numerous places. At one break, Extra Billy's horse tumbled in and floundered about, rider still attached. Smith extricated himself at the cost of a black eye for himself and a painful gash under a leg for his horse.

By sunup, Smith, his son, and the slave George had reached the Dover coal pits in Goochland County. They stopped there for breakfast at the house of Col. Christopher Tompkins, the mine supervisor. Fortified with a little whiskey, the governor recovered his accustomed bonhomie.[22] Fifteen miles behind Smith, his capital was about to change hands.

IN ANTICIPATION OF Captain Sulivane's final order, army engineers began rolling barrels of tar out along the length of Mayo's bridge. Just to make sure, they heaped up piles of pine knots and opened tins of kerosene. A lieutenant of engineers, seconded to Sulivane, awaited the captain's word to fire the bridge. It would be a tricky call. In the confusion of garbled communications that plagued the evacuation, it would be easy to overlook small units and some not so small that had not yet reached the bridge.

Civilians fleeing south mixed in with the soldiers and further complicated the army's progress. One of them was the fiery Irish editor John Mitchel, who had thrown his last thunderbolt from the *Examiner*. After kissing his family good-bye, he took his rifle and left for the headquarters of the reserves. With two companions, he made his way toward the stream of traffic funneling toward the bridge. When they reached their objective, an officer told them to cross immediately because the engineers were about to set it alight.[23]

John Jones, the fractious War Department clerk-diarist, had no intention of crossing Mayo's bridge that morning. Awakened by Admiral Semmes's demolition work, he walked downtown on sidewalks covered with pulverized glass and streets running with liquor. His diary entry for the day recounted the looting at length. It did not indicate whether he reflected on the oracular lines he had written in his antebellum best-selling novel *Southern Scenes*. In it, Jones had written an eerily prophetic account of civil war in America, including a description of the rear guard of the southern army crossing the river to abandon its capital, though in his fiction it was Washington, not Richmond.[24]

Pvt. John Woods, a drummer in a Georgia regimental band, was almost overlooked, or so he said, along with the rest of his fellow musicians. Only twenty, he nevertheless had survived the Seven Days, Gettysburg, and other battles. He claimed, somewhat dubiously, that the evacuation took place so quietly in his part of the defense works that he and the band did not know of the retreat until they woke up Monday morning. Realizing the army had left camp, Woods rolled up his blanket, picked up his empty haversack and canteen, strapped his drum to his back, and set off for Richmond, in hopes he was not too late. He reached the city in time to see the aftermath of Semmes's journey up the river. It was a bittersweet sight, "all the vessels on the James River, Confederate and private, floating down the river on fire, cut loose from their moorings, drifting steadily, silently, serenely, without a pilot or a flag."[25]

By now, with the sun coming up, Confederate soldiers watching from the south bank could see that the fire had become general. It was consuming not just the rail bridges but also warehouses and stores along the waterfront as the wind blew the flames up from the river toward the Capitol. To observers watching from east of the fire, especially on Church Hill, where Patrick Henry had asked for liberty or death nearly a century before, the first flashes of sunshine "burnished the fringe of smoke with lurid and golden glory." To those in the west looking east toward the flames, the sun looked "like an immense ball of blood that emitted sullen rays of light, as if loth to shine over a scene so appalling."[26]

Ewell later laid responsibility for the worst of the fires at the feet of the mob. He swore that they set fire to a large mill far from the tobacco warehouses fired by his soldiers, and he further alleged that it was that burning mill, not the warehouses, that spread the destruction. Certainly, in the predawn confusion, some of the looters may have set some fires. But Ewell convinced few people that the great fire had nothing to do with his men or their deliberate demolition of the warehouses and bridges through military orders passed down the chain of command. Ewell did not anticipate the wind that spread these flames and made the destruction wholesale, and few people accepted his attempt to deflect the blame to alleged incendiaries among the plundering mob.

Black smoke billowing up in the center of the flames marked the site of the arsenal. It was located across the street from the Richmond & Petersburg depot, which caught fire when soldiers burned the railroad's adjoining bridge. In turn, the burning depot set fire to Gorgas's arsenal. Detonating shells in the midst of the black cloud gave it the appearance and sound of a summer thunderhead, with forked lightning flashing through it. On the river the navy's ships joined the chorus as the fire reached their guns and then their magazines. The two rail bridges lit up the lingering darkness like strings of campfires miraculously suspended by high arches across the water. In the rapids below, the rushing torrent reflected the flames that were eating into the commercial center of town.

That morning, Francis Lawley, the pro-southern reporter for the London *Times*, fled north on the rail line to Fredericksburg. Like the visitor from Ireland, Thomas Conolly, with whom he had planned to dine Sunday night, Frank Lawley had been a member of Parliament. More successful as a journalist than as a politician, he was one of numerous Englishmen who came to see the rebellion firsthand. He had sent a stream of pro-Confederate dispatches back to London, including a firsthand account of Gettysburg.[27] The evacuation disrupted his plans to dine with Conolly, but before he left, he saw enough to give feeling to his last column, an eyewitness account of anarchy in the streets of Richmond. In that report, he invoked Shakespeare through Ariel's words from *The Tempest*: "Hell is empty, and all the devils are here."

On Mayo's bridge, Sulivane strained to identify the parties of soldiers and wagons making their way toward him from different streets, converging on this one last escape route open to them. Among them rode the twenty-nine-year-old general of artillery Porter Alexander. He struggled to get his light batteries across the river, at least those that had enough horses fit to pull guns and caissons. While supervising this work, he noticed that a burning canal boat had drifted or been pushed underneath the bridge and lodged there. Flames shot up through cracks in the wooden flooring. Alexander and his staff galloped across, fearing they would be cut off, even though all their guns had not yet passed over. Just in time, soldiers pried the burning canal boat away from the bridge, and Alexander's last field artillery made it through.

In the distance, Sulivane could see, or thought he could see, Yankee regiments streaming in from east of town. Were the hooves he heard clattering on Main Street Confederate or Union? The buildings blocked his view. Not taking any chances, he called his small infantry guard to arms and pulled his advance picket back across the canal. The engineer lieutenant lit his torch of fat pine. Just as he was about to give the order, Sulivane realized it was not time yet. The horses and mules he heard were pulling the last train of Confederate ambulance wagons. They would be needed in the coming campaign. More men would suffer and die before war ended in Virginia.

The ambulances were not home free yet. A mass of pillagers crowded around and prevented the harried teamsters from reaching the bridge. Sulivane ordered a subordinate to stand firm until Martin Gary's rear guard arrived, and then he turned and spurred his horse forward into the mob. As his men watched, the crowd engulfed him, but he reappeared and momentarily cleared a path for the struggling ambulances. As he did, Gary's command galloped into sight and scattered the swarm of looters. It was a close-run thing: the officers at the head of the cavalrymen had to use the flat of their sabers to prod the looters aside.

Cornelius Carlton, on picket duty the previous night with the 24th Virginia Cavalry downstream from Richmond, reached town about daybreak. A dozen of his company deserted, but despite a bad fever, Carlton remained. "What a scramble," he noted in the terse diary entry he recorded Monday night about the scene at Mayo's bridge, amid the fires and explosions and looters. Near the bridge, "one man with a hand cart bears away half [a] hogshead [of] sugar, another rolls a barrel of flour, another has a bucket of brandy. What a crowd! I can hardly get through them."[28]

The horsemen reined up at the canal while their leader, a balding lawyer-turned-cavalryman, spoke to Sulivane. Martin Gary had been an extreme secessionist before the war, a profane and truculent partisan who afterward would channel his rage into white supremacist politics. For the moment, he was not about to give up the fight. "Touching his hat to me," Sulivane remembered, "he called out, 'All over, good-bye; blow her to h—ll,' and trotted over the bridge."[29]

Assured by Gary that no more Confederate units remained on the Richmond side, Sulivane began to discharge his final duty. The last infantry guard double-timed over from Richmond to the south side. Then Sulivane, with the engineer and one other officer, walked slowly to the island, setting light to the combustible material as they went, "leaving the north section of Mayo's bridge wrapped in flame and smoke."[30]

Halfway across, they paused and watched a troop of Union cavalry-men riding furiously down Main Street. When they reached Four-teenth Street, the riders wheeled and raced for the bridge. Thwarted by flames burning on both sides of the street, and more interested in reaching Capitol Square, they fired a few desultory shots at the three figures, more for form's sake than anything else.

Despite Gary's assurance, yet another southern unit, a group of pickets from the 2nd Virginia Regiment, turned up at the wrong end of the bridge. One of them, W. L. Timberlake, later swore they were the last Confederates to march over Mayo's bridge. "If any crossed after we did," he remembered, "they need have no fear of the other world, because they surely were fireproof."[31]

Timberlake's was not the only claim to being the last man. The chief engineer of the army was Walter Stevens, a New Yorker and West Point graduate who married a Louisiana woman and sided with the Confederacy. When the flames on the bridge were as high as a man, Stevens ran through them back to the Richmond side and then appeared through the fire safely on the south side. He told his men he wanted to be the last Confederate out of the city he had labored so hard to defend. But Stevens was disappointed. Just as he announced his reason for dashing through the fire, a civilian burst through the wall of flames behind him to take the dubious honor.[32]

It was about eight o'clock, and the sun was now well up in the sky and had burned through the early morning mist. Lieutenant Handy, watching from the south side of the river, said the flames blazing out of the trelliswork on the nearby railroad bridge were like diamonds on fire. General Ewell reined in his horse on the Manchester side and sat there holding a stout walking stick and wearing a worn black hat pulled down on his brow, "with firmly compressed lips and a keen lit-tle eye glancing from point to point with the greatest rapidity."[33]

Breckinridge was with him, dressed in civilian black with a cape draped over his shoulder. For months he had known the South's cause was lost, and he knew the price for treason that those he fought against might exact. Even so, he did not want the Confederacy to disband piecemeal but to surrender properly. Watching the literal ruin of his hopes for a southern republic, he feared that Davis would not countenance such an action.[34] Now that the city's defenders had cut themselves off from the pursuing Federals and had a chance to join Lee, Breckinridge could think of how the government in the next few days should bring things to an end. But he must also have thought of his invalid wife, Mary, left behind in the prostrate city laid out before him.

From the river's edge southward, a host of army wagons, caissons, and tired men on foot lined the road leading toward Lee. Soldiers intent on desertion—and there were hundreds of them—had fallen out of ranks on the other side of the bridge or skulked away as soon as they crossed. Anyone in uniform at the southern bridgehead meant to stick with the army, at least for a time. Most of the slaves who worked with the soldiers ran away before crossing the bridge.

It was not just soldiers who stood on the banks of the James and watched the city burn and their enemy stream in. A mass of civilian refugees crowded into the little town of Manchester. The saddest were women traveling in the opposite direction. They had come from the south and now sat on their trunks and carpetbags by the roadside as the soldiers marched past. The refugees had been driven out of their homes in Petersburg by Grant's invading army, and now they were denied Richmond by the flames engulfing Mayo's bridge.

After he saw the last of his batteries safely across, Porter Alexander cantered over to a low rise on the river's edge and watched the panorama. A Georgian who had graduated from West Point shortly before the war, Alexander had served as an artillerist in most of the battles fought by Lee's Army of Northern Virginia. At First Manassas, he had used the parlor of his distant in-law Wilmer McLean as an observation post. Now, four years later, he was about to begin the last march that would end in another parlor in another house where McLean had moved to escape the war at a place called Appomattox.[35]

"We turned to take our last look at the old city for which we had fought so long & so hard," Alexander remembered long after, with a

melancholy detachment he did not feel at the time. "It was a sad, a terrible & a solemn sight. I don't know that any moment in the whole war
impressed me more deeply with all its stern realities than this. The
whole river front seemed to be in flames, amid which occasional heavy
explosions were heard, & the black smoke spreading & hanging over
the city seemed to be full of dreadful portents. I rode on with a distinctly heavy heart & with a peculiar sort of feeling of orphanage."[36]

CHAPTER 9

CRUEL CATACLYSM

Monday, April 3, Morning

I am so overjoyed with this day's success of our arms, that I can hardly keep still enough to write.
—Lt. Col. Thomas Barker, 12th N.H. Regt.[1]

In the Union lines east of Richmond, even the most lackadaisical soldier, bored with the monotony of the trenches, could tell by Sunday that something out of the ordinary was afoot. For nearly a week, the Army of the James had carried out a campaign of deception to match what the Confederate defenders opposite it were doing. As each side drew down its strength to reinforce the bigger armies at Petersburg, it feared the other would detect its movements. Edward Ripley ordered the drum corps of his regiments to play reveille and tattoo in different parts of their bivouacs. At twenty-five, the boy colonel of the 9th Vermont found himself brevetted a brigadier general commanding the 1st Brigade of the XXIV Corps. Ripley told his soldiers to keep fires lit in the camps abandoned by units that slipped off to the south. The USCT regiments of the neighboring all-black XXV Corps received similar orders.[2]

During the day on Sunday, General Weitzel ordered his artillery to experiment with the effect of chain and solid shot against a mockup of the southern fortifications. The prototype his gunners used for target practice featured thickets of crudely sharpened stakes that could thwart infantrymen advancing over open ground while their enemies picked them off. Though the result of Weitzel's exercise was disappointing, it was not the make-work activity for idle gunners that it seemed. The nervous general knew he might be ordering his men to attack positions that bristled with such stakes and, even worse, were strewn with explosive antipersonnel mines.[3]

Using field glasses, Weitzel's observers had been able for months to peer into the city from their observation towers. On Sunday, the signalman on duty counted thirty-eight railcars of troops going south from Richmond to Petersburg. Where did they come from? Weitzel cabled a subordinate to ask the crucial question: "Do you know of anything to indicate that they left our front?"[4] They could have come in from western Virginia and made a quick transit through town. Or they could represent part of the force guarding the capital. It would make all the difference in the world to Weitzel if he had to assault a well-manned line of trenches.

He had received similar reports for days but could not be absolutely certain that the troop trains meant the Confederates were stripping the city's defenses. A cautious man, he told Grant that not enough southern soldiers had left to warrant an attack: "I would rather that their line be a little more denuded of soldiers before I make the attempt."[5] On Sunday afternoon, telegrams from headquarters at City Point apprised him of Grant's smashing success at Petersburg that morning. There was no question now that the culmination of the campaign was at hand.

CAPT. GEORGE BRUCE, who heard the peal of Richmond church bells earlier in the day, drew duty as officer of pickets for the 13th New Hampshire on Sunday evening. He could hear the brass bands and drum corps on both sides playing longer and with more vigor than usual. The dueling patriotic songs did not fade until around midnight. In the silence that followed, Bruce went out several times but learned nothing untoward from his men peering through the darkness toward the southern entrenchments. At one point, he saw a bright fire a long way to the south, but it died out. As he prepared to go out again at half past three, a pair of deserters came in from a Virginia regiment. They said the Confederates had evacuated the whole line.

Bruce reported this intelligence to Ripley at brigade headquarters and then returned to his pickets with orders to advance as soon as they could see. By now, though he could make out no lights from the southern lines, he plainly saw large fires in the direction of Richmond. Maybe the deserters were right. Perhaps they had not been sent by their officers to mislead their opponents, a routine trick both sides often employed. When the shock waves from Semmes's exploding ironclads rolled over his lines and removed all doubt, Bruce rushed four men forward to investigate. They ran back to confirm that the southern forts were completely deserted.

In the gray of predawn, Bruce advanced his soldiers to the Confederate picket line and halted. The skirmishers then carefully moved forward along the paths made by southern pickets through the minefields. Fortunately for Bruce's men, the Confederates had failed to remove the telltale markers for the mines. A small square of red fabric stuck in a notched stick let the pickets know where each explosive was buried. Yet it was slow enough going even when the light had strengthened and illuminated these markers.[6]

Back at headquarters, the terse cables Weitzel sent to Grant told the story. At 4:30 a.m. he reported that the Confederate positions to his front seemed to be abandoned. An hour later he telegraphed again: "Continual explosions and fires in enemy's lines. Large number of deserters. All report evacuation. I will move at daybreak."[7]

Other picket officers reported George Bruce's experience up and down the Union lines. Like Bruce, they reflected soberly on the losses they would have suffered if they had been ordered to attack through the minefields under fire. The sense of good fortune increased as Federal troops passed by the silent, looming muzzles of artillery pieces, hundreds of them, left in perfect working order, unspiked. The evacuation came too quickly for the Confederates to disable many of their guns, much less scare up enough transport to move them.

Charles Washburn's duties as a musician with the 13th New

Hampshire put him at the head of Edward Ripley's brigade. The drum corps played "Yankee Doodle" and other patriotic tunes as they marched. Washburn never dreamed that they would take Richmond with hardly a shot being fired. Writing exuberantly that night with a pencil he took from the library of the Virginia Capitol, Washburn said he was "perfectly *astonished* at our *bloodless* victory this morning." Almost bloodless. Weitzel estimated casualties for his command from late March to mid-April at ten killed, forty wounded, and forty captured. Though nearly all of these came in small actions probing the lines before the evacuation, at least one man died entering the city, an unlucky soldier in the 9th Vermont who stepped on a mine.[8]

By the time his men reached the inner Confederate batteries, Ripley was convinced the southerners would not even leave a rear guard to slow the Federal advance. There would be no battle of Richmond. The battle *for* Richmond had already been fought offstage, to the south around Petersburg. No matter, the often-thwarted Army of the James would be the Union force that would take the southern capital. Full of himself, Ripley rode up and down the column on his new black stallion exchanging congratulations with his officers. Years later he recalled that he stood up in his stirrups and sang an army marching song as he spurred his horse along.[9]

The men did the same. Long afterward, Frederick Chesson recalled when he and his friends in the 29th Connecticut first saw Richmond. "Right out there in the open in sight of that flaming city," he wrote, "we went wild with excitement of the place and hour—we yelled, we cheered, we sang, we prayed, we wept. We hugged each other and threw up our hats and danced and acted like lunatics for about fifteen minutes, and then we went into Richmond, colors flying."[10] Henry Grimes Marshall, a white officer with the all-black XXV Corps, was just as excited. After seeing the rail bridges burning, the whole waterfront in flames, and his regiments marching in with bands playing, he wrote home that same night, "I tell you my head is so full of the sights & sounds I have seen today that I don't know what to say."[11]

Another soldier, a sergeant named Clarke, had a grand view of the city. His 12th New Hampshire halted at the edge of town at Tree Hill Farm, the property of Unionist Franklin Stearns. From the vantage point of the farm, Clarke had an unobstructed view of the spectacle. The city, he wrote, "lies before us all in flames, and there has been a continual roar of bursting shells and exploding magazines all the morning."[12]

Most of the men in Clarke's unit used the forced halt to write letters home, aware that they were witnessing history in the making. The sergeant wrote his on a sheet torn from a ledger book left by a Georgia regiment. His companions found a peacock and cut off its tail to send feathers home as mementoes in their letters. More warlike souvenirs would soon flood the army mails to towns and farmhouses across the North.

As the lead units entered the city, a cavalry contingent stopped at the hospital complex on the plateau above the river. At the only recorded meeting of Confederate and Union army officers during the fall of Richmond, they completed the handover of the Chimborazo facility in short order. They consolidated the wards of southern patients to free up one division of the hospital for wounded northern soldiers.

Legend has it that Dr. McCaw, who knew one of the Union officers from before the war, ordered a tray of mint juleps brought out to give the occasion a touch of Virginia hospitality, no matter the gravity of the circumstances. The drinks were probably apocryphal, but it was true that his visitors offered McCaw immediate standing as a medical officer in the Union army. He accepted Federal protection and the written passes necessary to continue working at the hospital, but he declined the appointment. Lee had retreated but had not yet surrendered.[13]

EARLIER THAT MORNING, while the committee appointed to destroy liquor set about its work, the mayor attempted to fulfill the other wish expressed by the city council at its late-night meeting on Sunday. Joseph Mayo, accompanied by several others, rode east in a carriage in search of "the General Commanding the Army of the United States in front of the City of Richmond." That was the wording that appeared at the top of the document Mayo carried, because they did not know that Weitzel commanded the Army of the James.

They hoped to find the Union commander by the time they reached the line of trenches along the Osborne Turnpike, about two miles southeast of the city limits. As they rode, the last organized Confederate force on the north side of the James was rushing toward Mayo's bridge before it fell burning into the river. Under the South Carolinian Gen. Martin Gary, this troop of cavalry passed the mayor's carriage going out on its doleful mission. Depending on the perspective, the horsemen were the last gallant remnant defending the southern capital, fleeing in the face of its overwhelming, malignant foes, or they were the last guardians of a system that rested on human chattel slavery, forced to yield to the army of freedom.

As the South Carolina troopers swept by, they recognized the mission of the mayoral delegation, for the driver of the carriage was waving a piece of white cloth.

A few moments later, Maj. Atherton Stevens rode up at the head of an escort from Weitzel's headquarters, forty men of Companies E and H, 4th Massachusetts Cavalry. Near the point where the Osborne Turnpike merged with the New Market Road, they met the mayor's carriage. Mayo handed Stevens the surrender note. The major read it and assured the delegation the army intended to protect people and property. After the two parties briefly discussed the best way to accomplish that goal, Stevens instructed the mayor to accompany him into the city. A native of Cambridge, Massachusetts, Stevens had turned thirty-nine the day before. Receiving the note surrendering the Confederate capital was a welcome belated birthday present but not the last one for him that day.[14]

Shortly afterward, Mary Fontaine saw the first northern soldier reach the portico of City Hall. As she watched from her window nearby, the streets filled with hurrying people and soon the cry of "Yankees" rose up to her. "I did not move, I could not, but watched the blue horseman ride to the City Hall, enter with his sword knocking the ground at every step, and threw the great doors open, and take possession of our beautiful city." Inside, while the members of Mayo's party watched, Stevens dictated orders to protect the inhabitants and their possessions. The first task was fighting the fire, and the major asked the surrender delegation to help him mobilize residents for that task.[15]

The surrender note, written in another hand but signed by Joseph Mayo with his distinctive, slashing initial letter "J," took up a mere twelve lines on a half-sheet of ruled paper. "The Army of the Confederate States having been withdrawn from the City of Richmond," it read, "as Mayor of the City I request that an organized body of troops under a proper officer be sent into the City to preserve order and protect the women & children and the property until the United States Government may take formal possession of it."[16] In one sentence Mayo committed the act he had sworn never to do.

FOR FOUR YEARS she had waited for this moment. The piazza at the back of her Church Hill mansion looked down on a spectacular sweep of the James as it flowed past the city. It was that same bend in the river that supposedly had reminded William Byrd of Richmond-upon-Thames a century and a half before. On this morning, the view took in the fires that stretched along the riverfront and the necklace of flames that had been Mayo's bridge. Even more electrifying, in the early morning light, she saw Union regiments race one another toward Capitol Square. Elizabeth Van Lew—wealthy spinster, abolitionist, local pariah, and bane of the Confederate provost marshal—exulted at the sight of blue-coated soldiers streaming unopposed into her city. "Oh, army of my country," she later exclaimed, "how glorious was your welcome!"[17]

Van Lew's father had made his fortune in the hardware business and sent his daughter to school in Philadelphia. Before the war, the family hosted the smartest parties and the most cosmopolitan visitors to the Virginia capital. Poe recited "The Raven" in the Van Lew parlor. Jenny Lind sang there at the height of her popularity. "Pleasing, pale blonde" Elizabeth Van Lew impressed visiting feminist Fredrika Bremer with the intensity of her compassion for the slaves.[18] Vivacious and willful, she wore her hair in ringlets and perhaps put off aspiring suitors for her hand and her inheritance with those flashing blue eyes, angular features, and sharp tongue.

The war gave her a purpose. When captured Union soldiers began to fill the converted warehouses along the waterfront, Van Lew took them books and food. She graduated to smuggling notes in and out of Libby Prison and then to hiding escaped Yankees and helping them reach their own lines. Their plight grieved her, and their frequent deaths in captivity spurred her on. "I meet everywhere," she lamented, "the unplaned, rough coffins of the wretched prisoners."[19] In public, she dressed oddly, talked to herself, and cultivated the impression of feeblemindedness so that children taunted her as "Crazy Bet." A holy fool for the Union.

Benjamin Butler, the vindictive Union general most despised by the South for his real and imagined treatment of Confederate civilians, called her "my secret correspondent."[20] Grant later said she had given him the best intelligence he ever received from Richmond.

Her Confederate neighbors tolerated her prison work and suspected worse of her. But neither they nor the provost marshal's ferrets ever caught her in the espionage at which she excelled. Toward the end, she began to receive anonymous threats. One bore a skull and crossbones and warned, "Look out! Look out! Look out! Your house is going at last. FIRE."[21]

They did not cow her. A niece who lived with her said all Sunday night she took in Yankee prisoners who had escaped their jailers in the confusion of the evacuation. She defied the threats against her house. "Auntie went out on the front porch," wrote Annie Randolph Van Lew later that day, "and said if this house goes every house in the neighborhood should follow."[22]

When a troop of soldiers arrived on Church Hill to protect Van Lew from vengeful Confederates, they discovered a large Union flag waving over the mansion. If these guardians sent by Grant had any question about which house they were meant to protect, Old Glory resolved the doubt.

Like her neighbors, in the days to come Van Lew would write about

To defend against Union gunboats downstream from Richmond, the Confederates guarded the river approaches with cannon of very large caliber, like this one along the bluff at Trent's Reach. (Library of Congress)

On the evening of April 1, the gruff Confederate provost marshal Isaac Carrington knew his orders to burn government-owned tobacco and military assets would soon have to be carried out. (Cook Collection, Valentine Richmond History Center)

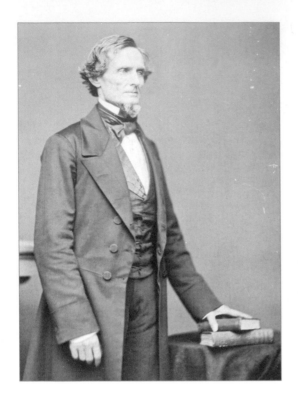

Jefferson Davis struggled with ill health as well as dismal tidings from the front during his last days in Richmond. Unwilling to accept the imminent prospect of defeat, he put off evacuation as long as possible. (National Archives)

The Union army erected signal towers in its fortifications outside Richmond and Petersburg that let it look behind the Confederate lines. A photographer stands in the right foreground with his apparatus on a wagon. (Library of Congress)

Richmond mayor Joseph Mayo wore the high starched collar, cravat, and brass-buttoned waistcoat of a former time. His notions of municipal government were equally old fashioned. (Cook Collection, Valentine Richmond History Center)

When Grant's army broke Lee's defenses around Petersburg on April 2 and compelled the Confederates to abandon that city and Richmond, the southern army had no time to bury its dead, like this soldier at Fort Mahone, photographed shortly after the Union victory. (Library of Congress)

Maj. Gen. Godfrey Weitzel commanded the Army of the James when it occupied Richmond with hardly a shot fired on April 3. During his short time as Federal military commander there, he ran afoul of Secretary of War Edwin Stanton. (National Archives)

Using wagons, like this one photographed the previous September, the Union army's field telegraph service gave Grant a valuable source of nearly instantaneous information from his commanders, spread out in an arc from northeast of Richmond down to Petersburg twenty miles to the south and beyond. On April 3, however, Godfrey Weitzel's men did not take enough wire with them to make the connection into Richmond. A courier therefore took Weitzel's electrifying dispatch on the city's fall back to field headquarters, where the telegraph operators sent it at the speed of light to City Point, Washington, and points north. (National Archives)

The double-turreted monitor USS Onondaga, *photographed here on the James River below Richmond, helped clear mines and open a passage to the city for President Lincoln on April 4.*

(Library of Congress)

It was one more improbability in a catalog of wonders during the spring of 1865 that Abraham Lincoln should visit Richmond as soon as he did — on the day after it fell but not before it ceased to burn.

(National Archives)

John Moncure Daniel (LEFT), *the fiery editor of the* Richmond Examiner, *died three days before the evacuation, in the mistaken belief that Lee had won a great victory in the trenches around Petersburg. Susan Hoge* (RIGHT), *wife of Presbyterian minister Moses Drury Hoge, was no friend of the North, but she conceded the day after Richmond burned that "the yankees put a stop to [looting] and made the negroes work to put the fire out & they worked hard themselves."* (Both photographs: Virginia Historical Society)

When the Union armies began to surround Richmond in the autumn of 1864, a photographer captured this encampment of the 5th Pennsylvania Cavalry near the city. (Library of Congress)

Nicknamed "Bison," John Minor Botts, seated at center and surrounded by his family, was the most prominent and vocal Unionist politician from Richmond. Briefly imprisoned for his views in 1862, he bided his time in sullen neutrality on his farm in Culpeper County.
(Library of Congress)

Neither Engine No. 3 nor any of the rest of Richmond's inadequate fire-fighting equipment was of much use in battling the flames on April 3. (Library of Congress)

The most famous Unionist in Richmond, Elizabeth Van Lew feigned feeblemindedness as a cover for her espionage activities. (Cook Collection, Valentine Richmond History Center)

Thomas Morris Chester, the only African American journalist with the Union army outside Richmond, sent dozens of firsthand reports to his readers in Philadelphia, describing conditions in the fallen Confederate capital. (University Archives, Cheyney University of Pennsylvania)

Irascible, bluff Maj. Gen. Edward O. C. Ord replaced Godfrey Weitzel as Federal commander in Richmond on April 13. Here he poses on the porch of his headquarters, the former White House of the Confederacy, resting his hand on the surrender table that he had purchased from Wilmer McLean at Appomattox Court House. (National Archives)

the fall of the city. Though she described the same events, the adjectives she used were different. The thundering explosions of the gunboats and arsenals, she said, "lend a mighty language to the scene." She grieved that so much of her city burned, yet she could not contain her joy. The fires of Richmond, she exclaimed, "filled the sky with clouds of smoke as incense from the land for its deliverance. What a moment! Avenging wrath appeased in flames!"[23]

Less conspicuous white Richmonders than Van Lew also welcomed the Union army. Most of these were literally as well as socially beneath her, for many were poorer residents who lived and worked down the hill from her mansion, along the waterfront directly on the line of march into town taken by most Union regiments. "The citizens are very kind and give the boys a hearty welcome," wrote James Hane, of the 81st New York. "Old flags that were hid they brought out and [were] flowing to the breeze." The New Hampshire musician Charles Washburn met "citizens *crying for joy* at the sight of the old *flag*. This I saw in several instances."[24]

So many northern soldiers wrote home about being greeted by long-hidden Union flags that even discounting for exaggeration, there must have been some truth to the claim. It was certainly true of Rachel Lewis, who hid a flag behind a parlor mirror during the war and brought it out that morning. It was not the Stars and Stripes but a banner she had made of silk and wool, with an image of George Washington riding his horse and carrying an American Revolutionary flag painted on linen. Though it commemorated Washington's victory at Yorktown, it served just as well to welcome the Union army into Richmond.[25]

William Rowley, a native New Yorker who moved to Virginia just before the war, awaited the army as eagerly as Lewis. The farm he rented east of town, just beyond the city limits, lay on the Union line of march. It had been convenient the year before when he and other Unionists surreptitiously moved Col. Ulric Dahlgren's body, to the chagrin of Confederate authorities. On that occasion, Rowley's two-horse wagon transported the metal coffin, covered with a load of young peach trees, through the Confederate picket line to a secret burial site outside town. Rowley's delight at the entry of Weitzel's army on Monday morning, however, was dampened when black cavalrymen stole one of the same bay mares and the wagon that had carried the Dahlgren coffin.[26]

The response of people like William Rowley and Rachel Lewis astonished Charles Morrell. "Imagine yourself as I did several times," the Yankee soldier wrote his brother, "to get . . . about a dozen offering, or poking a glass of water at you the same time, and as many more trying to get ahold of your hand to have a shake." Some of those glasses did not contain water. Charles Francis Adams, Jr., scion of a famous family and colonel of the black 5th Massachusetts Cavalry that stole Rowley's cart and horse, cursed civilians for forcing liquor on his men. A great deal of drunkenness resulted, he said. But the behavior of the Union soldiers was generally good, and the cynical Adams saw no sign of bloodshed or violence committed by any man in blue.[27]

Sgt. Edwin Ware marched into the city with the 13th New Hampshire behind Charles Washburn's drum corps. The reception of the people bowled him over. "Crowds of whites and negroes lined the side walks and filled the windows. Many of the ladies were waving handkerchiefs and nearly all looked pleasant and smiling. The negroes and many of the lower class of white were perfectly extravagant in their expressions of delight."[28]

Capt. Linus Sherman of the 9th Vermont probably was closer to the mark when he wrote his brother the next day. "People generally are glad to see us here," he perceived, "not, I suppose from much of a real union sentiment but because they have suffered so much."[29] Sherman's more gullible comrades would soon discover that the cheers of some civilians at the sight of blue uniforms did not speak for most Richmonders. They seethed with a hatred borne of four years of conflict and annealed by the fire that threatened to consume their city, a loathing shared across the South, a loathing that would not subside as quickly as the fire. Indeed, it would last for generations.

CHAPTER 10

REQUIEM FOR
BURIED HOPES

Monday, April 3, Morning

There were Yankee flags flying on all sides.
—Henri Garidel[1]

Confederate Richmonders described the reception of the Union soldiers in different words. For the most part, they agreed with Confederate soldier and novelist John Esten Cooke, who remembered a stern, unsmiling, conquering host "met by a huge crowd of dirty and jabbering negroes and outcasts."[2] Judith McGuire, the refugee from northern Virginia, spoke of "cringing loyalty" expressed by a vulgar, motley band of men and women of the least respectability.[3] "No one who was not here will ever fully appreciate the horrors of that day," agreed Mary Fontaine. "Our Richmond servants were completely crazed," she sniffed, using the standard euphemism for slaves, "they danced and shouted, men hugged each other, and women kissed, and such a scene of confusion you have never seen."[4] Writing that evening, Kate Mason Rowland vowed with impotent defiance that it would have been "better [to] lay the whole city in ashes than give the enemy one munition of war."[5]

Henri Garidel, the homesick Louisianan, had hoped to get away with the other departing members of the government but he waited too long. Caught under Union occupation for a second time—he had witnessed it in New Orleans—he returned to his boardinghouse and shut himself in his garret room. Almost physically prostrated by the fall of the city, he recorded his observations in his journal. "It made your heart bleed," he cried, "to see with what joy the [Union] army was received by the population, particularly the Negroes."[6]

The young Baptist preacher Alfred Dickinson gathered his wife and children for family devotions after breakfast on Monday. They lived on the far western edge of town, but over their prayers they heard the repeated explosions from the arsenal. The sounds startled Fannie, but she suppressed her emotions for the sake of the children. Afterward, she continued hiding their possessions from the looters they expected at the doorstep at any moment. When she heard martial music and cheering, she went to an upstairs window and was outraged to see "a Yankee crowd marching up Broad Street with the stars and stripes."[7]

In their anguish, Confederate Richmonders expressed their greatest resentment for neighbors whose outward allegiance changed overnight. It was humiliating to Fannie Dickinson to learn that neighbors who had professed southern patriotism suddenly let it be known that they had been Unionists all along. Such sentiments especially aggrieved her when they came from a neighbor whose son had died in Confederate service. "Union men began to show themselves," moaned Judith McGuire, "treason walked abroad."[8]

Many, like Dickinson and McGuire, observed the Union soldiers with a mixture of fear and scorn. In their agony that morning, they had not yet forsaken the Confederate cause. A journalist who marched in with Weitzel's army wrote, "There was no mistaking the curl of their lips and the flash of their eyes."[9]

Within hours, Confederate women began to swallow their pride, if not their opinions. As early as Monday afternoon, they began to inundate Frederick Manning, the harried Union provost marshal, with requests for soldiers to stand guard outside their homes. He tried to convince them there was no need but eventually consented to post sentries outside some houses. Julia Reed was less lucky. She loathed having to go in person to petition the "things," as she called Union soldiers, for protection.[10] It was necessary, she claimed, because black men had cursed her mother and threatened to burn down her house unless she gave them food. The provost marshal still denied her request for special guards and told her troops assigned to patrol the street corners would keep the peace.

Some women who went to the provost marshal to seek guards made this task seem a reproach to the occupiers. "We passed the sentinel," wrote Judith McGuire haughtily about going to City Hall, "and an officer escorted us to the room in which we were to ask our country's foe to allow us to remain undisturbed in our own houses."[11]

Constance Cary, an auburn-haired belle, accomplished fiction writer, and fiancée of Jefferson Davis's secretary, also went to secure a Federal guard to protect her family's property. She described the scene as she walked through the occupied capital: "Already the town wore the aspect of one in the Middle Ages smitten by pestilence. The streets filled with smoke and flying fire were empty of the respectable class of inhabitants, the doors and shutters of every house tight closed."[12] With houses like Cary's closed to the outside world, wrote another southern chronicler, the Federal army could be excused in the first days of occupation for thinking it had marched into "a city of the dead."[13]

Time seemed to stand still. "Such a long, long, day!" confided Kate Rowland to her diary on Monday evening.[14] Fear of occupation by the enemy and shock at the looting and burning prolonged the agony of Confederate civilians. Not having his watch, remembered John Leyburn, he could not judge the passage of time. "At last, when I thought it must be toward four o'clock in the afternoon, I inquired of the time, and found to my astonishment that it was only twelve o'clock. It seemed as if that day would never end."[15] "It seemed to me the day would never end," echoed Fannie Dickinson, "it was so filled with strange events, strange sights and strange sounds. . . ." The compression of these events oppressed her. "It was only day before yesterday that we heard of the certainty of the Yankees' approach, yet the time appears as years, so much has been crowded into that short space."[16]

IF THE REACTION of white Richmonders varied, no ambiguity clouded the minds of the majority of black residents. The absence of whites from the streets left them largely in the possession of black people, a change noticed by observers of every political stripe. A white commentator sneered that the capital "seemed in a night to have been transformed into an African city."[17] The crowds that greeted the Union troops included some poor whites but were mostly African American. "The pious old negroes, male and female," wrote black reporter Thomas Chester, "indulged in such expressions [as] 'You've come at last' . . . 'Jesus has opened the way.'" He later remarked that there were many whites on the streets, "but they were lost in the great concourse of American citizens of African descent."[18]

Some time before dawn, the slave pens that held runaways and others for sale were thrown open, and the inmates walked out free men and women. They did not need to be coaxed out of their cells. According to tradition, the people at Lumpkin's jail were the first to sing the words *"Slavery chain done broke at last! / Broke at last! Broke at last! / Slavery chain done broke at last! / Gonna praise God till I die!"*[19]

The joy of the freed people was great indeed. One of them even attributed a miraculous cure to the detonations of Confederate ordnance that rocked the city. A black girl who suffered poor vision and had become blind some months earlier swore that the shock of the exploding arsenal restored her sight. Thomas Chester interviewed her and believed her story of impaired eyesight "wonderfully improved."[20]

No Union soldier was prouder than the Rev. Garland White, chaplain of the 28th USCT. He knew what the crowds of cheering freed people were feeling. He had been in their place. Thirty-five years earlier he had been born in Richmond. As a boy he was sold to Robert Toombs, U.S. senator from Georgia, later Confederate secretary of state. Before the war White ran away. With secession, he recruited African Americans for the Union army. As he marched through town at the head of his regiment, White beamed at the ecstatic greetings of the city's black residents. "It appeared to me," he wrote, that in Richmond that day "all the colored people in the world had collected."[21]

As the soldiers marched in formation west on Broad Street, freed people pressed forward to touch their liberators, to embrace them as if they were their own flesh and blood. Looking back down the column, White saw some of them tugging at one blue uniform sleeve after another. The soldiers came from every state, North and South. Maybe they would know about a son or daughter sold away from home years before. Few enslaved families remained untouched by the sales that had kept the wheels of slavery lubricated at the cost of separating loved ones. His comrades, White observed with a mixture of pride and pain, were too disciplined to break ranks in order to answer the questions, poignant though they were. His heart went out to these suffering people, now at last released from bondage.

When the regiment reached Camp Lee on the edge of town, the throng followed. The soldiers stopped there, stacked their arms, and eagerly shook the hard, callused hands of these grateful people, slaves only hours before. The officers and men of the 28th USCT called on White to address the crowd. It seemed natural, for the preacher was a gifted exhorter and a native son, come home in glory. He gladly proclaimed "freedom to all mankind" but was so overcome with emotion that he had to step down. At that point, his fellow soldiers brought him an aged woman from the crowd who wanted to speak to him. She quizzed him on his own life story and then said, "This is your mother, Garland, whom you are now talking to, who has spent twenty years of grief about her son."[22]

WHILE FEDERAL TROOPS were streaming into the city, Raphael Semmes and his sailors arrived on their wooden steamers, the last organized Confederate force to reach the capital. They passed the burning hulk of William Parker's *Patrick Henry* near the wharf at Rocketts and saw the Confederate navy yards on fire on either side of the river. The flames that were beginning to consume the business district loomed before them. Semmes wisely docked his vessels on the south side of the river. He could see that Mayo's bridge, just ahead, was a mass of flames. More disconcerting was the presence of the enemy so uncomfortably close. The streets were filling with blue-coated soldiers. Landing on the Richmond side ensured a quick capture.

As soon as they docked, the admiral ordered his men to set fire to their steamers and push them out into the current. Armed and under the command of Semmes and his captains, the group nevertheless was no more prepared for further escape than the crowd of civilian refugees who had crossed the bridge and were milling about at its southern end. The sailors had no horses or mules, and the army's mounted rear guard had disappeared down the road toward Lee's retreating army.

When he recalled the scene at leisure years after, Semmes could still conjure up his anger at his boss. Navy Secretary Mallory had kept him in the dark to the last minute and then expected him to convert his men into infantry and join Lee without providing maps, directions, or transport. At the time, the admiral did not have the luxury of indulging his resentment. He knew the Federal horsemen clearly visible across the river would soon turn their attention to him and his men if they remained in Manchester.

At the railroad workshops a few blocks away, Semmes found a string of passenger cars filled with frightened civilians, walking wounded from the army hospitals, and government clerks. They seemed to expect someone to appear as if by magic with an engine to tow them to safety. There was an engine, but it was not attached to the cars, had no fire in its furnace, no fuel to burn, and no one to operate it.

Semmes could supply the know-how with a dozen steam engineers from his ironclads. The admiral made a cold, quick decision. He told his men to order the people out of the cars. Lee needed all the armed men he could find, not a crowd of frightened refugees. The sailors coupled the engine to the cars, tore down a picket fence for fuel, and fired up the boiler. The engine crept forward. Then it stopped, unable to pull the cars up even a slight incline. Because the rail line ran parallel to the river before turning southwest, the train had stalled while still in view of the Federal occupiers. To their discomfort, the sailors could see long lines of Union troops snaking through the streets.

Semmes knew he was temporarily safe, because the Federal army had to consolidate its position in the city, and the bridges were ablaze like the business district surrounding them. That would not last. The admiral considered uncoupling the cars to see if the engine could pull at least some of them to safety. Then his men found a second engine in one of the workshops. With two engines they raised enough steam finally to pull the cars along the waterfront, past the burning city, and at last to make the turn away from the river that would take them toward Danville and the fugitive Confederate government.[23]

BEFORE THE MORNING was over, a dispute began over who first raised the United States flag over the Confederate capital. Mary Fontaine sorrowfully recounted seeing one episode. "I . . . watched two blue figures on the Capitol, white men, I saw them unfurl a tiny flag, and then I sank on my knees, and the bitter, bitter tears came in a torrent." The two were Maj. E. E. Graves and Maj. Atherton Stevens, the aides to Weitzel who rode in with his headquarters cavalry to receive the surrender of the city fathers.[24] The tiny flag that Fontaine saw was one of two small cavalry guidons belonging to Companies E and H of the 4th Massachusetts Cavalry that the two majors hoisted on the flagpoles on the Capitol roof.

Some time after the horse soldiers claimed Thomas Jefferson's Capitol for the Union, Weitzel's staff galloped onto the square. Lt. Johnston de Peyster and Lt. Loomis Langdon raced up to the roof and lowered the little flags left by Stevens and Graves. In their place they raised a large national standard. De Peyster made much of his feat after the war, but Langdon graciously recognized Stevens as the first Union officer to place the national flag over Richmond.

There is no dispute that Stevens and Graves were the first Union officers to accomplish that feat, but another claimant, a southerner, had done the same before them. His name was Richard Forrester, and he was a pale-skinned youth of seventeen, the grandson of a free woman of color, Nelly Forrester. His grandfather was none other than Gustavus Myers, lawyer, pillar of the Virginia Historical Society, president of congregation Beth Shalome, state legislator, and defense attorney for numerous slaves brought before Mayor Mayo's court.

Forrester, a legislative page, had saved the Union flag that the state discarded when Virginia seceded and kept it under his bed throughout the war. Early Monday morning, he ran up to the Capitol roof and unfurled the flag, but he was accosted as he came down the stairs by Royal Prescott, a lieutenant of the 13th New Hampshire. Prescott interrogated the youth and asked him to write out his name on a page torn from a pocket memorandum book. Because Forrester then retrieved the flag and presented it to Prescott, Majors Stevens and Graves saw no United States flag on the roof when they arrived.[25]

Grant's reaction to the first-flag dispute might be inferred from action he took later. That summer he received a collection of $460 from patriotic northern citizens with a request to present the money to the soldier who first raised the flag over Richmond. With a hint of disdain, Grant said that "as Richmond was not taken by assault," he thought it best to divide the money among three men who distinguished themselves in the very real battle for Petersburg.[26]

Whoever could claim first rights, the effect of the flag was electric. Sally Putnam watched it while the fire burned and heard the strains of the national anthem. Instead of the patriotic thrill of former days, she recalled, "now only the most bitter and crushing recollections awoke within us, as upon our quickened hearing fell the strains of 'The Star Spangled Banner.' For us it was a requiem for buried hopes."[27]

Union soldiers also began arguing over which unit was first to reach the city. Men in the division commanded by Charles Devens, a brave, three-times-wounded, but inept political general from Massachusetts, claimed the honor of being the first organized Union infantry to reach the city limits. Disputing that claim, black troops said they, and not Devens's white soldiers, first passed over the border between Henrico County and Richmond. Thomas Chester, the African American journalist who marched in with the USCTs, supported their claim. They were ordered to stop before entering the city proper, and they did. But they were already on the spot to cheer Devens's men who came after them. That evening August Kautz, a vain, plodding commander with the XXV Corps, wrote with a curious mix of racism and pride, "I marched in at the head of my Division of niggers among the first to enter."[28]

The report that black troops of the USCTs were first to enter Richmond was especially welcome to many in the North. In Washington, Gen. Benjamin Butler, former commander of the Army of the James, told a crowd it was divine retribution that black soldiers were the first to liberate Richmond. Despite the sense of poetic justice that the story represented to many northerners, it probably was an exaggeration. The point at which the 36th USCT stopped and cheered the passing white regiments of Devens's division was certainly in the outskirts of Richmond. But it was at the point where the Osborne Turnpike and the New Market Road converge just below the city, not within the city limits.[29] For days in the columns of newspapers—and for decades to come in Union soldiers' memoirs—the issue of whose regiment got to Richmond first remained a hot one.

Godfrey Weitzel took special pride in the black soldiers under his command, and his report is instructive. He wrote that the escort for Majors Stevens and Graves, forty men of the 4th Massachusetts Cavalry attached to his headquarters, were the first unit into Richmond. After them came the pickets of the XXIV Corps. Which of the regular infantry regiments came next was, he admitted, "a matter of dispute."[30]

As with the argument over the flag, it was of no military significance which regiment was first. Whether black units technically were first to step over the city line or not, they had earned a large share of the credit for capturing the southern capital. What was significant was the hostility between the black and white soldiers and what it portended for the future. Indeed, when the black regiments stopped and stacked their arms on the outskirts, their drum corps played patriotic tunes, and they cheered loudly when Devens's white soldiers marched past them into the city. But the white soldiers "failed to respond, either from exhaustion or a want of courtesy."[31]

THE UNION ARMY had its hands full with occupying the burning city but nevertheless sent a small mounted force to probe to the west in pursuit of the Confederate rear guard. Sgt. Leander Bossuot of the 20th New York Cavalry was still euphoric when he wrote a clumsy but proud account to his sister two days later. "Our Company and Co B was the first Co of Calv that went in to the City[.] we went in on a charge you Bet[.] we Paroled the city all threw."[32]

Twelve miles west of town, Bossuot's small unit caught up with part of the southern rear guard still on the wrong side of the river. A much larger body of cavalry than the New Yorkers, the southerners refused to offer battle but hurried on toward a point where they could cross over and reach Lee on the south side. The Union horsemen were left with two canal boats overloaded with supplies that would never reach the Confederate army.[33]

By morning, residents of the countryside north and west of town had heard enough of rumors and distant explosions to confirm the evacuation. The Rev. Cornelius Walker saw Confederate soldiers going away from Richmond to the north and supposed they were going home. Yet he rationalized that they might be making their way to rendezvous with the army by a roundabout route. When he heard that Federal troops would soon be in Richmond, he walked to a neighbor's house. On the way there, he noticed another neighbor's slave out in the fields plowing, "but when I came back the ploughs were standing in the furrows & the driver gone."[34]

Farther afield, out in the countryside west of town, residents had not heard of Lee's retreat or of Richmond's fall. On his son's plantation, Edmund Ruffin worried about the grave state of Confederate affairs, still ignorant of the great changes in the capital. The curmudgeon of agrarian reform and secession, who had fired one of the first shots at Fort Sumter, contemplated the ruin of the southern republic. On the very day of Richmond's burning and occupation, he made one more gesture of solidarity with the cause. As a further contribution to Treasury Secretary Trenholm's plea for donations to the government, he sent his gold patent-lever stopwatch.[35] There was no way for him to know that Trenholm had fled the capital and Weitzel's army had taken possession of it.

GODFREY WEITZEL RODE into Richmond with his staff along the Osborne Turnpike, the same route taken an hour earlier by his headquarters cavalry. The general's entourage passed the point where Stevens and Graves accepted the surrender note from Mayo. Weitzel could see the infantry regiments coming up behind him. By the time the party reached the outskirts, joyful black Richmonders and poor whites were mobbing the Union soldiers as liberators. One of his aides wearing a full uniform attracted most of the attention of the delirious well-wishers, while the less resplendently attired major general escaped their notice.

At City Hall, Mayo and Weitzel repeated the symbolic handing over of Richmond.[36] The general went immediately across the road to the governor's mansion. There, in Extra Billy Smith's former residence, he took a blank U.S. Military Telegraph form in hand. With what must have been intense pleasure, he wrote "Richmond Va" in the space provided at the top of the form. "We took possession of Richmond at 8.15 a.m.," he began his dispatch to Grant. "I captured many guns &c. The rebels evidently left in great haste. The city is on fire in two places. I am using every effort to put out the fire. A great many people are here and the whole is a mob. We were received everywhere with enthusiastic expressions of joy."[37]

Weitzel gave the paper to an orderly and told the man to ride hell for leather. It was only three miles back to the closest telegraph at XXIV Corps headquarters east of town. From there his terse message would be sent at the speed of light to the whole country, but Weitzel had no time to think of that. Through his adjutant general, he issued an order assuring the inhabitants that he had come "to restore to them the blessings of peace, prosperity and freedom, under the flag of the Union." He also warned them to stay in their houses and off the public streets.[38]

He or someone on his staff had probably composed the order before entering the city. What they could not have prepared for in advance was the immediate task of fighting the fire that threatened to level the capital. Indeed, as the general wrote his message, flames were setting alight the roof of the governor's mansion over his head. Weitzel and his men were about to witness a scene of destruction that would stay with them as long as they lived and would come to symbolize the end of the Confederacy. From its ashes, however, there would arise conflicting interpretations of what it all meant—for Richmond, for the South, for the reunited nation, and for the future.

CHAPTER 11

BURNING

Monday, April 3, Morning to Afternoon

Richmond burning and no alarm.

—Mary Burrows Fontaine[1]

Capitol Square, the center of Richmond civic life, now became a refuge for traumatized civilians as well as a trophy for Union occupiers. On the square distilled all the terror and anguish that afflicted white Richmonders that morning. The large shade trees dotted throughout the steeply sloping lower half of the square had just begun to bud, their new leaves not yet unfurled. Beneath their branches, Richmonders were accustomed to promenading through the grassy lawns along gravel walks with neat cobblestone and brick borders. Laid out decades before, the landscaping plan for this classical republican space was at last coming to maturity, a fitting context for Thomas Crawford's bronze representation of the first president on the level, upper half of the square. Designed by the sculptor in Rome among the crumbling vestiges of Diocletian's monumental baths, the statue was now fated to tower over another spectacle of dissolution.

Before the morning was out, Union cavalrymen and terrified residents trampled the grass and the gravel paths. Above the chaos at ground level, flaming cinders seared and scorched the trees. Rising above them all, "amid this carnival of ruin, stood the great statue of Washington, against which firebrands thumped and rattled."[2]

As the fire spread, more and more dispossessed citizens sought refuge on the lawn. Merchants who lived above their stores in the crowded streets near the Capitol tried to salvage a few possessions by dragging them to the square. In the predawn hours, most people hurrying through the streets with bundles under their arms or balanced on their heads had been looters. Now, with blue-coated troops streaming in and the thieves cowed by the threat of summary punishment, anyone bearing a burden through the streets most likely owned it. With each minute that passed, haphazard accretions grew all over the square: piles of clothes and bedding, furniture and kitchenware, carpets, mirrors, heirlooms, and jumbled sacks of possessions mixed promiscuously together with their stupefied owners.

They still were not safe. "Men, women, and children crowded into the square of the Capitol for a breath of pure air; but it was not to be obtained even there, and one traversed the green slopes blinded by cinders and struggling for breath."[3] The sick and lame, brought there on litters by friends and family, lay helpless on the lawn. Airborne embers fell so thickly that refugees had to brush them off their clothing or risk catching fire, as some of the unattended piles of belongings did in the midst of the hoped-for sanctuary.

It was not a scene the people huddled there ever imagined for their city. "And thus, on this thronged theatre, unnaturally illuminated, and in an auditorium of almost unearthly sounds, expired much of the pride, the luxury, the licentiousness and the cruelty of Richmond."[4] So wrote Edward Pollard, the embittered and suddenly unemployed editor of the *Examiner*, sounding for all the world like one of his northern adversaries, who would now delight in describing the immolation of his city, his newspaper, and his cause.

THE FIRE HAD begun at the warehouses where soldiers carried out Ewell's disputed and now universally despised order. It radiated outward, and a rising wind from the south blew the flames away from the river and up through the commercial center of town toward Capitol Square. With the last disciplined Confederate force gone and the Union army not yet in firm control, the conflagration devoured hundreds of buildings. To an eyewitness, the sun seemed malevolent as it shone through the smoke, "like a great beacon of woe, or the awful unlashed eye of an avenging Deity."[5]

The flames spread so rapidly that before the Union army arrived, most citizens looked on the spectacle, helpless and paralyzed. Father Louis-Hippolyte Gache, S.J., the French-born Confederate chaplain of a Louisiana regiment, saw them standing in front of their houses and congregating from unthreatened parts of the city just to watch: "Everywhere there was grim silence, drawn faces and a sense of hopelessness and horror. . . . This very silence was all the more impressive for being suddenly broken again and again by the detonation of whole arsenals as the fire spread."[6] A resident of Franklin Street recalled the "death-like silence" that day: "No cries of fire, no ringing of fire bells, no rattling by of engines, not even the shrieks of women and children, for all seemed dumb with terror, and shrank pale and mute into their dwellings."[7] Mary Fontaine, who had watched the first Union soldiers raise the Stars and Stripes over the Capitol, agreed. "I watched those silent, awful fires," she wrote, "all like myself were watching them, paralyzed and breathless."[8]

After the second, formal surrender at City Hall, Godfrey Weitzel took up a position at the top of the steps on the east side of the Capitol to assess the situation. From there he and his staff looked down on what one of them called "a gigantic crater of fire."[9] With the pitiful refugees huddling below him on the square and the flames roaring toward the Capitol, Weitzel could understand the terror. He had a special, personal respect for the power of fire: his first wife had died horribly from burns when her dress caught fire from a candle. It would only have been human for him to remember that wrenching loss as he watched the fires destroy property and, for all he knew, burn countless innocent people to death trapped in the narrow streets below him.

His task was simultaneously to establish military rule and fight the fire. He proclaimed martial law and appointed his chief of staff, an impetuous attorney from Maine, Brig. Gen. George Shepley, as the military governor of Richmond. Experienced from doing the same job in occupied New Orleans, where the taint of corruption hung about him, Shepley quickly issued a string of orders—but not without first reminding everyone who had started the fire. He announced that the first duty of the Union army "will be to save the city, doomed to destruction by the armies of the rebellion." From his headquarters at the former Davis mansion, Shepley instructed the provost marshal, Lt. Col. Frederick Manning, to organize a force of soldiers to help the local fire brigade. Contradicting an earlier order from Weitzel admonishing civilians to stay at home, Manning appealed to all able-bodied citizens to lend the soldiers a hand.[10]

The chief engineer of the fire brigade was nowhere to be found. The next most senior officer, John Rodgers, stepped into the breach and worked side by side with the soldiers and impressed civilians. There was little equipment to aid them, only two steam fire engines, four worthless hand engines, and a large amount of hose that some sources say had been chopped up by saboteurs. Company G of the 13th New Hampshire was detailed to guard the hydrant, engine, and the remaining fire hose that vandals had not cut.[11]

By then, midmorning, the fire was far out of control and threatened the whole city. At the foot of the square, only the stone Custom House survived intact while flames reduced every building around it to ashes and rubble. None of the banks escaped—not the Bank of the Commonwealth, not the Farmers' Bank, not the Bank of Virginia, not the Bank of Richmond, not the Exchange Bank where Elizabeth Smith had dispatched the state-owned silver from the governor's mansion for safekeeping. J. B. Jones, the War Department clerk, counted them up two days later. "The burnt district," he declared, "includes all the banks, money-changers, and principal speculators and extortioners. This seems like a decree from above!"[12]

Only one building on Capitol Square burned, but it was an unfortunate loss—the State Court House. After he accompanied the mayor to surrender the city, Judge John Meredith hurried back to the court-house and helped cart out files of pending cases and most of the order books. He was not able to save the will books or the deed books, how-ever, or the records of the Supreme Court of Appeals, or those of Hen-rico County, which surrounded Richmond to the north, or thousands of legal records moved from outlying counties for safekeeping. They all burned. One piece of furnishing alone was saved from the building, a water pitcher snatched from the flames by the janitor's son.[13] The loss of so many public papers would become a serious inconvenience for the future, but that morning few people other than Judge Mere-dith thought about legal documents.

For a time, the Spotswood Hotel was in danger, but a providential lull in the wind spared it. The Ballard House and the Exchange Hotel escaped. The American and Columbian hotels were not so lucky.

Shortly after the Union army arrived, the fire at the Confederate arsenal and laboratory began to set off thousands of artillery shells and cartridges. A prolonged series of explosions added one more terri-fying element to a day already filled with calamity. Some people thought the Confederate army had returned and was shelling the city and its occupiers. A northern soldier who entered the capital that morning said the people stayed well back from the burning buildings because of the explosions. "I tell you," confessed Charles Morrell, "it made brick and mortar tremble."[14]

Prominent among the victims of the fire were Richmond's cele-brated newspapers. Friends had hardly laid the exegete of southern rights, John Moncure Daniel, in his grave when the flames consumed his paper. In his will, Daniel left the *Examiner* to his business man-ager, Richard Walker, one of the city council members who refused to the last to accept the fact of Richmond's fall. Now Walker's inheri-tance was ashes.

"It would be weak and idle to deny or blind ourselves to facts which stare us in the face," the paper's last issue admitted. "We can-not disguise the probability that Richmond may soon be in the hands of the enemy."[15] By the time anyone cared to read those out-dated words, the lead type in which they had been set on Evacuation

Sunday and the press that had printed them were melting in the inferno that silenced the voice of last-ditch Confederate defiance. Though John Mitchel, the Irish nationalist who probably wrote those words, had fled with the southern army, his colleague Edward Pollard remained to witness the destruction of their paper. "In this mad fire, this wild, unnecessary destruction of their property," Pollard later wrote, seething with hatred for Jefferson Davis, "the citizens of Richmond had a fitting *souvenir* of the imprudence and recklessness of the departing Administration."[16]

The *Enquirer* and the *Dispatch* also burned. Only the *Whig* and the *Sentinel* offices escaped. The former office of the defunct *Southern Literary Messenger* was reduced to ashes. The religious papers suffered, too—the *Central Presbyterian*; the *Southern Churchman*, published by the Episcopalians; and the Baptist *Religious Herald*, consumed by the flames that its editor had recently warned would be the reward for Richmond sinners. The fire put a number of job printers out of business, though Edward Ayres saved all of his type and paper stock, by happy chance having moved them to another location the week before.[17]

The only house of worship to burn was Dr. Charles Read's United Presbyterian Church, but that secular temple of learning, the Mechanic's Institute, kept it company. The Confederate War Department had occupied the latter building. In addition to official papers that bureaucrats were not able to carry off, between three and four hundred captured Federal regimental flags went up in smoke there. The office of the Southern Express Company, which shipped parcels by rail, entirely burned. The fire consumed every package in a large consignment that remained in the building on Sunday. Four large canvases depicting scenes of Confederate glory at Fort Sumter, the first fruits of secession, were destroyed when the shop exhibiting them burned to the ground.[18]

Despite Charles Ellis's efforts, the depot of his railroad burned, as did that of the Richmond & Danville line. The depots and workshops of the Richmond, Fredericksburg & Potomac escaped. In part, the railroad owed its salvation to the fact that it ended a block north of Capitol Square, away from the zone of destruction. Even so, during the height of the blaze the line's buildings frequently caught fire from airborne cinders. With help from the 19th Wisconsin Regiment, Samuel Ruth organized a party to put them out. The railroad's superintendent of transportation, Ruth had spent time in jail earlier, accused of being a "pestilent Unionist" and passing information to the northern army. Ruth had indeed given valuable intelligence to Grant's army, intelligence that led to the destruction of his railroad's bridges near Fredericksburg. Unaccountably, the authorities released him before the evacuation, but on the day of the fire he worked to save, not destroy, his employer's property.[19]

Most of the saloons disappeared in the flames. The misfortune was not the loss of alcohol. The occupiers would not let anyone sell it for many days to come, anyway. More important, the saloons had also provided the main source of food for many people. Among the victims was Tom Griffin's establishment, where only two days before, Thomas Conolly paid royally for culinary luxuries to entertain his newfound Richmond friends.[20]

When the fire began, William Warren tried to move the inventory from his dry goods store on Cary Street. He was doomed: his shop stood almost next to the Shockoe tobacco warehouse, the first building to burn at the hands of Ewell's soldiers. With the help of his slaves, Warren managed to shift some of his stock into a side yard. But he could not move it far enough to safeguard it from both robbers and fire. His cousin should have been at the store to help, but to Warren's disgust, the younger man joined the looters. The frenzy of thieves breaking into stores, smashing windows, and carting off whatever struck their fancy, the heat from the rapidly spreading fire, and sheer exhaustion from trying to carry too much by himself finally overwhelmed him. He admitted he might have saved more if he had persevered, but he succeeded in saving only a few personal items, "& in perfect despair & desperation & [with] no one to help I gave up all and resigned myself to my fate."[21]

By the time the army began to fight the fire in a systematic fashion, nothing could be done for stores like Warren's close to the waterfront. Or for the bridges, by then dropping into the river with great hissing splashes, span after span. The explosions of artillery shells at the arsenal added another complication to thwart the firefighters. The soldiers finally saw their efforts begin to succeed about noon in one sector after they blew up the Trader's Bank to prevent the fire from spreading farther east along Main Street. Everywhere else they had to wait until the wind subsided and the flames ran out of fuel. Complete mastery over all sectors did not come before late afternoon, and small, contained fires flared up for days to come. The smoke would continue for weeks.[22]

Weitzel assigned his brother and aide-de-camp to round up men to help. As he rode past a house on Franklin Street that was threatened by flames, Capt. Lewis Weitzel stopped when a black man asked him to come inside and speak to his mistress. He did and learned from the woman that she needed help to move her invalid mother, the wife of Robert E. Lee, who had been superintendent of West Point when Godfrey Weitzel was a cadet. The captain placed three soldiers and an ambulance at her disposal, and they remained outside her house until the threat of fire receded.[23]

During Gen. George McClellan's failed 1862 attempt to take the city, the parapet on top of the hip roof of the governor's mansion offered a nighttime view of artillery flashes in the distance. Now that McClellan's successors had finally done what he could not, Elizabeth Smith, the wife of the incumbent governor, did not need to climb up to the roof to see flames. When she, her daughter, and two house-guests left the mansion about seven-thirty in the morning, the fires were racing toward them. Only the diligence of a few watchers on the rooftops—first Confederate ones and then Union—kept cinders from burning the building down.[24]

The fire then chased Smith out of the friend's dwelling where she first took refuge. She returned to the mansion on Capitol Square, but in the meantime, Gen. Charles Devens had made his divisional headquarters in the reception room and planned to board his staff in the house. In 1862, Devens had been wounded not far from Richmond at the battle of Fair Oaks. Perhaps he knew that Smith's husband had commanded a Virginia regiment opposite him in that fight. Even so, he graciously gave her permission to reoccupy the family quarters until she could find an alternative. She kept up a brave front, made light of her troubles, and told the new tenants of the mansion it was the second time she had been caught behind enemy lines. "She says she is getting used to the Yankees," wrote a bemused northern reporter a few hours later, surprised by her good cheer in the face of disaster.[25]

Like Smith, Susan Hoge presided over a large household, the parsonage at Fifth and Main, next door to her husband's Second Presbyterian Church. Moses Hoge had fled on the presidential train, fearing that his well-known views and prominence as chaplain to the Confederate Congress put him at risk of arrest. A wife for twenty-one years, Susan had buried four of her eight children, run a school in a teeming household that sometimes sheltered a dozen boys, and earned a reputation for having a sound head for business.

She organized the children and slaves to be ready to leave if the fire forced them out. She instructed everyone to put on two sets of clothes and assembled them in the parlor, each with a snack, a bottle of milk, and a change of clothes in a bundle for easy carrying. The roof caught fire three times from embers blown across from neighboring buildings, even though she had covered it with wet shawls and blankets. The church's sexton and a slave stayed on the roof putting out sparks as soon as they landed. Explosions from the arsenal smashed nearly all the windows in the house. A piece of shrapnel came through the study window but only broke a bottle of ink and knocked some books off the shelves.[26]

A dentist named Davidson who had been out before sunrise went down to Cary Street after breakfast to the Gallego Mills just when they began to burn. When this towering building was completely on fire, he returned home. There he watched from the upper story, as the roof of the mill collapsed in a shower of sparks and burning shingles. The wind carried them high over the street. Coals blew into his house through the open dormer windows. Davidson put out the fire inside but knew he had to go out on the roof to put out other smaller blazes before his shingles caught fire. His neighbors did the same. The rain of burning coals increased as the wind rose, and eventually Davidson and other homeowners in his block gave up and watched the fire consume their houses, powerless to prevent it.[27]

BY THE TIME the fire burned itself out, hundreds of buildings had disappeared, perhaps eight hundred, perhaps a thousand. The view from Main Street down to the river, and between Eighth and Fifteenth streets—in all more than twenty blocks—embraced an appalling vista "of smoking ruins, blackened walls and broken chimneys."[28] Just outside the limits of the burning, furniture and household goods choked the streets and were trampled in the mud. Despite initial fears that many civilians died in the fire, such was not the case. Less than a dozen perished at the most, counting even the tally of dubious secondhand stories. It took a full week to pass before the first body was recovered, charred beyond recognition, from the canal turning basin.

The 12th New Hampshire Volunteers battled the flames all Monday afternoon. Bone-tired by nightfall, Capt. John Prescott managed to summon the energy to scribble in his pocket notebook that "the inhabitants thank us for our efforts, while they curse their Gov. for setting [the] fire."[29] Prescott's terse assessment captured more than wishful thinking by a weary northern soldier hoping the residents would thank him for saving their city from complete destruction. Richmonders, even staunchly Confederate ones, agreed with him. Susan Hoge, no friend of the North, conceded that "the yankees put a stop to [looting] & made the negroes work to put the fire out & they worked hard themselves."[30]

With a bucket and tin basin, the banker George Washington Camp helped save one threatened block of shops. He described in scathing words how on the previous evening the pleas of residents opposed to burning the tobacco were rebuffed by an aide to Breckinridge. "There are hard words & harder feelings here I tell you," wrote Camp three days later.[31] John West went further, telling his mother that "the terrible conflagration started by the reckless wickedness of the retreating authorities involved me with hundreds of others in ruin, and this last act of vandalism, together with the uniform good conduct of the U.S. troops has changed the feeling of our whole people."[32]

Gratitude did not mean political conversion, however. West, after all, was a Unionist. His Confederate neighbors could at the same time—and without blinking at their contradictory opinions—be grateful that the Yankees fought the fire, blame Jefferson Davis for causing it, and still pray that Lee would return with a flaming sword and drive the enemy from their city. And they did blame the hapless Davis even though the wider, wind-borne destruction came, however inadvertently, from the military demolition wrought by soldiers following the chain of command, from Lee to Ewell, from Ewell to Carrington, and from Carrington to the men who held the torch to the warehouses and bridges.

It was too much to say, as the *Richmond Whig* crowed after it changed its political stripes under federal occupation, that "the Discipline of Fire . . . has preached with tongues of flame the gospel of Union."[33] Anna Deane acknowledged that northern soldiers were all that stood between her and the complete destruction of her city. And yet, she said, "as I write I can see the Yankee flag moving over our Capitol, my heart sickens with indignation, to think that we should ever have loved it."[34] Confederate Richmonders, even at this late hour, fervently prayed for the success of their harried army, wherever it was. On the afternoon of April 3, they did not know what the future held for them or that army. They sensed that the fall of Richmond meant the end of all their hopes, told themselves it was not so, and put their hopes in Lee.

CHAPTER 12

LET IT BURN

Monday, April 3, Afternoon to Evening

Babylon falls, and her temples and towers
Crumble to ashes before us
—A. J. H. Duganne, "Richmond Is Ours"[1]

Godfrey Weitzel knew he would move temporarily out of contact with headquarters when he entered Richmond, because his telegraph corps did not bring enough wire into the city on the first day. It was a small problem. He had only to send a courier back three miles to his lines of the night before to be in instant touch with City Point. From there, word could go to the field headquarters of the Union troops chasing Lee's army. Because of a glitch, probably human error and not the telegraph, Grant did not receive Weitzel's message the first time it was sent to him, but word quickly spread down and across the chain of command. One lowly officer who heard the news and spoke for all of them was the army surgeon Daniel Nelson, who, with his field hospital, followed the spoor of wounded men that marked the Confederate retreat west of Petersburg. "Richmond is fallen, is fallen," he repeated to his journal Monday evening. "That wicked city is fallen. Freedom justice and Religion may now shout for joy."[2] Then he returned to the task, now disconcertingly routine, of sawing off mangled limbs, for the fighting continued.

ONCE WEITZEL CONNECTED to the field telegraph east of Richmond, he was in touch not just with City Point but also with the whole country beyond. This was possible because once the campaign against Richmond and Petersburg had settled behind static lines in 1864, the army connected Grant by telegraph to Washington, D.C. This first required extending the line from the Federal capital all the way down the Eastern Shore of Maryland and Virginia. Then engineers ran it under the Chesapeake Bay at Cherrystone Point to Fort Monroe at the tip of the Virginia Peninsula and finally along the banks of the James to City Point. When Confederate raiders cut the line, resourceful Union engineers laid a submarine cable down the middle of the river, beyond the reach of saboteurs. Weitzel's message thus reached Washington only two hours after he dashed it off in Extra Billy Smith's house overlooking the fire down below. The news of Richmond's fall spread throughout the North the same day at lightning speed.[3]

The very first word reached Washington, in fact, not directly from Weitzel but through a cable sent by Abraham Lincoln from City Point headquarters, where he was visiting Grant. Right after they received that message, War Department clerks received another from Fort Monroe saying, "Turn down for Richmond." That was the telegrapher's shorthand request for the Washington office to turn down the armature spring on its machine to allow it to respond to the weaker signal coming from a more distant apparatus. When the Washington man did as asked, he received the historic report from Fort Monroe: "All right. Here is the first message for you in four years from Richmond, Va., April 3, 1865."[4] What followed was a recapitulation of Weitzel's report that he had taken the city that morning.

That was all anyone heard from the general all day long, for Weitzel was too busy fighting the fire to spare another courier to take further messages to the field telegraph. But one message was enough. As soon as they received the electric and electrifying news, the War Department telegraphers in Washington ran to the windows and shouted the word to passersby outside. Immediately, government workers took to the streets to celebrate.[5] They gathered in crowds in front of offices to cheer, hug one another, and demand speeches.

Politicians made happy capital of the occasion. To a crowd gathered in front of his office, Secretary of State William Seward asked rhetorically what he should say to the various foreign powers. He ran down the list of countries and couched his reply to his own question according to how helpful each nation had been during the war. Sometimes the crowd answered for him. When he got to France, whose meddling below the Rio Grande gave Seward a special headache, he asked, "What shall I say to the Emperor of the French?" A cocky voice in the throng answered, "To get out of Mexico!"[6]

A large crowd assembled outside the War Department and called on the secretary to address them and to read Weitzel's cable. They cheered each Union success and laughed with derision at each detail of Confederate defeat. The loudest cheers greeted the news that Richmond was on fire. At the mention that Union soldiers were helping put out the flames, they roared, "Let it burn, let it burn."[7]

At the Willard Hotel the crowd spotted Vice President Andrew Johnson and urged him to speak. It was the first public address since his disastrous performance at the inauguration ceremony in the Senate chamber the month before. On that occasion the combined effects of typhoid fever and whiskey produced such a rambling, incoherent discourse that Lincoln prevented Johnson from speaking again to the crowd outside.[8]

At the Willard, the vice president began on a harsh note and hammered it without subtlety. He reminded the audience of a scene in the Senate at the beginning of the war when he was, he said, the only southern senator to resist the allures of treason. Someone had asked him then what fellow Tennessean Andrew Jackson would have done about the secessionists. Johnson had said that "he would hang them as high as Haman." Now, he said, to prolonged cheers, "humble as I am, when you ask me what I would do, my reply is, I would arrest them; I would try them; I would convict them, and I would hang them."[9]

Gen. Benjamin Butler also spoke to the crowd. Quarrelsome and inept as a commander, called "Beast" by Confederates for his treatment of civilians and "Spoons" for allegedly stealing silverware, he did reward loyalty and displayed great solicitude for the black soldiers under his command. His comments at the Willard were based on garbled telegrams from the front and added to the confusion about which Union forces first entered the city and which raised the first flag. It was, he told the throng, an instance of divine retribution "that the corps of colored troops, under the gallant Weitzel, was the first to plant the flag of freedom over the rebel Capitol."[10] Although the USCTs claimed to be the first regiments into Richmond, they never claimed to have raised the first flag. Butler's remarks conflating the two issues just muddied the disputes.

By nightfall the spontaneous revelry of midday began to take on a more organized, though still boisterous, tenor. Fireworks lit up the sky. Military bands competed with one another. Bonfires burned in the streets. People waved flags of every size. Fireworks, church bells, and nonstop cheering punctuated the celebrations. The White House was ablaze with light. But with Lincoln at the front, it could not compare to other displays.

At the Patent Office a huge gas-lit sign proclaimed, "Union." At the Capitol a more grandiloquent illumination bore a verse from Psalms 118: "This is the Lord's Doing; It is Marvellous in our Eyes." Chinese lanterns and illuminated mottoes decorated the banking houses, which also highlighted the percentage yields of war bonds, demonstrating that patriotism and profit were not mutually contradictory. The Treasury, State, and War departments vied with one another for the grandest display. Candles at each window made a dazzling effect at the normally dingy War Department building. At the Treasury, a gas-lit transparency displayed a giant greenback, the almighty dollar triumphant.[11]

In New York City, George Templeton Strong, prominent lawyer and leading figure at the U.S. Sanitary Commission, walked down Wall Street on Monday morning to read the bulletin board in front of the *Commercial Advertiser*. He arrived just at the moment a clerk painted in oversized letters on a large sheet of brown paper the news that Richmond had fallen. A devout churchman, Strong rushed to Trinity Church to ask the rector for permission to ring the bells. "Men embraced and hugged each other, kissed each other, retreated into doorways to dry their eyes and came out again to flourish their hats and hurrah," he wrote. "There will be many sore throats in New York tomorrow."[12] After the example of Trinity, church bells pealed all over the city for half an hour, from Wall Street to Harlem. In the soldiers' hospital, freed prisoners from Andersonville, too ill to shout, feebly waved bouquets of flowers to show their happiness.[13]

The rage for flags exhausted the supply. The Stars and Stripes festooned every public building and most private ones. Miniature flags bedecked railway cars and horse-drawn wagons and carriages. Ferries draped their railings with bunting. From the waterfront to the hotels along Broadway, and on to the mansions of the rich farther up Manhattan, red, white, and blue fabric covered the city. Ten thousand or more joyfully sang "The Battle Hymn of the Republic." The people of New York celebrated Richmond's fall so intensely precisely because it was the seat of Confederate government and power, the symbol of all they had been fighting for four years: "They wanted its lines of defence broken and its fortifications captured—they wanted Jeff. Davis driven out or hanged at his door post, and Gen. Lee swept from his entrenchments."[14]

Because of multiple extras printed by the papers and notices posted like the one George Strong saw, a large meeting, "the result of spontaneous patriotic combustion," assembled in front of the Merchants' Exchange in Wall Street. A speaker addressing the multitude said the leaders of the rebellion should be exiled: "I would be generous and provide them with a steamboat, and let them go to . . ." At that point, voices in the crowd interrupted him with cries of "Hell," "Hell," "Hell." Thousands cheered, danced, huzzahed, and shouted themselves hoarse. After hearing the obligatory patriotic utterances from selected leaders, the people took off their hats, and with the chimes of Trinity floating above them, sang the Doxology in unison in an extraordinary outpouring of emotion. "Who can ever forget the day?" asked the New York Independent. "Pentecost fell upon Wall Street till the bewildered inhabitants suddenly spake in unknown tongues—singing the doxology to the tune of 'Old Hundred!' "[15]

In Philadelphia the fire engine companies sent their steamers, hose carriers, and hand engines into the streets to add their whistles and bells to the cacophony around Independence Hall. In Boston, epicenter of abolition, they celebrated with equal abandon at Faneuil Hall. The newspaper in Annapolis heralded the death of "Richmond, the Moloch of the rebellion." A handbill that reflected sentiment all over the North proclaimed, "Babylon has Fallen!! . . . Richmond, the proud, the defiant stronghold of treason and head-quarters of traitors has been humiliated."[16]

In Chicago, patriots congratulated themselves: "Of all the places hateful to God and man, Richmond has been, for four long years, the most abhorred and detested."[17] Enterprising merchants along the shore of Lake Michigan, destined to lose their own stores in a much greater fire six years later, immediately began to offer sale prices in honor of the burning of the enemy capital. For days the front pages of northern papers were filled with maps of Richmond, diagrams of Capitol Square, and lengthy eyewitness accounts, some by reporters who arrived with the army, others by those who flocked as quickly as they could to the site of this great culminating news story of the war.

Reactions in those parts of the shrinking Confederacy not yet occupied were necessarily different. Out in mountainous southwestern Virginia, Capt. Edward Guerrant, a young Kentucky Confederate, put on a brave front, trying to convince himself all was not lost. "Other nations have lost their capitols & triumphed," he wrote plaintively in his diary when the telegraph tapped out the words of doom about Richmond. "Why may not we?"[18] William Nalle, a farmer in Culpeper County, ninety miles northwest of Richmond, was closer to the capital than Guerrant but did not learn the news until a day later. When he heard, the pragmatic Nalle doubted the news just as he did another report that France had belatedly recognized the Confederacy. He just went on harrowing his fields, for spring planting had to go on, whatever the news from Richmond.[19]

Edmund Ruffin, the most famous fire-eating secessionist in the

South, feared the fall of Richmond meant "the vindictive & atrocious enemy" would soon occupy all of Virginia.[20] Two weeks later, after those fears were realized, he put his son's musket to his mouth and pulled the trigger with a forked stick. Catherine Edmondston, when she heard the news down in North Carolina, was prostrate. "I sit stunned & am unable to look forward to a single day," she wrote.[21]

The news took a little longer to cross the ocean. That marvel of the age, the transatlantic telegraph cable, was only then being laid, and so word of Richmond's fall raced across the sea, at the speed not of electricity but of steamship. The fate of the South was no less important to many people in London and Paris for being so far away from the action. One of them, John Reuben Thompson, former editor of the *Southern Literary Messenger*, had left Richmond in 1864 to write for the *Index*, a London newspaper subsidized by the Confederacy to sway English opinion.

As a spokesman for the South, the ardent Richmond-born poet made his mark in the British capital. Fashionable parlors were opened to him, and he was often in the company of Tennyson, Dickens, and the Brownings. In early April, Thompson viewed the Oxford-Cambridge boat race along the Thames with a vast throng basking in the sunshine of a perfect English spring afternoon. That evening he enjoyed the repartee across the dinner table at a friend's country house, enlivened by the brilliant chancellor of the exchequer, William Gladstone. The conversation would have lost its sparkle for the Virginian had he known that at the same hour Lee had reached Appomattox.

On the 15th of the month, the news about Richmond reached London. It swirled through the clubs of St. James's and the drawing rooms of the West End. Thompson, already weakened by tuberculosis, was prostrate. A few days later he received a letter his sister had written from Richmond the same day Weitzel's soldiers marched in. From her he learned that the fire had consumed their family business and—far worse tidings for a literary man—that all of his books had burned.[22]

RICHMOND'S FIRST EVENING under Union control passed without incident. "By nightfall," remembered southern apologist T. C. DeLeon, "the proud Capital of the Southern Confederacy was only a Federal barrack!"[23] Just to make sure of its control, the army rounded up hundreds of Confederate deserters and stragglers throughout the day and put them in Castle Thunder and Libby Prison—the "Hotel de Libby" in the sneering phrase of a northern journalist who watched with glee.[24]

By evening every citizen felt the effect of martial law administered by the provost marshal, Lt. Col. Frederick Manning, "a very youthful and worried and busy looking man," in the words of a Confederate petitioner.[25] He made his office in the Capitol in the same quarters occupied by his southern predecessor, Isaac Carrington. Just as under Confederate rule, no one could leave the city without a pass. Manning's signature on these coveted bits of paper became so much in demand that it quickly deteriorated to a blurry line. The provost marshal warned soldiers against insulting residents, but he also declared he would not tolerate treasonable speech or insults to the Union army or flag. Anyone attempting to plunder public or private property risked summary punishment. Residents not burned out of their houses were told to stay inside. Meetings were forbidden.[26]

Many civilians had fled across Mayo's bridge before it disappeared in flames, or left the city to the north and west. Even so, most remained, and the fire dispossessed many of them. Residents burned out of their homes bedded down on the grounds of the Capitol and on its portico and steps. Col. William Kreutzer's 98th New York Volunteers stacked arms in front of City Hall across from the north edge of the square. Looking through the cast-iron fence, through gateposts molded to represent ancient Roman fasces, Kreutzer remembered watching as these unfortunate people spilled over the grounds and, in his condescending words, "like unclean beasts lay down and slept."[27]

Brig. Gen. Edward Ripley, taking no chances, turned out his staff for a tour of the city in the small hours of the morning. After the exhausting, exhilarating day they had just lived through, they cannot have relished the order to saddle up at 2 a.m. As they rode from one end of the city to the other, though, they saw nothing to alarm them, heard nothing but "the clatter of our horses' hoofs and the jingle of our sabres."[28] No one was abroad in the silent gloom but Union sentries scattered on alternate street corners to protect the houses and property of their former enemies.

One of those enemies, Lucy Fletcher, the mother of five, had served as a hospital volunteer and lost a brother and a brother-in-law killed in action. She sat up all night in a large armchair, unable to sleep, telling herself she would never take the oath of loyalty to the United States. Scribbling in her diary before drifting off to sleep toward morning, she wrote, "I looked out in the moonlight, and saw the guard passing to & fro and heard no sound to break the *unusual* stillness but his measured tread."[29]

Thomas Chester, the Philadelphia reporter, took special pleasure in the knowledge that African American soldiers were among the guards who stood watch over the property of "these would-be man sellers."[30] Some of them who now wore the blue uniform, indeed, had once been inmates of the nearby slave jails.

At Chimborazo, northerners and southerners wounded in the last battles around Richmond passed the night together. No sound broke the stillness, recalled the matron, Phoebe Pember. Not, that is, until she was awakened by a gang of men breaking into her pantry. The hospital was under Union control, but in the confusion of the first day, no guards had been posted. Pember accosted the men and immediately recognized them as "hospital rats," slang for malingerers. They knew where she stored her cache of medicinal whiskey and wanted it. The ringleader grabbed her by the shoulder and "called me a name that a decent woman seldom hears and even a wicked one resents." Before he could push her aside, Pember put her hand in her pocket and cocked the pistol she carried. She said, no doubt with more bravado in her memoir than she felt at the time, "if *one* bullet is lost, there are five more ready, and the room is too small for even a woman to miss six times."[31]

On one thing both Union and Confederate witnesses agreed: the exceptional quiet of that first night under occupation. No train whistles or squealing brakes, no familiar chiming of the hours by the state bell or the police station bell. Worn out, spent, exhausted, prostrate with grief or tired from celebrating, Richmonders black and white slept that night.

Witnesses also remarked on the contrast between darkness and light in different parts of town. With the gasworks shut down and candles in short supply, it was uncommonly dark everywhere away from the Burned District. There, however, one could see faintly by the light of the remaining embers. Now and then a smothered part of the fire flared up briefly and flashed through the smoke that still rose in great clouds from the precincts below Capitol Square. A New Hampshire officer recalled looking south from the governor's mansion and seeing "a lake of liquid flame agitated by a gentle wind. The spectral walls, edged here and there with tufts of flame flickering in the breeze, were all that remained."[32] With the bitterness of an eyewitness, Confederate editor Edward Pollard remembered, "a strange quiet fell upon the blackened city . . . the quiet of a great desolation."[33]

CHAPTER 13

UPON THE WINGS
OF LIGHTNING

Tuesday, April 4

Thank God that I have lived to see this!
—Abraham Lincoln[1]

On Tuesday morning, stunned residents began to venture down to the waterfront. They gawked at the devastation. A few began to think about rebuilding. Along the wharf at Rocketts, a group of freedmen labored under the supervision of a Union officer to remove debris from the canal, the first fitful effort at reconstruction. Nearby, a reporter picked his way through the rubble, still burning in many places and smoking everywhere. Tall, genial, and handsome, a gifted musician and, for a journalist, unnaturally abstemious—no alcohol, no tobacco—Charles Coffin seemed prudish to some of his colleagues. But this New Hampshire farm boy had an eye for detail and turned it to good effect for the *Boston Morning Journal*. Though the army rejected him because of a bad foot, he was present at First Manassas and reported on every major battle in the East through four years of fighting. Anticipating the end to the campaign, on Friday he had told his readers "the last flicker of a candle is sometimes its brightest flame."[2] He believed his own copy and rode into town alone on Monday on the heels of Weitzel's regiments.

At midafternoon Coffin and the work crew in the canal were among the few spectators to see a shallow-draft admiral's barge, really just a big rowboat, coming up the river.[3] With its twelve long oars flashing in the sunlight, it approached the shore bearing an unmistakable figure dressed in black trousers, a long black overcoat, and a tall black silk hat. Abraham Lincoln had come to Richmond.

THAT THE PRESIDENT of the United States should appear so soon after the city's fall was one more improbability in a catalog of wonders that spring. In his second inaugural address delivered in Washington barely three weeks before, Lincoln had spoken of "malice toward none." He looked forward to the end of the fighting, to reconstructing a broken nation, and to peace. Before any of that happened, he longed to visit the front, and so he accepted at once when Julia Grant suggested to her husband that he invite the president to army headquarters. At the end of March, Lincoln and his wife took the steamer *River Queen* from Washington down to City Point, the teeming depot on the James River that supplied Grant's army outside Richmond and Petersburg.

City Point displayed the North's industrial might in all of its potency for waging war. Ships clogged the shoreline bringing in the prodigious quantities of food, fodder, and munitions that were necessary to feed the army of more than a hundred thousand strong tightening the noose around the capital region. The scene could only thrill any northern patriot and fill any southern one who saw it with foreboding.

To observers there, the president seemed fatigued. He had begun to look old. His sunken cheeks, loss of weight, and heavily lined face gave those close to him real concern about his health. But he did not want to disappoint the desire of ordinary soldiers to pay their respects, and he made himself available to them.

He was also troubled by his wife's emotional state. Away from the White House, Mary Lincoln became even more ill at ease than usual. She thought the officers' wives at City Point did not sufficiently defer to her. One day, in a particularly brutal manner, she berated Mary

Ord, the wife of one of Grant's favorite generals. That night she scolded her husband in front of chagrined dinner guests for allegedly flirting with Mary Ord. Only when she decided to return to Washington on the first of April did the president begin to relax.[4]

Like Grant, Lincoln hoped the spring campaign would end the war swiftly, and he wanted to be nearby when it did. At eleven o'clock Sunday, just as church services were beginning in Richmond, he enthusiastically cabled Edwin Stanton about the smashing Union victories that morning at Petersburg. The next day, at the same hour Weitzel entered Richmond, Lincoln set out from City Point with his son Tad to visit Grant at the scene of his triumph twenty miles below the capital. When he learned from his commander that Richmond had been evacuated, he announced he would go there, too.[5]

On his return to City Point, he found a telegram from Stanton begging him not to put himself at risk. For the good of the nation, Stanton pleaded, the president should not expose himself to harm. The Confederates were still dangerous enemies. Lincoln's reply gave his secretary of war cold comfort and perhaps a few more gray hairs in his long beard: "I will take care of myself."[6]

That night, when reports came in confirming details of Richmond's fall, Adm. David Porter, the senior naval officer present, remembered the president exclaiming, "Thank God that I have lived to see this! It seems to me that I have been dreaming a horrid dream for four years, and now the nightmare is gone. I want to see Richmond."[7] Though Porter wrote down his recollections years later, the words he put into Lincoln's mouth did fairly express the president's state of mind. Lincoln repeated his desire to visit the Confederate capital, and his wish set in train a series of near-disasters that dogged his progress and threatened more than once to end in tragedy.

Knowing the determination of the commander in chief, Porter ordered his ships to begin removing the obstructions that choked the river. Arrogant, brash, and prickly, prone to squabbling with his colleagues, Porter nevertheless in this instance attended to his duty with dispatch. Most important, he instructed his sailors to sweep for torpedoes, as marine mines were called then, and place a buoy carrying a red flag at each suspicious spot. "My ambition," the Confederate officer in charge of that stretch of the river had said, was "to fill the waters of the James as full of torpedoes as they were of catfish."[8] All day Sunday he had supervised his men arming more mines, but fortunately for Lincoln's ships, he did not have a chance to launch this latest batch of explosives before the evacuation.

Enough other mines already infested the river, though, to make Porter's sailors jittery. Under a clear sky Monday night, with moonlight reflecting on the surface of the James, they began their dangerous task. The navy knew the Confederates had created some mines they could detonate remotely by battery as well as by contact, so it also sent men along the shore with shears to cut any electric wires they found. The sailors eliminated other mines by blowing them up, with explosions of sobering power. So-called drift torpedoes remained a threat. These were submerged mines connected by multiple wires to drifting wood on the surface. If the wires became entangled in the propeller of a passing ship, they would detonate the charge.[9]

On Tuesday morning, while the Army of the Potomac pursued Lee's forces westward and Federal troops in Richmond turned from fighting fires to restoring order, the president and his son Tad boarded the *River Queen*. Porter's flagship, *Malvern*, a fast side-wheel steamer, accompanied it, as did the gunboat *Bat*, a former blockade runner that had been commissioned into Federal service. The *Malvern*, in the vanguard, swept for mines that had escaped detection the night before. The transport *Columbus* followed with the president's cavalry escort and his carriage, a four-horse ambulance.

About midday, the flotilla reached the first line of Confederate obstructions a mile below Chaffin's Bluff and successfully passed by. On either side of the James, southern fortifications, peppered with dozens of large-caliber artillery pieces, rose up in impressive ranks. One of the sailors said they stretched "from rivers edge across country some places as far as the eye can reach."[10] Now abandoned, they were impotent. Not so the danger below. Above the first line of obstacles, many Confederate mines remained, despite efforts to sweep them. Lincoln trusted his sailors to clear a path, but Porter did not share his chief's nonchalance. It would not have made him feel any better if he knew then what he learned two days later—that at Chaffin's Bluff his ships passed over a huge mine containing more than seventeen hundred pounds of gunpowder that his men had failed to neutralize.[11]

Drewry's Bluff, seven miles below Richmond, marked the second line of obstructions, and there serious problems began. To restrict passage, the Confederates had sunk steamships across the river, leaving only their rotting wheelhouses protruding above the surface and a gap of fifty feet to allow flag-of-truce boats to pass.[12] Even before reaching this point, Porter had to leave the *Bat* behind when it ran into trouble. Its modern design—shallow draft, steel hull, and two large oscillating engines—had not saved it from being captured on its first blockade run, and it was of no help at all now to its new Federal owners.

The *Columbus* fell behind, too. Then the sailors discovered that the *Malvern* and *River Queen* were too large to squeeze past the Drewry's Bluff barrier. But Lincoln would not turn back. He transferred to the admiral's barge, normally propelled by twelve oarsmen. To give more speed, the small steam tug *Glance* took the barge in tow. The tug carried the president's guard of thirty marines, a skimpy force for protecting the commander in chief on a visit to the enemy capital, not yet, as far as anyone in Lincoln's party knew, completely under firm Federal control.

Months of conflict had clotted that stretch of river with the debris of war. On either side, wrecked shipping and dead horses floated by, and below the danger from mines was ever present. Lincoln laughed away the hazards and joked that it was Porter's fault they were on the river in the first place. The admiral risked all these mines, the president teased, because he was afraid to ride to Richmond on horseback. Escape from the confines of Washington had done Lincoln good. The thrill of being on hand when his armies achieved their final victories made them all the sweeter.

Shortly after Drewry's Bluff, the president's party caught its first sight of the city, a pall of smoke still hanging over it. The barge passed the remnants of the ironclads that Admiral Semmes had destroyed with thundering explosions only the morning before. The smoke-stacks of the *Virginia II* protruded above the surface, as did the ruined paddle wheels of another vessel.

The one operational steamer that remained intact at Richmond was the flag-of-truce ship *Allison,* which two days before had carried Robert Ould and his last batch of Yankee captives to the final prisoner exchange. The *Allison* came down the river Tuesday under Union command before the president's party reached the city. Just as it reached the *Glance* pulling the admiral's barge, it ran against an obstruction. Then, when the tug tried to help free the *Allison,* it ran aground.

Lincoln insisted on continuing without escort. He had not come this far to be frustrated. Now even his marine guard on the tug had to be left behind, just as his cavalry guard had been when they abandoned the stranded *Columbus.* To make matters worse, the barge ran aground before they reached the shore. It was not a happy moment for the proud admiral. Porter admitted later he had hoped to make a grand naval entrance into Richmond with his gunboats.[13] But his fleet of four ships carrying hundreds of soldiers, sailors, and marines had been reduced by one mishap after another to a single open boat propelled only by muscle power. It was certainly a dramatic approach but hardly what Porter had in mind.

In a week filled with symbols and portents, Lincoln's boat made landfall within sight of Libby Prison. Few people beyond the locals had heard of this building before the war when it was a plain ship chandler's warehouse. But thanks to newspaper accounts describing it as a dungeon for Union officers, its name now resonated with a malignant power throughout the North. By a quirk of geography, the prison inmates—now all southerners—were among the privileged few to gape at the same incongruous sight as the work crew of freedmen and Coffin, the solitary northern journalist. Coffin made it sound as though the newly freed slaves, simple men in his description, were first dumbfounded at the sight and then went wild with joy. They may have been unlettered, but they were no more astonished than the newspaperman when he first caught sight of Lincoln.

The army had alerted Weitzel about Lincoln's intentions, but no guard of honor appeared to greet the president, because no one expected him until later in the day. It was not Weitzel's fault, but it only confirmed Porter's belief that the commander was weak and ineffectual. Despite the confusion, word of the impending visit leaked out, and when the admiral's barge arrived, news sped through town, "as if upon the wings of lightning."[14]

ONCE THE PARTY made it safely to shore, one of the army officers formed up a vanguard of six sailors, distinctive in their blue jackets and round blue caps. Each of them carried a short naval carbine. After them came Lincoln, Tad, Admiral Porter, Charles Coffin, and two officers. The remaining six sailors formed the rear guard. Coffin later sketched the makeup of the procession for artist Thomas Nast, whose drawing of the scene thrilled thousands of northern newspaper readers.[15]

Lincoln towered over the other members of his party and the crush of well-wishers. In the warmth of the sun and with the crowd pressing close around him, he took off his overcoat. Every so often he lifted up his hat to wipe big drops of sweat from his forehead. Dust and smoke made the weather even more stifling, while the pungent scent of burned tobacco mingled with an acrid, charred aftertaste.[16]

Lincoln knew Weitzel had established his headquarters at Davis's house, the White House of the Confederacy three blocks north of Capitol Square, and made it the destination of his march through the ruins. Each step of the way, his party attracted more followers. The freedmen crowded around to shake the president's hand or just touch him. The most affecting moment came when, in a gesture of respect, Lincoln took off his hat as an old man prayed for God to bless the president. At another point, a woman exclaimed, "I know that I am free, for I have seen Father Abraham." Yet another shouted, "I'd rather see him than see Jesus."[17]

As the crowd clustering around Lincoln moved through town, some of the freed people, overjoyed at seeing him, shouted out that the president had arrived. In the confusion, rumors swirled through the city ahead of the party. According to one, the army had captured Jefferson Davis and brought him back to town. Some people therefore believed the shouts meant that Davis had returned, and they cried out, "Hang him! Hang him!"[18]

Thomas Chester kept an eye out for residents who were hostile to the apparition from the North. "Those who lived in the finest houses either stood motionless upon their steps or merely peeped through the window-blinds, with a very few exceptions," he noted. "The Secesh-inhabitants still have some hope for their tumbling cause."[19]

Kate Mason Rowland counted herself among the latter. Her bitterness at southern defeat and her hatred of Yankees would long outlast the fighting. She dismissed Lincoln's visit to the Confederate White House. Better that Davis's mansion had been lost in the fire, she wrote, than be violated by the Union president: "He harangued the mob of Jews, negroes & Yankees from the Presidential Mansion. What a pity it was not burnt too!" Constance Cary, whose prolific writing after the war would idealize the Old South, put similar tones in a letter written that day: "I looked over at the President's house, and saw the porch crowded with Union soldiers and politicians, the street in front filled with curious gaping negroes who have appeared in swarms like seventeen-year locusts."[20]

Weitzel met Lincoln on the street in front of the mansion and escorted him up the steps to loud cheering from the crowd. Thomas Chester was overcome at the sight of Lincoln in the former capital of the slave republic. As the president climbed the steps, he turned and bowed to the crowd to acknowledge them. This mark of respect from the Great Emancipator electrified the gathering until, Chester wrote, with his emotions overcoming his usual cynicism, "it seemed as if the echoes would reach the abode of those patriot spirits who had died without witnessing the sight."[21]

Inside, Lincoln was relieved to sit down and rest in Jefferson Davis's easy chair, an image whose symbolism captivated northern reporters. It bemused them, too, that upstairs they found Varina Davis's knickknacks still on the bureaus and mantels. The calling cards of the French consul and Richmond luminaries remained in a vase in the entry hall, though not for long. Journalists reported to their readers that in the parlors the damask curtains, French plate mirrors, marble-top tables, Italian mantels, and rosewood furniture gave the house a level of taste and refinement equal to the mansions of well-to-do New Yorkers. For the first few days, before too many souvenir hunters had passed through, the house retained the air of having just been abandoned by its residents.[22]

So many officers crowded the parlors of the main floor that they spilled out through the open, triple-hung French windows onto the wide porch facing the garden behind the house. In spite of the shabbiness of wartime Richmond, the garden appeared remarkably well kept. The remaining stock of Davis's liquor soon attracted the attention of the jubilant soldiers and sailors, who sarcastically toasted the absent Confederate leader. Lincoln contented himself with a glass of water and good-naturedly shook hands with every one of the men in uniform.[23] They had sworn to protect the Constitution of the republic, and he was grateful to them for their dedication, happy to share their moment of triumph and accept their hearty congratulations.

The journalists on the scene reported these and many other superficial details of this exuberant, unplanned reception of the president in the house of his adversary. They were giddy, like the army officers, who still could hardly believe that only two days before, formidable military obstacles separated them from the Confederate capital. They were so ecstatic about their victory that they misjudged the crowds, and one of them even wrote that Lincoln's reception augured well for the rapid reconstruction of the Union.[24]

William Merriam of the *New York Herald* made the most accurate prediction on the spot. "No one incident of all this drama," he said, "will so attract and fix the attention of the American people and the civilized world as the appearance to-day in the city of Richmond— erased capital of infernal traitors—of Abraham Lincoln."[25] He inadvertently hinted at the real import of Lincoln's visit when he said that just after the reception the president attended a private conference. The reporter would have to wait a day to understand how important that conversation was. In the meantime, Merriam and the others at the White House of the Confederacy basked in the triumph of their commander in chief and in Union victory.

ON LEAVING THE mansion, Lincoln stepped into a carriage drawn by four horses and toured the city with a cavalry escort and a large retinue of mounted officers. As the carriage drove slowly through the crowds, army bands played patriotic tunes and artillery fired blank charges in salute. Most of the throng consisted of former slaves, free but a day, and their joy could not be contained. Garidel, the Creole Confederate from New Orleans, saw the president's entourage pass in front of his boardinghouse, "followed by the entire Negro population of Richmond who were shouting hurrahs. Their cheers were filling the air. I have never seen such an outpouring." They hailed the president and ran alongside his carriage as it drove through the cobblestone streets. One woman shouted at the top of her voice, "Jesus Christ has come at last."[26]

When the cavalcade reached Capitol Square, the base of the Washington statue teemed with a mass of humanity straining to catch sight of Lincoln. In one of the statue's hands a soldier had placed a flag, and the Stars and Stripes fluttered in the breeze above Lincoln's head as he spoke to the crowd. Farther down the square, another flag, a cavalry guidon like the one Majors Stevens and Graves had first attached to the Capitol roof, adorned the smaller statue of Henry Clay. Lincoln told the other passengers in the carriage that he was sorely tempted to climb to the roof and personally raise his own flag over the Capitol.[27]

To the impoverishment of posterity, no one had the presence of mind to write down the exact words Lincoln spoke at the statue. The sense of them, though, shines through in a memoir written much later and, more plainly and powerfully, in a secondhand account written at the time. You can, he supposedly told them, according to Admiral Porter's recollections, "cast off the name of slave and trample upon it. . . . Liberty is your birthright. God gave it to you as he gave it to others, and it is a sin that you have been deprived of it for so many years."[28] Lelian Cook, a young woman living with Moses and Susan Hoge, did not see Lincoln, but she did note his visit in her diary that day. "I heard he made an address to the colored people" when he stopped on Capitol Square, "telling them they were free, and had no master now but God."[29]

The president and his party made a brief tour of the Capitol, which showed the neglect of wartime and the disarray of hasty evacuation. Pine desks and chairs were scattered around the plainly furnished legislative chambers. Homemade rag carpets and a multitude of spittoons covered the floors. The tall, triple-decker cast-iron stove, stamped with the British coat of arms by its London manufacturer, had warmed the colonial House of Burgesses in Williamsburg and served the same purpose for the Confederate legislature.[30]

Looters and relic hunters had already begun to pick over the spoils. They hacked off pieces of desks and stripped the fabric covering from chairs. Rubbish lined the corridors, and in every room official documents covered the floors. Outside, the warm spring breeze blew $1,000 Confederate bonds across the lawn, and no one cared.

After leaving the square, Lincoln's entourage toured the Burned District and then the prisons, whose reputations had seared the northern consciousness since early in the war. Seeing the prisoners—now all Confederate—prompted Weitzel to ask Lincoln how to treat the conquered southerners. This was a signal moment, as the commander in chief stood in the ashes of the defeated capital and considered how to respond to his commander on the spot groping for the right policy. He did not want to tie Weitzel's hands by issuing specific orders, but he did suggest a tone and an attitude. That much comes through clearly in the different accounts of this conversation when Lincoln suggested that Weitzel "let them down easy." A few days later, the general reminded Lincoln that "you spoke of not pressing little points. You said you would not order me, but if you were in my place you would not press them." Long after, he wrote that Lincoln said, "If I were in your place, I'd let 'em up easy, let 'em up easy."[31]

Whatever the precise words, it was a magnanimous sentiment, perhaps even premature. Lincoln may have been moved by his reception and by the threadbare state of the people he saw in Richmond, but Lee was still in the field. People sensed that the fall of the Confederate citadel meant the end, and yet no one knew what the outcome on the battlefield would be.

LINCOLN INTENDED TO stay in Richmond overnight, but the army advised him it was not yet safe enough. By late afternoon, the navy solved the problem when the *Malvern* finally made its way upriver past the obstacles and mines and dropped anchor off the Rocketts landing. As Lincoln stepped into the barge to be rowed out to the flagship for the night, an old woman on the quay greeted him with a good-natured shout: "Don't drown, Massa Abe, for God's sake!"[32]

Though Porter breathed easier once he had the president safely on board the *Malvern*, Lincoln's whereabouts were widely known in town. Twice, suspicious men hailed the ship and asked to come aboard to speak to him but then disappeared. Another emissary apparently got through. This one came from the manager of the New Richmond Theatre, an irrepressible scapegrace named Richard D'Orsay Ogden. He had been called many names in his time, including "a fawning sycophant, with just enough brains to know how to fascinate a frail woman and keep himself from the clutches of the conscript officer."[33] The *Examiner* had delighted in mangling his name as "D'Ogden" and charged that he had made "the temple of Thespis a cess-pool of excrement and foul vapours."[34] The taunts just made him more popular.

Imprisoned briefly by the Confederates for draft-dodging, Ogden was back at his post when the city changed hands, and received military permission to reopen two days after the fire. He planned to sprinkle northern patriotic songs throughout the performance, knowing that Union soldiers would make up nearly the whole audience. Weitzel, Shepley, Kautz, and other generals received personal invitations and accepted. Another went to the most important northern luminary in town.[35] Perhaps Odgen knew of the president's fondness for theater of all kinds, from blackface minstrel shows to his beloved Shakespeare. Lincoln declined the offer.

CHAPTER 14

A WEEK IN APRIL

Tuesday, April 4, to Saturday, April 8

Nothing new here. The fires are out and perfect quiet reigns.
—Maj. Gen. Godfrey Weitzel[1]

Godfrey Weitzel warmly detested his superior, Maj. Gen. Edward O. C. Ord. In March, Ord had taken part of the Army of the James south to reinforce Grant's hammer blows against the Confederates at Petersburg. Not a talented administrator or strategist, Ord was in his element on the battlefield and repaid Grant's confidence with tactical élan. Before his field headquarters moved beyond the reach of the telegraph, the irascible, bluff Ord sent a rapid-fire burst of orders back to Weitzel in Richmond. "Let food and necessaries come to the city. Register the white men. Appoint a military commission for the punishment of offenses against law and order. Organize a police force. Start gas and water companies and protect all inhabitants in their property who come forward and take the oath of allegiance." On second thought, Ord decided he ought to clarify the last sentence: "By property, persons are not meant."[2]

Weitzel did not need Ord's advice. He found chaos when he entered the burning city, and on the faces of the civilians, he saw fear and relief, indescribable joy and inconsolable distress. But he was far more experienced than his twenty-nine years suggested. Indeed, he had had a taste of civil administration as acting mayor of Union-occupied New Orleans. He knew he needed to establish order as a first step to making Richmond militarily secure. He had to make sure his forces were prepared for all contingencies, including possible Confederate counterattack. On Wednesday, the chief of artillery of the XXIV Corps received instructions for the disposition of caissons and guns in the event of an assault and orders to "hold the place at all hazards."[3] With this and similar orders, Weitzel's officers deployed their men to assure they kept the prize that had fallen into their laps with hardly a shot fired.

In retrospect these commands proved unnecessary, but at the time it was better to be overly cautious. No one knew for sure where Lee was, only that the familiar rumble of artillery from the direction of Petersburg had faded into the southwest with the contending armies. Appomattox was still just a name on a map, not yet the eponymous end to a turbulent historical epoch.

As WEITZEL'S MILITARY governor in Richmond, Brig. Gen. George Shepley promulgated a list of rules outlining the duties of his regime and the responsibilities of the residents. He put civilians on notice that anyone selling or giving liquor to a soldier faced summary punishment. He designated district provost marshals and appointed Edward Ripley, the young Vermont colonel, now brigadier general, in command of all troops doing guard duty in the city.

As a first measure, they opened registry books to enroll white male inhabitants. A further register, recording administration of the oath of allegiance, separated political sheep from goats. The oath would become a source of contention in the coming days. Whether to take it would cause intense anguish for Richmonders still reluctant to abandon hope for the Confederacy. Ripley recommended a military commission to sort out the status of inmates in the various jails and prisons. He was right to suspect that some of them were there for Union sympathies rather than common crimes.[4]

On Wednesday the fire department began pulling down the

scorched, unstable remains of brick buildings. The army assigned a detail of USCTs to help with the task, and it was none too soon. Already a teetering wall had collapsed on some boys hunting for scrap iron and seriously injured them, and a falling brick had gashed the head of a fireman helping to demolish a burned warehouse. Passersby would be making narrow escapes from tumbling masonry for days to come.

Rumors about Confederate and foreign gold caused a special headache. People knew about the train that left after midnight on Sunday, with its gold and its guard of midshipmen. Each time the story was recounted, the amount and nature of the treasure varied. But did any bullion or coins remain behind? That question intrigued residents in the wake of the fire and for a long time after. In the destitution of occupied Richmond, the prospect of instant riches was a tantalizing dream. The army posted guards at the sites of the burned banks to deter scavengers who had begun crawling over the ruins on Monday. The day after the fire, a soldier dug up a strongbox from the site of the Trader's Bank, blown up by the army to arrest the flames. Tales that the box contained gold owned by foreigners emboldened more treasure seekers.[5]

Like most prosperous cities before the war, Richmond had boasted of gas lighting for homes, businesses, and streetlamps. People learned how dependent they were when the gas had to be turned off because of damage to the pipes during the fire. Outside the Burned District, where smoldering embers gave off a ghostly, erratic glow on Monday night, the city was plunged into darkness. Shepley hired a large force of black men to clear away the rubble and expose broken gas mains for repair. The army pushed ahead with the work, not for the convenience of households but to provide nighttime lighting for security and military construction. The waterworks were still out of commission and under an armed guard because of an unwarranted fear of sabotage.[6]

The fire consumed the wooden superstructure of the two railroad bridges spanning the James. It only slightly damaged the masonry of the high stone piers that supported the Richmond & Petersburg line, but the footings of the Danville bridge would take longer to rebuild.

On Monday evening after the worst of the fire subsided, engineers began to build a pontoon bridge with the canvas boats, trestles, and other bridging material they brought in by wagon train. They started from the north side of the river, just downstream from the ruins of Mayo's bridge. It took thirty-five boats, spaced fifteen to twenty feet apart, to reach the island in the middle of the river and a further twenty-five to reach the south side. The engineers completed their task within two days, and as soon as they were done, they began planning a second string of pontoons to ease the flow of traffic.[7]

The U.S. Military Railroad Service jumped into action with the evacuation. It had been maintaining lines from City Point to Grant's army in front of Petersburg and had prepared for the breakthrough by stockpiling timber, rails, and rolling stock. The engineers needed all the matériel at their command in their frantic effort to exploit the decrepit captured lines running west to supply Grant's men pursuing Lee's army. Rotten ties, worn-out rails, and the need to convert the gauge of the track demanded intense labor. The service also had orders to reopen the line to Richmond. On Thursday, an inventory of assets that had survived the fire revealed that though the bridges were destroyed, forty-two engines, hundreds of cars, and fully equipped machine repair shops remained in good order. By Friday, two regular passenger trains began a daily run from the main base at City Point across to Petersburg and then up to Manchester on the south bank of the river opposite the capital.[8]

Supplying its forces at Richmond was the army's main objective in opening passage to the city by water. Along the waterfront, quartermasters employed about a thousand black workers in return for room and board. Some cleared debris. Others gathered up abandoned naval stores and machinery. Still others repaired the docks to receive the resupply ships. By Thursday, dozens of schooners and steamers contracted by the army had put in at the wharves between Seventeenth and Eighteenth streets. Nearly all carried military stores or provisions for sutlers, the traders authorized by the army to sell to soldiers from their mobile canteens.[9]

By the end of the first week, a rudimentary steamer service connected the capital with City Point and from there with the outside world. It cost nonmilitary passengers a dollar each way, and everyone, military and civilian, had to show a pass from the provost marshal. It was still too dangerous to sail at night. Buoys with red flags marked the location of disabled but still dangerous mines, and the sound of engineers blowing up others sporadically punctuated the week after the fire. There were plenty of nonexplosive impediments to avoid as well. Hardly a day passed without a ship suffering from some form of damage from running into obstructions.[10]

All of these tasks—deploying troops, setting up a system of provost guards and passes, and repairing bridges, railroads, and utilities—were enough to keep Weitzel busy for days, but he was well trained for the job. The more subtle problems of dealing with a sullen, conquered people were not so amenable to the empirical talents of a straightforward West Point engineer. Nor were the niceties of dealing with multiple superiors.

BOTH SIDES EXAGGERATED conditions with liberal use of words like "starvation." Before the evacuation, Confederates cursed the Union stranglehold and agreed with Robert Kean, the War Department bureaucrat, who blamed the Yankees in late March for the city's "rapidly approaching a state of famine." Conditions were bad enough without the hyperbole. If people were not literally starving, there was widespread hunger and deprivation. Stealing food and envy of those who had it became the principal activity and the dominant emotion of many civilians. A northerner who arrived with Weitzel's army spoke of the "gaunt figures, sharp features and general attenuated appearance" of supplicants for free food. The New York Tribune's reporter agreed that no one was starving but said, "Everybody was pinched."[11]

The New Orleans Confederate Henri Garidel probably had a typical experience. He had complained almost daily about pitiful, badly cooked food at his boardinghouse before the evacuation. He wrote of "our miserable breakfast of gruel and biscuits" during the first few days of occupation. By the end of the first week of Union rule, though, he noted with approval the appearance of better-quality fried biscuits and real coffee.[12]

The destruction of supplies in the fire, a nearly total absence of food for sale in the markets, and the lack of greenbacks temporarily increased the suffering of the population after occupation. Restrictions on movement of civilians in and out of the city made the shortages worse. "No one will touch Confederate Notes," lamented Margaret Brown Wight on Sunday night as she anticipated with a peculiarly practical dread how to find enough to eat—and how to pay for it—when the city changed hands the next day.[13]

If there was one topic on which conquerors and conquered could agree, it was the need to supply the daily bread of the population. From the instant of Federal occupation, a crowd of hungry people besieged army officers at the Capitol, clamoring for food. The army did not authorize Weitzel to give rations to civilians, but he improvised by using the proceeds from selling tobacco that had survived the fire to purchase food for the poor.[14]

Two private philanthropies became essential to the daily strategy of many for finding their next meal. Normally, the U.S. Sanitary Commission provided food, medicine, stationery and stamps, and other non-army-issue comforts for Union soldiers. On Monday, the commission drove its wagons into the capital with the army, set up headquarters in the former house of Chief Justice John Marshall, and began to aid poor Richmonders.[15]

The U.S. Christian Commission had done similar work providing food, stoves, and regimental chapels for northern soldiers. It circumvented the army's red tape to give nourishment for body and soul. Now the commission's agent, E. F. Williams, began to distribute food to needy civilians, hospital patients, and prisoners. The commission distributed newspapers and religious tracts, but Richmonders probably valued most the eight thousand rations that Williams gave out in his first four days of operation.[16]

In this work, the Christian Commission received the willing assistance of the Richmond YMCA and its president, William Munford.[17] Munford had headed a Confederate poor relief committee during the war and continued in that role with Federal blessing. His organization divided the city into thirty districts, each with a committee of citizens appointed to pass judgment on the merits of individuals seeking relief.

As hunger overcame pride, even staunch Confederate families applied for help from the relief agencies. To their Union benefactors, some appeared ungrateful. One woman resented taking handouts but listed pork, brown sugar, black tea, grits, and crackers among the free provisions her mother received from the hated men from the North. Thomas Chester saw Confederates like her accepting charity from their conquerors with bad grace and called it "a spectacle of mingled destitution and ingratitude."[18] Black Richmonders endured the privation with their Confederate neighbors. Despite their poverty, however, a northern journalist told his readers, "they submit with far better grace than the whites. They have a word and a smile for our soldiers; the whites cannot do either."[19]

Despite the generosity of the relief agencies, there never seemed to be quite enough food to meet the need. Crowds of destitute women gathered outside the office of the Christian Commission. On one occasion, Col. Dexter Clapp of the 38th USCT leaned out a second-floor window and pleaded with them. He implored those who could go another day to refrain from drawing down his limited supplies until the next morning, when he hoped to have enough food for everyone. When this small open-air drama attracted the attention of two reporters, Clapp pressed them into helping him.[20]

THOUGH THE FIRE consumed most of the newspapers, the *Whig* resumed publication the next day. It could do so in the first place because the flames spared its building and in the second because the army allowed it. While the fire was still burning out his competitors, *Whig* proprietor William Ira Smith approached the military governor about resuming publication. General Shepley agreed, as long as the paper published thoroughgoing Union sentiments. That was not an obstacle for Smith. On Tuesday afternoon the first issue appeared under the title *Evening Whig*. With headlines like "Continued Retreat of the Enemy," it ran no risk of offending Shepley's political sensibilities. A brief note in the first issue by an anonymous local Unionist set the tone by calling Confederate rule the most tyrannical since "darkness was changed into light."[21]

Because so few Richmonders owned greenbacks, the newspaper accepted IOUs in Federal currency, due in thirty days. In exchange for these chits, the purchaser received a modest single sheet, four columns wide. It bore the same logo as before. Above the proprietor's name appeared the Virginia state seal, showing the female figure of victory standing with her foot on the neck of a prostrate representation of royalty. Above the figures appeared the state's motto, *Sic Semper Tyrannis*—"Thus Always to Tyrants." During the Confederate years, the paper had carried an additional legend, "The Constitution— State Rights." That addition was nowhere to be seen on this newest and very pro-Union incarnation of the newspaper, which eagerly promised to promote loyalty to the United States. It hinted that it would soon secure one of the most illustrious Unionists in the state as editor. Readers understood the paper to be referring to former congressman John Minor Botts, who bided his time on his farm in Culpeper County.

The main topics of interest, of course, were the war and the fire. Because no one could glean conclusive news about Grant's pursuit of Lee that week—just hopeful but uncertain reports from the Union point of view—the paper printed speculation about the fighting and out-of-date stories from northern papers. The outcome of the fire, however, was all too obvious. From its first issue, the reborn *Evening Whig* began to assemble accounts of the damage that had turned Richmond's business quarter into "an amphitheatre of crumbling walls and tottering chimneys."[22]

The newspaper made certain to heap blame on the departed Davis administration and tell its readers how enraged all their neighbors were at the wanton destruction of private property. Though it was stridently pro-Union, the *Evening Whig* did not exaggerate when it described the widespread anger of Richmonders, even staunch Confederates, at the decisions that had led to the burning of their city. They still revered the South's commanding general, and even though most people understood that soldiers ultimately under Lee's command had lit the fires, the southern president got the blame. A visitor from Baltimore summed it up neatly: Davis had "alienated entirely the good will of the people. But Lee is fairly idolized & his word is law."[23]

In its first issues, the *Evening Whig* tried to describe the enormous loss of property. "For the distance of half a mile from the north side of Main street to the river," it proclaimed, "and between 8th and 15th streets, embracing upwards of twenty blocks, [the scene] presents one waste of smoking ruins, blackened walls and broken chimneys."[24] Brick, iron, and granite debris piled up in huge mounds. The disappearance of familiar landmarks made it difficult to point out exactly where a particular store had stood. Before the work crews began, cross streets were hard to make out, distinguishable only by small openings through the rubble. Because most insurance companies had their offices in the business district, their loss would compound the problems of rebuilding.

One business that skipped fewer beats in the transition to Federal rule than even the resourceful *Evening Whig* was prostitution. On Saturday evening, Richmond whores had cursed the nearly worthless Confederate currency they received for their services. Two nights later they found an abundance of new customers with pockets full of greenbacks. The densest concentration of brothels just east of Capitol Square, including the most notorious bawdy houses along the one-block stretch of Locust Alley, escaped the fire. That meant the women were able to ply their trade among the uniformed newcomers without the inconvenience of having to find new places of business.

Their good fortune alarmed Union army doctors. Two days after the fire, Norton Folsom, surgeon of the 45th USCT, reckoned conservatively that there were a hundred brothels in town and a thousand prostitutes, "many of them fully diseased."[25] He lobbied for a system to subject the women to medical inspection, though not their clients. He proposed to issue licenses to those who were free of infection and to establish hospitals for those who could be treated.

At least one Washington physician saw an opportunity and began advertising to Richmonders in the newspaper, under the heading "A Friend in Need." In the coded phrases of the day, he said he had made "certain diseases" his special study and had cured many patients of both sexes. All such promises at that stage of medical science were false, and soldiers on both sides took home with them, wittingly or not, the scourge of gonorrhea and syphilis to infect their wives and sweethearts. One study suggested these amounted to a third of all veterans.[26]

Right behind the brothels and the *Evening Whig*, the exuberant Richard D'Orsay Ogden reopened his theater on Wednesday. In the absence of gas lighting, his actors made do with masses of tallow candles. The provost marshal supplied a strong guard to deter unruly behavior among the patrons, nearly all of them in uniform. Ogden wasted no time toadying to the occupiers and could not believe his luck that Lincoln was in town the night he reopened his theater.[27]

Though the president declined his invitation, nearly all the general officers turned out. Ogden draped the theater profusely with American flags, to the vocal delight of the audience. John Prescott, an army captain from New Hampshire who had helped battle the fire, was surprised to hear so many patriotic Union songs sung in the dim and flickering candlelight. "We cheered them lustily," he wrote later that night.[28]

The next night Buckley and Budd's United Minstrels and Brass Band resumed performances at the Varieties Opera House on Franklin Street. Harry Budd and Billy Lewis were accustomed to eliciting guffaws from theatergoers at their stereotyped black characters. They knew their lines would go down just as well before a Federal audience. Budd appeared again as "Julius Crow, the Boot Black," but they were true to their promise of original skits and burlesques. Lewis realized that a new regime called for new political jokes, and so he sang a just-composed song celebrating Grant's pursuit of Lee: " 'Twas then Bob Lee rode up his lines, / And, rising in his saddle, / He waved his sword and gave command / To right face and skedaddle."[29] Lewis sang this doggerel for the first time on April 8, the first Saturday of Union rule, when no one in Richmond yet knew the fate of Lee's army

The newspaper joined the vaudevillians in ridiculing the former regime. On Friday it ran a notice set in black-bordered type to mimic an obituary. Under the headline "DIED," it read: "At the late residence of his father, J. Davis, Richmond, Virginia, SOUTHERN CONFEDERACY, aged 4 years. Death caused by strangulation. No funeral."[30]

CHAPTER 15

A WHIRLWIND SWEEPING

Tuesday, April 4, to Saturday, April 8

> *You would be sadly grieved to see the desolation of our beautiful City.*
>
> —Margaret Keeling Ellis[1]

The evidence of collective and public loss was easy enough to see, but less apparent, individual losses were what distressed Richmonders most. Elizabeth Smith returned to the governor's mansion the afternoon of the fire at the invitation of General Devens, commander of the XXIV Corps. She discovered that thieves had broken into the closets and stolen linens, glassware, and china. It was a wonder they did not take more, given the opportunities for theft. One of the boxes she had hurriedly packed the day before contained nothing of value, but she was pained all the same to see that someone had rifled it. When she looked more closely at this assortment of mismatched bits of crockery with purely sentimental associations, she was overjoyed to find that the vandals had passed them up for the more practical boxes of hoarded groceries.[2]

The minister of the United Presbyterian Church was less fortunate. Dr. Charles Read was absent from the city on the day of evacuation, and as soon as he heard of Richmond's fall, he hurried back to find out about his congregation. He walked all the way from

Cartersville, forty miles up the James River to the west. His feet were so blistered by the time he reached the capital that he could not put his boots back on once he removed them. When he arrived, he discovered that both his house and his church had burned, an unhappy distinction he shared with no other man of the cloth in Richmond.[3]

Robert Powers, a druggist, was luckier. He had been imprisoned and then exonerated during the war on a charge of selling whiskey under a bogus doctor's prescription. The fire stopped half a block from his drugstore at Fifteenth and Main streets. When the explosion of the powder dump woke him early Monday morning, he walked with a slave to the store, braving the flames that raged just yards away. They threw the firearms he had kept there into the river to avoid trouble with the Union occupiers. Then he locked the store, for what it was worth, and went home to breakfast. The next day, Powers received permission to open for business. As a druggist, he had a useful stock to sell and was therefore one of the first merchants to reopen.[4]

Newspaper publisher John Wesley Lewellen, formerly of the *Enquirer*, lost everything but the clothes on his back. Even so, he said on Wednesday he would not "exchange my condition and peace for all the wealth of the world and war." He hoped for the chance to publish a paper again but did not know if he would be allowed to do so. Nevertheless, he wrote a friend, conveniently ignoring his support of the Confederacy, "come what may, my skirts are clean of helping to bring about this horrid war."[5]

Burnham Wardwell was hopeful, too. An ice dealer from Maine who had sheltered escaped prisoners of war and helped the Van Lew spy network, Wardwell had left Richmond after briefly being imprisoned for his politics. He returned the first week of occupation and in a tiny newspaper notice invited his old friends to come visit him at his new office. Perhaps he planned to sound them out on prospects for reopening his ice business. Whatever his plan, he was full of ambition to get even with his persecutors. It may have given him a thrill of satisfaction to stake out as his new office address the same slave jail where he spent two months in 1862 with John Minor Botts and Franklin Stearns for political offenses.[6]

In the first week after the fire, though, aside from Powers's drugstore, there was little business activity beyond that hawked by prostitutes, the theater, and a horde of Union army sutlers, all of whom catered to the occupiers and their plentiful greenbacks.

MATERIAL LOSSES COULD be replaced but not the human ones. It was a time of turning inward, of grieving for lost loved ones, of consoling family and friends. In rural Georgia long after the occupation of Richmond ceased to be national news, Amanda Fitzpatrick opened a letter and read the words she had feared: "As you in all probability have not heard of the death of your husband . . ." The letter was from William Fields, a Virginia private. On the morning of the evacuation, Fields had ridden into Richmond on one of the last hospital trains with another wounded soldier, Amanda's husband, Marion. Just before the rail bridge burned, their train was shunted across the river to Manchester, where Maria Clopton took charge of Fitzpatrick, Fields, and other wounded Confederates. Continuing her compassionate work as she had done all during the war, she organized a private hospital at her daughter's house as the Confederates fled and the Federal army marched in. Like the hospital matron at Chimborazo, Phoebe Pember, Clopton negotiated with Federal officers to care for her patients under the occupation.[7]

The attention did Fitzpatrick no good. "There wer ladies with him all the tim and surgeons," wrote Fields, "but his wright thy was shatered all to pieces an recovery was impossible as it was so high up that it could not be taken off." Fitzpatrick died on Thursday. Just before he breathed his last, he sang a verse of an Isaac Watts hymn from the Primitive Baptist and Sacred Harp hymnals, "Jesus can make a dying bed / Feel soft as downy pillows are."[8]

When the city changed hands, thousands of Confederate soldiers, like Fitzpatrick, too ill or wounded to be moved, remained in the military hospital at Chimborazo. The only thing that changed for them was the knowledge of southern defeat. And now sick and wounded men from the northern army shared their hospital. The day after the fire, Kate Rowland resumed her visits to the wards and sang patriotic songs to wounded Confederates to keep up their spirits. The subversive music seemed to cheer them up. It was good for her morale as well. Hearing the men laugh and joke, she could hardly believe that "we were all *prisoners*. . . . I pick up a book, & try to think it all a dream—this ghastly phantom of Yankee Doodle in our midst!"[9]

Rowland's neighbors were too disturbed to think of singing. So many had family members with the Confederate army, and every hour brought rumors with the names of those who had been wounded or killed. Lee's invalid wife may have been amused at erroneous newspaper reports that she was dying. But she must have been distraught to see the account that listed her son among the dead. That too turned out to be false, but it cannot have eased her mind in the days before news of Appomattox reached Richmond.

In ADDITION TO its efforts to feed the hungry and police the city, the army tried to win over the affections of civilians. Privately, many white residents had to agree with the words that Frances Hunt, a Confederate teenager, wrote on Tuesday: "The yankees are behaving very well considering it is them."[10] If the *Evening Whig* could be believed, the city's own Armory Band serenaded General Weitzel at the Davis mansion. By Friday evening, even though smoke still rose from the ruins, musicians played in the center of town. The strains of "The Star-Spangled Banner" wafted over the city, in place of "Dixie" and, as the paper described them, "other now obsolete ditties."[11] The music gave an entirely misleading aura to the occupied city. "As I close my letter," wrote an overly sanguine northern journalist on Friday, "bands are playing in the Capitol Square, the moon shines brilliantly overhead, and the scene seems not at all one of war."[12]

In fact, much of what the single Unionist newspaper in town described was of no interest to the majority of the white population. Most refused to give credence to anything it printed. Few attended the open-air concerts. It did nothing to foster a feeling of reconciliation when the paper printed the words to the national anthem, allegedly for the benefit of those who had "forgotten" them.

People were too distressed over the plight of Lee's army and the fate of their loved ones in gray to read blithe reports of doings in northern cities. They were in no mood to hear the southern cause lampooned at the local theaters, and they did not care to be reminded by the paper that Edwin Booth, who had played in Richmond before the war, had just completed a hundred consecutive performances of *Hamlet* in New York City. They resented the brash Yankee merchants who sold their wares exclusively for greenbacks to Union soldiers under slogans like "Clear Away the Wreck." As far as they were concerned, advertisements in the *Evening Whig* by Brooks Brothers and other New York stores willing to ship goods to soldiers in Richmond might just as well have promoted trade with the moon.

When the army began to organize parades through the city, the reaction of white Richmonders was predictable. The first review took place on April 8, the first Saturday of occupation. It involved the 3rd Division of the XXIV Corps, under the command of General Devens, the current occupant of the governor's mansion. Spectators lined Main Street and leaned out their windows to watch infantry regiments, artillery batteries, and cavalry squadrons pass by.[13] The most a Union observer could say for their reaction was pitiful indeed. They viewed the pageant, he opined, "with silent interest, from their sidewalks, doors and windows; and if they did not openly rejoice at the appearance of the 'Old Flag of the Union,' there were no expressions that could be construed into derision or contempt for it."[14] Another acknowledged the difficulty in divining Confederate opinion. "The people of Richmond feel intensely," he admitted. "It is easy to get at their feelings, but more difficult to find out their opinions."[15]

The Federal occupiers, of course, did not rely solely on band concerts and free rations to ensure acceptance of their rule. Those bayonets gleaming in the Saturday sunlight had other uses than as ornaments on parade. One of the most important activities of the provost marshal was to enlist local Unionists as detectives to help squelch any possibility of southern resurgence. There were plenty of volunteers among the Union spies and sympathizers who had suffered under Confederate rule.

One was John, the brother of Elizabeth Van Lew, who received a pass to return to Richmond on Wednesday, the third day of occupation. Another secret Unionist and friend of the Van Lews was William Lohmann, the German grocer and restaurateur, who had held a Confederate army commission and had helped spirit Colonel Dahlgren's corpse out of town the year before. He spent Evacuation Sunday confined to Castle Thunder but later joined John Van Lew in the detective ranks.[16] It was time to repay their persecutors.

A BLIZZARD OF paper covered the streets everywhere in the central part of town that the fire did not reach, accentuating the city's forlorn appearance. "A whirlwind sweeping through dead leaves in autumn scattered them no more wildly than official documents, pamphlets, &c., were scattered on Monday morning," opined the *Evening Whig*. "Confederate bonds, Confederate notes, bank checks, bills, flecked and whitened the streets in every direction—all so worthless that the boys would not pick them up."[17]

Historic documents as well as memoranda written within the past week swirled promiscuously through Capitol Square. Letters of George Washington and two-hundred-year-old colonial indentures fluttered in the breeze. The meager collections of the Virginia Historical Society suffered, too. A moribund institution with no permanent home, the society had been evicted from its rooms in the Mechanic's Institute by the Confederate War Department. It was a providential dispossession, because the fire turned the institute's building and its contents to ashes. The society's books were temporarily lodged in the Custom House, the only building below Capitol Square to survive the flames, but part of its tiny store of historical manuscripts fared less well. Attorney Gustavus Myers, long an officer of the society, moved some of them to a bank vault, where they met their fiery end.[18]

Secretary of War Edwin Stanton cared nothing for old deeds and wills, but he did take a keen interest in the papers of the Confederacy. He did not want them left to the relic hunters and ordered Weitzel to gather them up for shipment to Washington.

Stanton, in fact, was not content to leave much to the army. As soon as he received Weitzel's first, electrifying telegram on Monday, he sent a messenger to the house of Assistant Secretary Charles Dana with orders to pack for Richmond.[19] The cynical Dana had come a long way from his youthful stint of teaching at the Brook Farm socialist community. He had built Horace Greeley's *New York Tribune* into a national power and even retained Karl Marx, then in English exile, as a correspondent for the paper. Sometimes, without Dana's knowledge, Marx farmed out the work to Friedrich Engels, giving the founding fathers of communism a brief American platform. Headstrong and self-confident, Dana eventually broke with Greeley. During the war he suppressed his independent nature when it meant that as Stanton's assistant he could exert influence at the highest levels, even serving as a go-between dealing with Grant and Lincoln.[20]

Dana arrived just after midday Wednesday, barely forty-eight hours after the fire burned at its hottest. On the way upriver, his ship passed Admiral Porter's barge being towed back down to City Point by tug, with Abraham Lincoln sitting serenely in the stern.[21] The *Malvern* remained moored at the Richmond wharf, and the president was content to descend the river in the same unpretentious manner in which he had arrived.

From the first day of Union occupation, Stanton used the telegraph to micromanage Weitzel. With the demands of putting out the fire, restoring public order, ensuring a food supply for the civilian population, and deploying his troops in the event of a counterattack, Weitzel did not welcome the cables that originated in the War Department a hundred miles to the north. With Dana on the scene, he would be even more under Stanton's microscope.

THE FIRST TOURISTS arrived barely twenty-four hours after Weitzel's soldiers marched in. When the news reached him in Norfolk, Virginia, Adm. David Farragut decided on an unauthorized visit to Richmond, taking a group of officers and their wives with him. He was as impetuous in this instance as he had been in his bold, reckless victories at New Orleans and Mobile Bay. The party's steamer reached Varina

Landing, on the James downstream from the capital, at dawn on Tuesday. Two hours on horseback brought the group to Weitzel's headquarters at the Davis mansion.

After touring the city, they returned by water on Robert Ould's flag-of-truce steamer *Allison*, the only Confederate vessel left intact at the Richmond docks. The admiral heard that his adoptive brother, Admiral Porter, was bringing the president up the river and thought it would be a lark to greet him steaming downstream. It required some cajoling to persuade the *Allison*'s captain to risk his vessel against the mines that still infested the channel.

One of the party, Gen. George Gordon, took a souvenir with him from the Davis mansion, a small, grotesque sculpture of an alligator eating an eagle, supposedly a metaphor for southern victory. Northern papers made much of this odd trophy.[22] They did not mention that another of Farragut's party, Emma Doane, the wife of the ship's purser, selected a much more symbolic object from headquarters: she boldly took the surrender note that Mayo had given to Weitzel.[23]

The news of Richmond's fall drew journalists from all over the North. The lucky ones were already at the front, behind the lines at City Point, or with the army just outside the Confederate capital. Charles Coffin, the reporter who had seen Lincoln arrive, was with Weitzel east of town, but the general forbade him to enter Richmond until Monday afternoon. Thomas Chester marched in the same day with his beloved USCT regiments, former slaves exacting retribution from former owners.

In Washington, when the news broke, Charles Page of the *New York Tribune* and two fellow journalists railed at the ban on press passes to the Virginia capital. But they did not just complain; they finagled their way onto a transport and reached the city on Wednesday.[24] Page's colleague, the radical journalist Whitelaw Reid, said their ship was filled with sutlers, merchants, and "parasites that feed upon great armies, who wanted to dig for money around the garbage of Richmond."[25]

A *New York Times* correspondent did not exaggerate by much when he wrote from the southern capital at the end of the week that it would take a long time before people in the North were sated with news about Richmond.[26] A colleague argued that the city "has become to loyal Americans in the course of the last four years as strange and foreign a place as Rome or Constantinople."[27] Northern papers filled their pages with such dispatches sent by as many journalists as could make their way to the fallen citadel.

The city also attracted photographers. Alexander Gardner and his staff arrived on Thursday, three days after the fire. By Friday, Mathew Brady was also in town with a full complement of assistants and equipment.[28] It was not the first time he lagged behind his competitor and former employee to record a famous scene. His men went to work like Gardner's, photographing views of the Capitol towering over the Burned District. One blurry image even captured the smoke still rising from the ruins behind a row of cavalry horses tied up to the iron railing around Capitol Square, something difficult to accomplish in the era of very slow shutter speeds.

Unfortunately for posterity, Gardner missed by only one day the chance to capture the image of Lincoln in the defeated Confederate capital. But he and Brady and other cameramen made an indelible record of nearly every other dramatic view to be seen there. One of the best was A. J. Russell, a captain with the U.S. Military Railroads, who documented the logistical achievements of Grant's army and the record of destruction in Richmond. Despite the slow development process and awkward, bulky camera equipment, these photographers exposed vast quantities of wet collodion glass plate negatives to memorialize the Richmond moonscape. Altogether, they captured at least three hundred images of the first few weeks of Union occupation.[29]

Two leading periodicals of the day, *Harper's* and *Frank Leslie's Illustrated Newspaper*, sent artists to sketch the same scenes. Back in New York, engravers translated these views into their own medium for publication.[30] The locals did not leave all the graphic opportunities to outsiders. Four days after their first issue, the enterprising staff at the *Evening Whig* were selling a lithograph map of the city that delineated the Burned District. At fifty cents a copy, it was meant as a souvenir for Union soldiers. Few residents of Richmond had U.S. money to lavish on anything inedible.[31] Demand in the North for images of the fallen city exceeded the meager supply. Entrepreneurs posted appeals in the Richmond newspaper for photographers, and for a time pictures of the ruins provided a handsome income to those who could produce them.

Because of the demand, images of the Burned District have left a powerful but distorted impression on every generation of Americans since then. They captured the main surviving buildings and monuments, Davis's house, the Capitol, City Hall, Libby Prison, the governor's mansion. The cameramen, however, focused mainly and repeatedly on the destruction, the gaunt, fire-blackened brick walls, the rubble that had once been prosperous mills and counting houses, and the ranks of stone pillars that had borne rail lines across the James. In one sequence, Gardner created a giant panorama of five plates giving a sweeping view from Capitol Square down through masses of ruin and rubble to the riverfront. This was the Richmond that the northern public paid to see. It reinforced their sense of triumph over their foe, and it showed graphically the stern punishment meted out to the enemy's capital, even if by the hands of that enemy's own soldiers.

In fact, only about 10 percent of the area of the city burned. Away from the commercial precincts, the majority of housing survived, but it was pictures of devastation that people in the North craved. The view from the ruined canal turning basin, where legislators had frantically scrambled for space on the last packet boats, gave an especially impressive picture of destruction. This perspective was perhaps the one most widely reproduced. Though misleading as to the proportion of the city destroyed, it did reflect the fact that nine-tenths of the business district went up in smoke, and with it most of the jobs. As Whitelaw Reid told his abolitionist audience, "Richmond is today a city of aristocratic residences, without the business heart that should support them."[32]

Long before the war, architect Henry Exall left his native England for Virginia. He designed many of the houses built in Richmond during the last prosperous decade of peace, though perhaps not quite as many as half of them, as one admirer claimed. He was a director of Hollywood Cemetery and the architect of a handsome block of town houses behind the governor's mansion.[33]

On the day of the fire, Exall was at the portico of the Capitol and helped put out a blaze that started at one of the windows. Afterward, he offered his services once more to his adopted home, "To those who have the courage to begin at once to repair the damage done our devoted city."[34] He hoped former clients would count themselves among this bold and forward-looking class and informed them they could find his new office temporarily next to the Spotswood Hotel. Fittingly, it looked out over the sea of rubble that was still smoking when he placed his expectant announcement in the *Evening Whig,* five days after he watched the fire consume many of his earlier commissions.

A DIFFERENT FORM of reconstruction began throughout the region, one far more difficult to accomplish than the rebuilding Exall imagined. The first signs from the employer's perspective were marked down in ledgers kept by every household that owned slaves. Typical were the accounts on James Wickham's plantation north of town, which dutifully kept track of childbirths in the quarters. Wickham's ledger, like many others, listed the mother's name, the sex of the child, the child's name, and the date of birth.

The last sheet of the ledger he used for this purpose recorded the last African American born in bondage on the plantation, a boy, name not given, brought into the world by his mother, Fannie, a week before slavery died. A week after Fannie's son came into the world, Wickham no longer needed to keep the register, for he no longer owned the people. But he did need to come to grips with some new system of labor if work was to proceed. Without missing a day, Wickham shifted to wage labor. Starting on April 3, the day of the fire, he began listing agreements with his former slaves, retaining most of them for $6 a month.[35] The working out of new labor relations, not to speak of new social relations, between the races would not be so easily decided elsewhere in Virginia and the South as they seemed to be at the stroke of Wickham's pen.

On the day after the fire, the Bureau of Colored Troops in Washington opened a branch office in Richmond. In all, the army detached eleven officers under a major general for this duty. Their number suggests they expected better luck signing up blacks than Major Turner of the ill-starred Confederate effort had experienced. They were not disappointed. Virginians of African descent volunteered that first week at the rate of two to three hundred per day, a clear sign of the political sympathies of black Richmonders.[36]

At the prisons that now warehoused hundreds of Confederate soldiers, blacks could see tangible evidence of the changes sweeping over the South. One elderly man spotted two white civilians being led under guard to Libby. He recognized them as men who used to patrol the streets to arrest African Americans without identity papers. He turned to a companion and said with great satisfaction, "Guess they won't pick us up and put us in the *cage* any more."[37]

On Thursday morning word circulated about a "Jubilee Meeting" to be held that afternoon in the African Baptist Church, a large building that could seat more than a thousand worshipers. By the appointed time, the church was crammed full with twice that many black Richmonders and soldiers wearing the uniform of the United States Colored Troops. Hundreds more outside edged close to the open windows to hear.[38] The choice of hymns was no accident. The singing grew especially emphatic when the congregation began a song by Isaac Watts, whose words also came on that same day to the lips of the dying Confederate sergeant, Marion Fitzpatrick. Later, with the words "I'm going to join in this army; / I'm going to join in this army of my Lord," wrote a white northerner at the church, "the smiles of the spectators could hardly be repressed."[39]

Before that day, no black man had been permitted to preach from the high pulpit. Chaplain David Stevens of the 35th USCT was the first African American clergyman to break the barrier. Thomas Chester, the black reporter from Philadelphia, called the meeting to order. It was a proud moment for him. The people cheered him noisily as he congratulated them "upon the triumph of liberty in Richmond, and urged them, as redeemed freemen, to assume the duties and responsibilities belonging to the change."[40]

THE DAY AFTER Godfrey Weitzel arrived in the capital, the military telegraph clicked out an order from Grant to "arrest all editors and proprietors of Richmond papers." Grant further cautioned that the provost marshal should carry out the arrests quietly to prevent any of the targeted men that remained from escaping. Despite the precaution, Weitzel's soldiers did not snare them all.[41]

Though most of his colleagues had fled, Edward Pollard remained behind. Reporters for northern papers recognized this badly dressed man with the red beard and one arm in a sling as the famous *Examiner* editor. They pointed out with ridicule that a warehouse holding three thousand copies of his woefully out-of-date book on the war had survived the fire but his newspaper had not.

"Unmolested and saucy," Pollard strutted about the streets, defiantly refusing to take the oath of allegiance. On Thursday he was observed dining at the Spotswood across the room from Charles Dana, neither man apparently aware of the other's presence. With his mentor John Moncure Daniel dead only a week, the chief surviving emblem of southern journalistic defiance elicited different sentiments from his print adversaries. One called him the liveliest secessionist editor, pitied him, and reminded readers that the Virginian inadvertently had done the North a favor with his scathing denunciations of the Davis government.[42]

His effrontery in persisting with his southern rights opinions, though, offended other Yankees. By the end of the week, the army decided it could no longer tolerate the notorious firebrand. It arrested him on Saturday and expelled him from the city. The *New York Times* correspondent had Pollard in mind when he crowed that the Richmond editors "have found the last ditch of the rebellion, and have tumbled into it."[43] But Pollard meant to have the last laugh.

CHAPTER 16

PRAYERS FOR
THE PRESIDENT

Tuesday, April 4, to Sunday, April 9

*Through all this strain of anguish ran like a gleam of gold the
mad vain hope that Lee would yet make a stand somewhere.*
—Constance Cary[1]

In the first days of occupation, the *Evening Whig* flaunted its new
colors by praising the benefits of Union victory. It touted cheap
food, sound money, a benevolent government, and even brass band
concerts on Capitol Square as the blessings of Yankee rule. But in trying to determine the opinions of white Richmonders, the newspaper
and some of the less astute northern officers in town mistook acquiescence for approval.

"The population of Richmond moved mechanically before their
new masters," wrote Edward Pollard about the time just before the
conquerors expelled him from the capital. "But there was, for some
days, an undercurrent of eager, excited thought which the Federals did
not perceive. . . . Thus it was told in whispers that Gen. Lee had won a
great victory on his retreat."[2] Kate Rowland wrote with fervent hope
on Monday evening, the first under Union control, "I believe Lee will
yet give them a lesson."[3] On Wednesday another rumor of Confederate victory raced through town, and in the Hoge household young

Lelian Cook confessed that "we almost forgot the Yankees were here."[4]

In the Army of Northern Virginia, fading away toward Appomattox, a committed remnant kept hope alive. William Gordon McCabe wrote defiantly from the retreating band: "Hungry, wet, with blistered feet, without sleep, they have stood by their guns & fought with a desperation, a superb courage that I never dreamed of. . . . They will go with Genl. Lee as long as the Battle-Cross floats on the field."[5]

In Danville, his temporary capital near the North Carolina border, Jefferson Davis tried to rally the faithful. "We have now entered upon a new phase of a struggle," he urged them with an optimistic view of Richmond's loss that took the breath away. "Relieved from the necessity of guarding cities and particular points, important but not vital to our defense, with an army free to move from point to point . . . nothing is now needed to render our triumph certain but the exhibition of our own unquenchable resolve. Let us but will it, and we are free."[6]

Davis only deluded himself about his fleeting parody of a government. And McCabe surrendered with the others just two days after he wrote that hopeful letter from the field. But neither Davis, nor McCabe, nor all those white Richmonders moving about like automatons knew what the outcome would be in the first week after the city's fall. It is no surprise, then, that defiant residents of the capital moved the struggle from the battlefield to another, unexpected arena, and they did it from the very beginning of Federal occupation.

AT MOMENTS OF crisis throughout the war, Richmonders looked to their churches. The first Sunday of April 1865 had begun like so many before it. Before they learned that the government would evacuate their city that night, pastors once more fervently led their flocks in prayer for the victory of southern arms. Then, when the city fell, people instinctively went to their houses of worship for solace and there gave the first collective expression of their despair. At one service "the Litany was *sobbed* out by the whole congregation." At another, after the minister prayed for wounded soldiers, there was a pause, and the sound of weeping filled the church.[7]

On Thursday, the fourth day of occupation, Edward Ripley summoned ministers to the house he had commandeered as his headquarters. The Vermont officer wanted to discuss reopening the churches for regular services on Sunday. It amused Ripley, at twenty-five a cocky, very young brevet brigadier general, to be waited on by two dozen eminent divines, most of them old enough to be his father. He sparred with Charles Minnigerode, the St. Paul's rector, who represented, however diplomatically, the unrepentant face of resistance to Federal rule. With a German accent still detectable in his voice, Minnigerode lectured Ripley about the inability of Episcopal churches to change the wording of their liturgy without permission of their bishop. He was inconveniently out of touch in Canada.

Ripley told the clergyman his church was welcome to hold services on Sunday, but he warned him the army would allow no disloyal words to be spoken. He then dismissed the clerics and strode across the hall to another parlor where theater managers had gathered to seek permission to reopen their establishments. When that meeting ended, the Vermont Yankee thought he had neatly disposed of both issues, sacred and profane, when he had only witnessed the opening move in a test of wits with the clergymen.[8]

The next day he received a letter from Minnigerode. The minister who had often dined with Jefferson Davis—indeed who had baptized Davis during the war and told him, "I look upon you as God's chosen instrument"—proved to be a more formidable adversary than the young general had realized.[9] When he sat down to compose his letter—probably right after the meeting at Ripley's headquarters, perhaps with colleagues, perhaps alone—Minnigerode must have realized he was ratcheting up the hostility between conquered and conqueror to a dangerous degree. "He was one of the Prussian refugees of 1848," wrote a northern journalist who contrasted Minnigerode's opinions in Germany and in Richmond, "and, though a hot Jacobin there, became a more bitter secessionist here."[10]

In the middle of a communion service earlier in the war, a messenger had come to him with the shocking news that his son had been killed in battle. The minister learned later that there had been a mixup: it was not his son who had died. But the scene recurred when word came that the same son had been killed in the first hours of Lee's retreat. When the minister wrote his letter to Ripley, he had this heavy burden weighing on his mind. Only later did he learn that his son, though wounded and permanently crippled, had not died.

Minnigerode began his letter by reminding Ripley that the Episcopal churches of Virginia had continued to pray for the president of the United States in 1861, even after the lower South seceded. Their liturgy required it and they obeyed. After Virginia seceded, political expediency compelled them to omit the reference. But they did not substitute an explicit prayer for the president of the Confederate States until much later when a conference of southern Episcopal churches formally ordered it. It would only be fair that they be allowed a similar flexibility in 1865.

"If it is the purpose of the United States Government to heal dissensions and promote peace," he slyly argued, then the army should permit him and his fellow Episcopal ministers "quietly to use our own ritual, omitting everything which could have the least tendency to give offense."[11] Minnigerode knew about the generous sentiments Lincoln had expressed to Weitzel three days before on the issue of treating the defeated southerners. He also cited Lincoln's willingness to forgo a required oath of allegiance. This leniency in political matters, the minister said, should apply even more in regard to something as innocent as public prayers.

Minnigerode's argument carried the day. He persuaded the army to accept his formula. The Episcopal churches would omit the prescribed, customary prayer for Davis and add one, not for Lincoln by name, but for those in authority generally. For the rest of the week, Richmonders were preoccupied with picking over their ruined property, wondering where they would find their next meal, and most of all, worrying and praying about loved ones with the southern army. Then the prayer issue came to the fore dramatically on the first Sabbath under occupation, for it was Palm Sunday, the beginning of Holy Week. Northern

reporters in Richmond went to church that day, and what they observed filled many column inches in metropolitan dailies across the
North. While Lee was meeting with Grant at Appomattox, in happy
ignorance the loyal Confederate civilians of Richmond continued to
pray silently for their general's success. But it was the public prayers
that elicited the most comment.

LIKE THE SUNDAY before, April 9 dawned mild and cloudless. The pop-
ulace walked to church to the sound of tolling bells. The distant rumble of cannon no longer competed with the bells or the uplifting
chords of organ music. Though all of the churches and synagogues
but one had survived the fire, they were close to the ruins that still
smoldered and sent up thin streams of smoke. On that Sunday morning worshipers making their way to services could see what a week's
misfortunes had wrought. Even in the houses of God they could smell
the acrid scent of ruin.

At Monumental Church, the Episcopal rector preached on a text
from the Gospel of Matthew: "Come unto me all ye that labor and are
heavy laden, and I will give you rest." He omitted the prayer for the
president and substituted the phrase "bless all Christian rulers and
magistrates."[12] The Presbyterians, who did not have the same stric-
tures about the form for prayers, nevertheless echoed the defiance of
the Episcopalians. Moses Drury Hoge had fled with the Confederate
government, but two colleagues stood in his pulpit at Second Presbyterian that day. In the morning, William Brown prayed for "all who
are in rightful authority over us." In the afternoon service, Charles
Read, burned out of his own church, prayed for "kings and rulers."[13]

At St. Paul's, the congregation once again consisted mostly of
women in deep mourning, women mocked by a northern observer as
"dark Richmond beauties, haughty and thinly clothed." One of them
wore her colonel's gold braid on her arm. Of the dozen or so officers
who attended in Confederate gray, several bore empty uniform
sleeves or pant legs. The congregation followed the responsive readings with tremulous voices, and Minnigerode glossed rapidly over the
prescribed verse, "They who take up the sword shall perish by the

sword." The sight of these sad and forlorn parishioners reminded a northern visitor "of the captive Jews holding worship in their gutted Temple." During the service, the sobbing was audible and frequent. "The fact is, Richmond is heart-broken," Uriah Painter wrote as he described the scene for his readers in Philadelphia. "They are subjugated, and know it and feel it. They have lost their all, but hug their pride closer and closer as their troubles thicken and their relatives and friends are swept away."[14]

The Unionist *Evening Whig* gave a cheerful interpretation of what happened, or rather of what did not happen. Omitting the phrase "President of the Confederate States," while retaining only a blessing on "all in authority," was acceptable to the newspaper, just as Minnigerode had hoped. "As the United States is the power 'in authority,' " blithely reasoned the editor, "here the prayer for the President of the United States was, of course, implied if not said."[15]

It was nothing of the sort. Most people who worshiped at the Episcopal churches recognized the political struggle being acted out before them. "Neither President was prayed for," wrote Confederate loyalist Judith McGuire; "in compliance with some arrangement with the Federal authorities, the prayer was used as for all in authority! How fervently did we all pray for our own President! Thank God, our silent prayers are free from Federal authority."[16] The African American journalist Thomas Chester shared few opinions with McGuire, but they agreed on what was happening that morning. She recognized the prayer as a compromise, and so did he. But he thought it imprudently let the clergy avoid overt sedition by the narrowest margin: "They prayed for the Powers that be, but it was evident that they meant Jeff."[17]

No ambiguity showed its face at the black churches, whatever their white ministers said. "We came together," a black pastor told a visitor, "and gave thanks with all our hearts and prayed for Abraham Lincoln."[18] At the largest house of worship, the African Baptist Church on Broad Street, they prayed for him "with Amens that made the very walls ring."[19]

In Washington the secretary of war exploded when he read the cable sent that evening by Charles Dana, his assistant secretary and agent on the spot. The telegraph wire fairly sizzled with Stanton's sarcastic message to General Weitzel. He could not conceive how a Union officer could allow the Episcopal churches to omit the prayer said for Lincoln in northern churches of that denomination.[20] Worse, Dana had reported that the former Confederate assistant secretary of war, John Campbell, had had a hand in the matter. Stanton demanded a prompt report from Weitzel and forbade him to have anything to do with Campbell.

Weitzel was indignant. In an impertinent reply that bordered on insubordination, he asked Stanton if he expected him to impose a prescribed loyal prayer on Jews, Roman Catholics, or others with a liturgical form of worship. On hearing the next day that his explanation was not satisfactory, Weitzel cabled the War Department again. This time he begged permission to ask Lincoln to intervene. The president could tell Stanton exactly what he had said to his commander in Richmond. Only then, suggested the audacious Weitzel, could Stanton correctly interpret the general's actions.[21]

The president did absolve Weitzel from error. "I do not remember hearing prayers spoken of while I was in Richmond," Lincoln assured him, "but I have no doubt you have acted in what appeared to you to be the spirit and temper manifested by me while there."[22] It was a fleeting vindication. By then the young general had incurred Stanton's wrath and was a marked man. Already, on Wednesday, the secretary of war had ended a telegram to Grant with the ominous query "Had not Weitzel better have duty elsewhere than Richmond?"[23] And now the prayer issue exploded. Weitzel did not fully appreciate his perilous state, but he was in no doubt about the difficulty of occupying a hostile city while trying to please his masters in Washington.

Unlike Lincoln, Stanton was not mollified. He was determined to humble the Episcopalians. They must acknowledge who was in charge. He ordered Weitzel to run a notice in the newspaper. When it appeared, the editor of the *Whig*, seeing now what he had not seen before, admonished the clergy to comply.[24] Confederate civilians did not see it in the same light. "An order came out in this morning's papers that the prayers for the President of the United States must be used," wrote one. "How could we do it?"[25] They knew nothing of the furious row brewing between the secretary of war and the local Union commander, but they suspected the mailed hand of Stanton behind the printed ultimatum.

The stiff-necked Episcopal clergymen would not bend. On Good Friday their churches remained shut, and for them there were no Easter services in 1865.

THAT, HOWEVER, is getting ahead of events. The prayer issue reflected the continuing resistance of civilians to Union rule, but it was only a superficial expression of a defiance that showed itself in a more ominous manner on the first full day of occupation. Therefore, it is necessary to go back nearly a week before that Palm Sunday and examine a conversation that took place when Lincoln came to Richmond the day after the fire, on Tuesday, April 4.

Overshadowed by the wild celebration of the freedmen in the streets and the self-congratulation of Union soldiers, a less public event transformed the president's visit from a symbol, however dramatic, to a catalyst of great portent and uncontrollable consequence. Even before the defeated Confederates used the Episcopal prayer to flaunt their defiance, they discovered almost serendipitously in Lincoln's presence a chance to maneuver for influence from their position of seemingly abject impotence.

In the crush of blue uniforms at the Davis mansion on Tuesday, a journalist unwittingly observed the opening scene of this controversy. William Merriam of the *New York Herald* was caught up like everyone present in the excitement of the moment. To shake the president's hand in the house of the defeated enemy leader hardly a day and a half after Davis fled was almost more than any of them could take in. In his euphoric dispatch written literally within minutes of the reception, Merriam briefly alluded to a private conference Lincoln had there. But after that fleeting reference, he moved on to other topics. The scene at the mansion and the president's tour of the city were certainly more interesting subjects on the surface.

By the next evening, Merriam realized he had overlooked the most important point about the visit to the White House of the Confederacy. In a subsequent dispatch, he corrected his account and described how Lincoln had heard the military governor, George Shepley, explain a meeting he and Weitzel had just had with "several prominent secessionists." Patiently listening, the president "indicated his sense of the magnitude of the propositions submitted for his consideration by great nervousness of manner, running his hands frequently through his hair and moving to and fro in the official chair of the late Jefferson Davis, in which he sat."[26] When he had heard what his generals told him, he agreed to a meeting. While jubilant Federal officers crowded the formal parlors and drank Davis's whiskey, Lincoln slipped away to a small adjoining room where he conferred briefly with one Confederate official—not several, as Merriam reported—and agreed to a further discussion the following day.

The man Lincoln met was John Archibald Campbell. His role in the overt resistance of the Episcopal clergy about prayer was minor. Not so his approach to the president. Indeed, it was the reason why he had stayed behind, at some personal risk, when all higher-ranking Confederate officials had fled.

While he waited for this chance, it would have been natural for Campbell to reflect on the events of 1861 and his part in them. Then he had remained a justice of the United States Supreme Court even after his native Alabama seceded. Hoping to avert war, he offered himself as an intermediary between Lincoln and Confederate emissaries sent to Washington. When his efforts failed to prevent hostilities at Fort Sumter, both sides suspected him of duplicity.[27] Enemies in the North called him a "clumsy Jesuit" who remained in Washington after "more candid traitors" had left only so that he could covertly supply the Confederates with intelligence.[28] But even after he threw in his lot with the South—indeed, even after he became assistant secretary of war—some Confederates questioned his loyalty to their side.

In February 1865, Campbell and two other Confederate peace commissioners had met with Lincoln at the Hampton Roads conference.

The two sides had agreed that a high-level discussion on terms to end the war might clear the air. It did. But it only showed that no negotiated end was possible. The one thing Davis would not give up was the one that Lincoln would not concede: southern independence. Campbell had wanted to continue the discussion then but was overruled by Davis.

Now, after a two-month hiatus, he had his chance to renew the conversation without having Davis around to thwart him a second time. He meant to repeat his role of negotiator, this time to speed the transition from war to peace. The sooner the fighting stopped, the better for all, especially for the defeated South. A friend, commenting on his iron constitution, said Campbell was happiest when he worked. He would have a lot to be happy about over the next few days.[29]

As the Federal army entered Richmond on Monday morning, Campbell had prudently stayed inside his house. The next morning, when he learned which officers were in charge and where to find them, he made the first move. He sought out the military governor, who, as luck would have it, was an acquaintance. George Shepley had distinguished himself as U.S. district attorney in Maine and argued before the Supreme Court when Campbell sat on the high bench. Shepley readily gave the former justice a pass that exempted him from arrest. With his personal safety assured, Campbell turned to his real business.

When the general mentioned that Lincoln was still at City Point headquarters, Campbell said he would like to talk to him. Shepley agreed to telegraph the president, but it proved unnecessary, because a few hours later Lincoln made his triumphal entry into Richmond. When the president reached Davis's house, Shepley told him about Campbell's request, and a staff officer went to fetch the southerner from his house nearby. The president seemed to expect him to bring a message authorized by the departed Davis government, but Campbell disabused him of that notion. He was there as a private citizen to urge the president to talk to some leading Virginians about how best to take the state out of the Confederacy, and thus speed an end to the war.

Lincoln had been worrying that his generals might win the war on the battlefield and then, exceeding their authority, botch negotiations for peace as the fighting ended.[30] Now it was the president himself and not his generals who gave the Confederates an unexpected opening. There, in Jefferson Davis's house, he agreed to meet Campbell again the next day and discuss what amounted to the details of reconstructing the Union. At the time, few people knew that meeting was the reason Lincoln stayed overnight on the *Malvern*, moored in the river at Richmond, but word would soon leak out.

The prospect of an imminent end to the war had exhilarated the president ever since he arrived at Grant's Virginia headquarters in late March. His reception by Union soldiers, especially by the wounded men he visited in hospitals, had touched him deeply. The improbable journey to Richmond only heightened his optimism. The welcome of the freedmen in the Confederate capital and the knowledge that final victory was within reach made him almost giddy with joy. He was eager to do whatever it took to hasten that day, even if it meant private, personal negotiation with Campbell.

After leaving the Davis mansion, Campbell doggedly sought out other prominent Richmonders to accompany him to meet Lincoln again the next day but came up shorthanded. Some had left town; others refused to go with him. Indefatigable, he did not let rejection stand in his way. He was not in the least downcast that only attorney Gustavus Myers turned up on Wednesday to go with him.[31]

That same Wednesday morning, Charles Page of the *New York Tribune* finagled his way to Richmond. He had missed the entry of the victorious army on Monday and Lincoln's arrival on Tuesday. But after he booked a room in the Spotswood and hurried up to the Davis mansion, he was just in time to see Campbell and Myers ride with Weitzel down to the river to see Lincoln on board the *Malvern*. Sensing the importance of the meeting, Page wrote a lengthy description of the scene for his readers that nicely captured the outward appearances. And yet, like William Merriam in his first dispatch of the day before, he completely misinterpreted what was happening.

Page described Campbell as "an elderly bald man, bowed, pale, and with a look on his face full of all disappointment and sadness, yet of great dignity. I could but note the contrast afforded by Weitzel, who, in full uniform, with sword at his loins, was to go with him to the President. It was the contrast between sorrow and joy, between bitter failure and glorious success, between a thwarted and broken conspirator, whose age precludes any honorable retrieval, and a soldier who, though not yet thirty, has served his country well. . . . The very courtesy of Weitzel's demeanor toward the old man but pointed the difference each must have felt in his consciousness."[32] In fact, it was Weitzel who had reached his zenith two days before when he rode into the burning city. His name was on everyone's lips in the North, but he was about to plunge into hot water. Campbell was not the frail, powerless figure he appeared to be.

On the ride to the wharf, skirting the gutted, smoking ruins of the Burned District, Campbell and Myers broached the subject of a mandatory oath of allegiance. Both were relieved at Weitzel's response. "When men take an oath reluctantly," he told them, with unimpeachable, soldierly common sense, "they are not apt to respect it."[33] As their carriage rattled past block after block of scorched rubble, the two civilians took some measure of reassurance on this point.

As soon as they went aboard the *Malvern*, Lincoln showed them a handwritten sheet of paper, which he read out loud, stopping frequently to elaborate on each of his points. Then he gave the paper to Campbell. This was likely the document that a naval officer had seen the president laboring over for hours before he retired the previous night.[34] It was unsigned and undated but listed three prerequisites for peace: restoration of Union authority in all states, no retreat on the abolition of slavery, and no end to hostilities short of complete dissolution of all Confederate armed forces.

These conditions did not surprise Campbell. They were, in fact, the ones Lincoln had stated to him and the other peace commissioners at the Hampton Roads conference in February. Myers told Lincoln the restrained behavior of Federal forces in Richmond had gone far to allay the apprehensions of residents. He hoped the army would not enforce an oath of allegiance, as that would undo all the good that had been done. The president told Myers he had never attached much importance to a mandatory declaration of allegiance and left it up to Weitzel. The general repeated what he had said in the carriage: he would not impose an oath. Campbell gave Lincoln a letter expressing the same concern, but it was unnecessary. His letter also urged an armistice—he called it "a military convention"—while the two sides negotiated terms.[35] Lincoln did not promise an armistice but agreed to think about it.

The meeting progressed with civility and even good humor. So far, it was going very well for the southerners. Then the president dropped a bombshell. He said he had been thinking about a way to convene the Virginia legislature to see if it would withdraw the state from the Confederacy. If it did, the fighting might end more quickly. For emphasis, Lincoln repeated himself and said he meant "the very Legislature which has been sitting . . . up yonder" and pointed toward the Capitol.[36] Campbell had suggested bringing together an undefined group of leading Virginians. It was Lincoln who proposed calling the legislators together as a body. Campbell was only too happy to agree.

The two southerners returned to the city in buoyant spirits. As they left the ship with Weitzel, Lincoln told the general he would write him the next day and indicated that he planned to authorize safe passage for the legislators to gather as he had just proposed. In a conversation back at headquarters at City Point that night, Lincoln hinted at his motivation. Marsena Patrick, the Union army's provost marshal general, had just returned from his own first visit to the capital, and he and the president shared their worries about the dangerous lack of order there. Patrick said they talked "fully and freely of Richmond Matters which appear to be in a bad State."[37] That troubling situation reinforced Lincoln's desire to convene the legislature in order to resolve the uncertainty and bring the fighting to an end as quickly as possible.

Later that day, Charles Dana got wind of the meeting on the *Malvern* and buttonholed Weitzel about it. All the southerners asked, Dana reported back to Stanton, "is an amnesty and a military convention, to cover appearances. Slavery they admit to be defunct. General

Weitzel, who was present, tells me that the President did not promise the amnesty, but told them he had the pardoning power, and would save any repentant sinner from hanging."[38]

Dana may have used the word "amnesty" to cover the issue of the loyalty oath that Myers raised. If so, that was a misleading usage. More important than that, Dana completely missed the most significant aspect of the meeting between Lincoln and the southerners. Or Weitzel withheld it from him. For, although Lincoln did not agree to an armistice, he had suggested something almost as dangerous, permission for the Virginia legislature to reconvene. He had not thought through the idea, and it offered a striking concession that Campbell seized.[39] Here was a measure of recognition that the jurist had not hoped for. Through his own actions, Lincoln showed how contingent were the circumstances surrounding the end of the war. And how dangerous, even for the victor.

By 1865 the weight of military power had made Union victory impossible to deny. The war that had rent the republic for four awful years and had sown death and misery for hundreds of thousands was about to end. How it came about was still subject to a thousand influences on the battlefield and in the minds of the opposing commanders. But when the president himself gave the Confederates of Richmond unlooked-for hope, the implications for peace and reconstruction of the Union took an unexpected turn.

LINCOLN SENT a letter to Weitzel the next day as he promised. It came to the general by the hand of former Minnesota senator Morton Wilkinson, one of the early tourists who rushed to gaze upon the ashes of Richmond. He was best known for demanding execution back in his home state of three hundred prisoners in the 1862 Sioux uprising. Incensed at Lincoln's relative leniency—the president agreed to hang only a tenth as many Indians—Wilkinson said the only hope for the country was "the death of the President and a new administration."[40]

The repellent Wilkinson now served Lincoln's purpose by being there to carry a message from City Point to the Federal commander at

Richmond. "It has been intimated to me," Lincoln wrote Weitzel with carefully chosen words that nevertheless had greater portent than the president realized, "that the gentlemen who have acted as the Legislature of Virginia, in support of the rebellion, may now . . . desire to assemble at Richmond, and take measures to withdraw the Virginia troops" from the Confederacy. He ordered Weitzel to aid this effort. "Allow Judge Campbell to see this," he added, "but do not make it public."[41]

Following orders, the next day Weitzel read the letter to Campbell. He met with a group of citizens and told them they could issue a call through the newspaper to assemble other Virginia leaders. He then sent out passes guaranteeing them safe conduct through Union lines.[42]

In a letter to selected Virginians, most of them former Confederate officials, Campbell said Lincoln authorized the legislature to reassemble. That much fairly reflected the president's wishes. But then Campbell went far beyond anything Lincoln had approved. "The object of the invitation," he ventured, "is for the government of Virginia to determine whether they will administer the laws in connection with the authorities of the United States. I understand from Mr. Lincoln, if this condition be fulfilled that no attempt would be made to establish or sustain any other authority."[43] In other words, he said Lincoln would recognize the Confederate state legislature and not the loyal Unionist body located at Alexandria, near Washington, D.C. Hardly an honest misinterpretation, this statement revealed Campbell's intention to extract more from Lincoln's leniency than the president meant to offer. His actions set off a controversy. If nothing else, they represented a bold attempt to undermine the Unionist government of Virginia waiting to move to Richmond.

If the contretemps over prayers angered Stanton, news of Lincoln's private negotiations with Campbell made him livid. Campbell had tried to insinuate himself into a position of power rather than accept the outcome dictated by the Union's military victory. Stanton would not tolerate it. Two days after meeting Lincoln, Campbell justified Stanton's suspicions when he urged Weitzel to endorse his diplomacy because "the spirit of the people is not broken." He hinted at the prospect of a long, sanguinary guerrilla war—he called it "a prolonged & embarrassing resistance"—if the Union commander did not support his effort.[44] Campbell's words sounded like a threat from the Federal perspective. That is certainly how Stanton interpreted them.

In the meantime, Lincoln wrote Grant that he did not think much would come of his conversations with Campbell. "Nothing I have done," he stressed, "or probably shall do, is to delay, hinder, or interfere with you in your work."[45] A day later he cabled Grant again: "Gen. Sheridan says 'If the thing is pressed I think that Lee will surrender.' Let the *thing* be pressed."[46] But the damage was done. Through his private diplomacy, Lincoln had set in train events that he could not control. He did not mention his diplomatic overture to his entourage as they sailed from City Point back to Washington. Instead, buoyed by his visit to Richmond and Grant's smashing victories, he regaled the others with readings from *Macbeth*.[47] But the news of his private talks did not stay private long.

Three days after the *Malvern* conference, a meeting of Richmonders gathered to hear Campbell report on "the terms upon which President Lincoln had expressed himself as willing that Virginia might return to the Union."[48] Campbell made a short speech to the group promising liberal terms from Lincoln. He went further. He urged them to seize the opportunity to form a committee of four to visit Lee and Grant, secure an armistice, and call a convention in Charlottesville, Virginia, declaring it neutral ground.[49] The group chose a delegation to inform the legislature and Governor Smith of Lincoln's terms. Although the meeting took place in the offices of the staunchly Unionist *Evening Whig*, the participants were all Confederate. In fact, they chose as chairman a former Confederate general, Joseph Reid Anderson, whose Tredegar iron foundry did more to sustain the war effort than any other firm in the South.

These plans were doomed, given what was happening south of the James River as Grant pursued Lee. But people in Richmond, both Confederate civilians and Union occupiers, did not know the outcome on the battlefield. There was as yet no word from Appomattox. The organizers of the meeting at the *Whig* offices, however, had to have been politically blind to think appointing Anderson would not stick in the throats of their occupiers.

Other groups of citizens met at the same time to discuss restoring Virginia to the Union. Some of these were consistent Union men, not former Confederates like most of Campbell's group. Northern journalists in town made their own observations. They thought it would be unjust if the authorities listened to the likes of Campbell and not to steadfast Union men of the John Minor Botts stripe.[50] The indignant Philadelphia reporter Uriah Painter said the soldiers were in favor of counting the names of men imprisoned in Richmond as a fair index of Union sentiment and wanted to teach the former Confederates "that rebellion is a crime to be atoned for, not an experiment to be tried at their pleasure."[51] Before any of these political maneuvers could take their next step, other events intervened.

CHAPTER 17

IMPORTANT COMMUNICATIONS

Sunday, April 9, to Friday, April 14

It will be a long time before the United States is greatly beloved, but it will be always obeyed.

—George Alfred Townsend[1]

On the evening of Palm Sunday, April 9, the officers of the side-wheel steamer *Malvern*, still moored in the river at Richmond, took their chairs out on deck to enjoy the mild night air. A waxing gibbous moon, nearly full, flooded the surface of the James with light. It had been a pleasant day. The scents of spring competed with the lingering, acrid residue of the great fire, the remnants of which still smoldered. The meeting on their ship between Lincoln and Campbell had been the subject of curiosity, but that was four days ago. Since then, gossip in the mess had shifted to other topics, not least the whereabouts of the two armies. The sailors were about to retire for the night when they heard a commotion onshore. When cannon began to fire, they sent a man to find out what was happening. The word came back: Lee had surrendered.[2]

At first, Confederates in and around the city took heart from the crash of artillery. People who had gone to bed flung open their shutters and leaned out the windows to catch the hopeful rumors spread by men who ran shouting through the streets. They cried out that Lee had returned and was attacking the Federal occupiers.[3] Deliverance was at hand. North of town, Cornelius Walker heard the cannon fire, too. "Can it be," the minister scribbled in his diary that night with hurried, sanguine strokes of his pen, "that the report of Lee & Johnston's victory is true, & that they are pressing the enemy back upon Richmond?"[4]

Others indulged equally fatuous hopes. After sorrowfully recording the evacuation of the capital, Alice Payne wrote with exuberant relief in her journal, "Great & good news the Capture of Sherman." She hated going back and crossing through that line with the dread truth in one word: "Mistake."[5] It was Lee who was captured. Henri Garidel lamented the news as he lay in his bed, despairing. "The shouts of joy of the Negroes," he moaned on Sunday night, "were making Richmond tremble as much as the cannon."[6] Thomas Chester, however, exulted at the cannonade, "the funeral service over a God-forsaken Confederacy, with the artillery of the Union army and Porter's fleet, to chaunt the requiem."[7]

Not to be outdone by the army, the fleet fired a hundred-gun salute at Drewry's Bluff when it heard the news. The next morning it repeated the performance. In reply, soldiers unlimbered artillery pieces at the base of the Capitol to thunder out another grand salute, also of a hundred guns. They did it again on Wednesday and in the process managed to break many of the windows in the much-abused Capitol that had survived the war and the fire.[8]

Over the next days, stories about the retreat and the surrender began to come back to town with returning paroled soldiers. Some of the first to return were men who had defended Richmond and then marched out to link up with the retreating Army of Northern Virginia. The small army that Ewell had ordered through the streets in the early hours of Monday, across Mayo's bridge, and on toward Lee, never made it to Appomattox. It came to grief at Sayler's Creek, about forty-five miles southwest of the capital. In that battle, the last major one in Virginia, Ewell and his other generals were captured, their command broken. The despondent Ewell looked as though he would die of despair. One soldier said he "stared at the ground, as if trying to avoid attention."[9]

William Basinger, the Savannah major who earlier vowed undying enmity toward the Yankees, had evacuated with his 18th Georgia from their entrenchments at Chaffin's Bluff on the river below Richmond. He had just written his mother, "The command enjoys excellent health. Tell the mothers, sisters &c, that the lads are all right."[10] Nine days later gave the lie to those rosy sentiments. They made a stand with the others at Sayler's Creek. Bullets pierced Basinger's coat many times. They shattered his pistol in one hand and his sword in the other. His men rallied in a bayonet charge and took a Union regiment's colors but in the end succumbed.

The casualty list was a bloody testament to the fight that yet remained in many Confederate units—and to its ultimate futility. Though Basinger survived with slight wounds, of his eighty-five effective soldiers, twenty-four died, twenty-eight were wounded, the rest taken prisoner. "I cannot think of the splendid conduct & of the losses of my noble little command," he scrawled in a letter written on a prison train headed for Washington, "without mingled emotions of admiration & grief."[11] The intensity of Basinger's feelings hinted at the strength and the durability of white southern loathing for their conquerors that would persist for years to come.

Fatigue and hunger overwhelmed the retreating Confederates as much as losses to enemy fire. Some just sat down on the roadsides to be overrun and captured by the pursuing army. Desertion ate at the strength of many regiments. It eroded the few small black units recruited for the southern army as they retreated with the rest of the Confederate forces from Richmond. By the time one of the companies reached Amelia Court House, the army's rendezvous point not quite half the distance to Appomattox, only the white captain and the African American corporal remained.[12]

Margaret Brown Wight surveyed the news from Appomattox and despaired. "We have certainly been thro' a furnace of fire. . . . Lands laid waste and desolate mills, farms burnt, dwelling houses, servants gone. Nearly all the horses taken. Confederate money nothing but waste paper . . . and all this for nothing, *nothing*."[13] Fanny Young was equally distraught. She could not bear to reflect on the losses, could not think what it all portended: "When the list of the dead & wounded come in, how many, how many will be gone! . . . If I dare to look into the future of all this, I almost go mad with horror & fear." In depression, she concluded, "What an immense thing a revolution is! & how silly ever to have attempted this! So many of our noble young men perished for nothing!"[14]

The North greeted news of the surrender with joy. At Trinity Church on Wall Street, war profiteers and patriots alike jammed the pews for a service of thanksgiving. They listened to the choir sing a Te Deum, heard prayers for the president, and filed out with the soaring promise of the Hallelujah Chorus resounding in their ears.[15] But the *New York Times* bluntly admitted that Appomattox failed to excite people as much as the fall of Richmond.[16] The earlier victory had been the first and grandest. It had been hoped for and even expected, but the news still burst on the world with great surprise. It had signaled the end to the war at last. Sated by the subsequent diet of triumphant news bulletins, including those describing the surrender, northerners could not imagine they would ever again hear news that could top Weitzel's telegram from Richmond on the memorable 3rd of April 1865. All that followed would be anticlimax.

LEE'S SURRENDER ENDED all hope of recovery and compelled Confederates to think about what kind of future lay in store. Yet, despite the surrender, incredibly, the Campbell initiative did not end. Indeed, it took on a life of its own. What began as an effort to hasten the withdrawal of Virginia from the Confederacy by removing the state's troops from the fight now became an attempt to restore power to the state's defunct Confederate legislature after the shooting stopped.

The former justice and his associates continued their efforts to reassemble the legislators, still with Federal military sanction. They ran an open letter in the newspaper. In their minds, Lee's surrender made the meeting of the General Assembly all the more urgent because "the matters to be submitted to the Legislature are the restoration of peace to the State of Virginia, and the adjustment of questions involving life, liberty and property."[17] Campbell placed his name alongside those of the thirty-four signatories, all prominent Virginians. Weitzel also lent his name giving authorization for the letter to be printed, and it appeared around town in handbill form as well.

A week after the *New York Tribune*'s journalist, Charles Page, compared Campbell and Weitzel as they left Davis's mansion to meet Lincoln, their circumstances were much altered. Now it was Campbell who had seized a measure of influence through his personal initiative with Lincoln, and it was Weitzel who had fallen afoul of the politics of governing Richmond. He and his XXV Corps left the city on April 13 for a temporary posting outside Petersburg in a dirty camp with a polluted stream for water. Shortly thereafter the army banished them to the dusty, lonely exile of a posting on the Rio Grande.[18]

It offended Weitzel greatly that Edward Ord, whom he thought entirely unfit, replaced him in Richmond. And he attributed his removal not to Secretary of War Edwin Stanton but to the influence of the defeated Confederates, those haughty aristocrats of the First Families of Virginia, who wished to be rid of his black soldiers. "But you know," he wrote to his patron, Gen. Benjamin Butler, "the negroes had to leave there, the smell was offensive to the F.F.V.'s."[19] In fact, though, it was Stanton after all.

John Coles Rutherfoord, the morose Virginia legislator who had seen the capital descend into chaos from the next-to-last canal boat to leave, reached his home fifteen miles to the west in Goochland County. During the next few days, he learned the results of the great fire from later refugees. He witnessed what he called a stampede of former slaves toward Richmond and Union rule. One group of black men left the county "threatening that they wd. return to set things right." Rutherfoord took the hint and buried his valuables.[20]

Though Rutherfoord lived in a part of central Virginia not yet occupied by the Union army, when word reached him of Appomattox, he knew it was only a matter of days before the men in blue uniforms arrived. Then he heard about the Campbell initiative from a delegation that brought him a guarantee of safe passage back to town for the meeting of the legislature sanctioned by Lincoln. There was no hope for the Confederacy, but Rutherfoord recognized the chance to thwart the loyalist Union government of Virginia itching to take over.

Opinion in the North was divided. The *New York Herald* likened Campbell's supporters to Egyptian mummies for being so out of touch that they considered it daring and magnanimous on their part to agree to readmit Virginia to the Union on the condition that slavery end. The paper nevertheless called Lincoln's overture to Campbell a shrewd decision because the Confederate legislators could not fail to be moved by the president's generosity.[21]

Journalist Whitelaw Reid would have none of it. A tall, handsome man with courtly manners and southern-style hair down to his shoulders, Reid was no Confederate sympathizer. The radical abolitionist finished his last Richmond dispatch with an admonition to any northerners inclined to leniency at the moment of triumph. He warned against a resurgence of Confederate sentiment. "In a community thus tainted, the iron hand must govern," he cautioned his readers. "Case it in velvet, if you will, but beneath must be the iron still. Above all, let us have no hasty patchings up of a reconstructed State Government."[22]

Stanton agreed. In his mind, the flap over the Episcopal prayers validated his distrust of the Richmonders. Now his unease about Lincoln's meetings with Campbell consumed him. Once the president returned to Washington, his war secretary argued with him to revoke the permission he had given to the legislators. Any recognition of Confederate officials, however slight, was dangerous. Campbell's action already proved that. Stanton's fear was confirmed when Charles Dana cabled him that Campbell and his committee had expanded the limited permission Lincoln gave them into an attempt to negotiate Virginia's relationship to the United States.[23]

In Alexandria the long-suffering Francis Pierpont waited for destiny. The loyalist governor of Virginia, reviled by Confederates and barely tolerated by his Union army protectors, expected any day word to come down that would allow him to go to Richmond in glory. Finally, Lincoln summoned him to the White House. "Please come up to see me at once," the president cabled him tersely.[24] The governor obliged, and they talked over the details of installing his regime in Jefferson's Capitol with the statue of Washington that a month before Pierpont had officiously asked Grant not to let his soldiers vandalize.

According to the governor, Lincoln fully reiterated his confidence in him. Perhaps. Pierpont would not have been happy to know that at the next cabinet meeting Lincoln damned his loyalist administration with faint praise, saying that it might be legal but it enjoyed scant support.[25] The date Lincoln summoned Pierpont was significant: it was April 10, after Appomattox had eliminated the value of the Campbell initiative, and not before.

ON WEDNESDAY MORNING, April 12, Lincoln cabled Weitzel. It was the day before the unlucky general was sent out of the city. The president wanted to know if there was any sign of the Virginia legislature gathering in response to his letter. "If there is any such sign, inform me what it is; if there is no such sign you may as [well] withdraw the offer."[26] He telegraphed the general again that evening with an entirely different tone, one shaped by the unanimous opposition of his cabinet and by Stanton's decisive influence in private. Lincoln knew the Virginia situation was impossible. Congress would never have approved, even if Campbell and his friends had not pushed for more authority than the president meant to give them.[27]

At the War Department the telegraph operator watched Lincoln write out his message to Weitzel, using a borrowed pen. The telegrapher opened his cipher book and hurriedly transcribed the cable for transmission, line by line. Finally convinced by Stanton, Lincoln informed Weitzel that Campbell had misinterpreted him. The southerner assumed the president meant to convene the Confederate legislature of Virginia as the legitimate authority to settle differences with the United States. "I have done no such thing," admonished Lincoln. "I spoke of them not as a Legislature, but as 'the gentlemen who

have *acted* as the Legislature of Virginia in support of the rebellion.' "
Because Campbell had misunderstood him, Lincoln continued, the
offer must be withdrawn: "Do not now allow them to assemble."[28]

Lincoln had been unwise. His earlier cables indicated that he did intend for the General Assembly of Virginia to convene under Federal
military protection. The president did not mean to give the legislators
any authority other than to take Virginia out of the Confederacy. But
he made the mistake of recognizing them as a corporate entity, and
that emboldened them. Campbell later argued that he did not mislead
either Lincoln or Weitzel and that it was Lincoln who brought up the
idea of the legislature. That was so, but Campbell and the Virginians
he convened went further than Lincoln wished, and tried to grab as
much power as they could.

The army officers in command in Richmond, cowed by Stanton's
fury and fearful of what Dana was saying about them, kept the president informed after he revoked his offer. On April 13, Weitzel's successor, Edward Ord, telegraphed the text of the notice that would
appear the next day in the city's paper: "Owing to recent events," it
read, with thundering understatement, "the call for the reassembling
of the gentlemen recently acting as the legislature of Va is rescinded."
Ulysses Grant told Ord to make only one change in the text, but it was
a significant one that revealed his political sensibilities. Strike the
word "call," he said, and substitute "permission."[29]

THE WAR THAT had dragged on for so long was suddenly ending. Richmond burned; Davis a fugitive; Lee a paroled prisoner. All in a week's
time. At last Lincoln could begin to think seriously about peacetime.
One of the last documents he endorsed before he left the office on the
evening of Good Friday, April 14, was a memorandum that, in its ordi-
nariness, summed up the state of affairs: "No pass is necessary now to
authorize any one to go to & return from Petersburg & Richmond.
People go & return just as they did before the war."[30]

Despite the finality of Appomattox, however, the Campbell initiative still would not die. Virginia's former U.S. senator R. M. T. Hunter
and the former Supreme Court justice went to Ord's office on Friday

On April 20, Mathew Brady finagled his way to photograph the Confederate commanding general, Robert E. Lee, on the porch of his rented town house on Franklin Street. (National Archives)

The Confederates managed to evacuate a number of trains from Richmond but had to leave many engines and hundreds of cars of rolling stock behind. Most of the cars survived the fire, but not this locomotive at the Richmond & Petersburg depot. (Library of Congress)

On the first evening of the occupation, Union army engineers began to throw the first line of pontoons across the James, just downstream from the scorched piers that were all that remained of Mayo's bridge. They later expanded the makeshift bridge into a double line of pontoons to provide a smoother traffic flow. (National Archives)

Clearly visible in this stereoscopic photograph looking toward the river from the base of Capitol Square, the Burned District towers over a row of Union cavalry mounts tied up to an iron fence. Surprisingly, given the slow shutter speeds of cameras at the time, smoke can still be seen rising from the ruins in the middle distance. (Library of Congress)

With the gaunt ruins of the Gallego mills in the background, stone piers from Mayo's bridge were the only remains of the city's single pedestrian and vehicular bridge, the wooden superstructure of which fell flaming into the river with great hissing splashes on April 3. (Library of Congress)

No one photographed President Lincoln during his dramatic visit to Richmond, and even if someone had, the newspapers of the North could not have reproduced the image. They relied instead on engravings, such as this one, to convey the reception of Lincoln in the former Confederate capital. (Frank Leslie's Illustrated Newspaper)

At the U.S. Christian Commission, large numbers of destitute people, like this group of largely African American Richmonders, applied for free food in the early days of the occupation. (Library of Congress)

Within days, the wharf at the Rocketts landing, just downstream from the last of the rapids, was back in action receiving supply ships for the Union army. The masts of sailing vessels are apparent in the right background, beyond an artillery park of abandoned Confederate cannon. (Library of Congress)

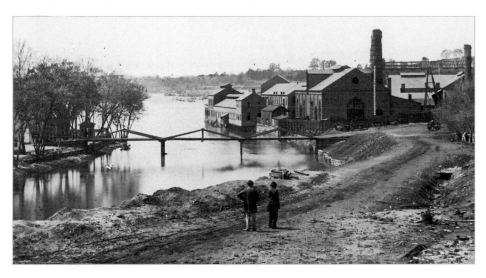

The Tredegar ironworks, just west of downtown, occupied the largest industrial complex in the Confederacy. It survived the fire largely intact. (Library of Congress)

Thomas Jefferson's neoclassical Virginia Capitol rises above the Burned District, showing that the fire stopped only when it ran out of combustible material at the base of Capitol Square. This photograph, taken from one of the broken windows of the Spotswood Hotel, shows the trees not yet fully leafed out, indicating that the time of the picture was not long after the evacuation. (Virginia Historical Society)

The Burned District in the commercial heart of Richmond, in all
more than twenty blocks, afforded an appalling vista "of smoking
ruins, blackened walls and broken chimneys." (Library of Congress)

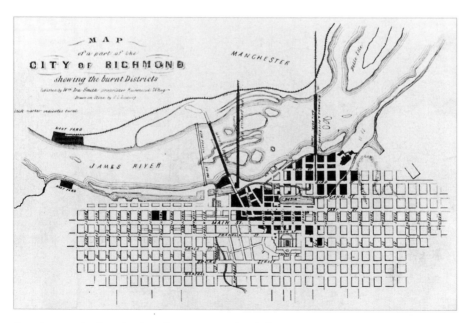

Exactly a week after the fire, the rejuvenated and thoroughly Unionist Richmond Evening
Whig *began selling souvenir lithograph maps to northern soldiers. Irritatingly oriented with
south at the top of the image, the map shows burned areas in black. Even from this perspective, which does not include all of the built-up areas of the city, it is apparent that the fire
consumed only a fraction of Richmond. Even so, that fraction constituted nine-tenths
of the business district and thus the greatest portion of the city's moneymaking capacity.*
(Virginia Historical Society)

One of the most impressive perspectives on the ruins left by the fire—and one of the most widely reproduced images—is this photograph taken from the south bank of the canal turning basin, showing the utter destruction of property between that point and the base of Capitol Square. (Library of Congress)

Prestigious Hollywood Cemetery was located on a bluff overlooking the falls of the James from the north bank of the river, just to the west of town. During the war no Richmonder erected a single marble tombstone in the cemetery, but rude wooden headboards marked the graves of thousands of soldiers. (Library of Congress)

In this photograph, Thomas Crawford's bronze equestrian statue of George Washington dominates the northern corner of Capitol Square. St. Paul's Episcopal Church is to the left. Remembering the fire many years later, a Union soldier wrote, "Amid this carnival of ruin, stood the great statue of Washington, against which fire-brands thumped and rattled."
(National Archives)

The largest auditorium in Richmond was at the African Church on Broad Street. On the first Thursday of the occupation, a Jubilee meeting filled the building to capacity, as freed slaves celebrated their liberation. The fact that the leaves on the trees in the churchyard are not fully out indicates that this picture was taken not many days after that tumultuous event. (Library of Congress)

A former U.S. Supreme Court justice, John Archibald Campbell was the highest-ranking Confederate official to remain in Richmond after the evacuation. His appearance showed the iron determination with which he boldly negotiated with Lincoln on the president's visit to the fallen southern capital. (Handy Studios Collection of the Supreme Court of the United States)

morning, April 14. It was Ord's first day on the job as replacement for
Weitzel. One of Grant's favorites, Ord had just returned from the
heady scenes at Appomattox Court House. He had been present in
Wilmer McLean's parlor when Grant and Lee met. After Lee signed
the terms of capitulation, Ord and other generals stripped the room of
furniture and furnishings for souvenirs. Nothing remained but the
carpet and the McLean girl's rag doll. Then a staff captain took the
doll, too.[31] Ord bought the marble-top surrender table and brought it
with him when he and his wife, Mary, moved into the former Davis
mansion in Richmond. Prematurely gray at forty-six, he scowled at
Mathew Brady's cameraman recording the house for posterity, but he
smiled on his late enemies. Ord was inclined to sympathize with the
defeated Confederates and intended to rule with a light and concilia-
tory hand.

Campbell and Hunter knew about the general's skepticism regarding black soldiers and his leniency toward southern whites. They
asked him for passes to go to Washington to confer with Lincoln, because they had not given up their quest for a voice in formalizing
peace and, they hoped, in reconstruction. Ord thought their request
had merit. He recommended that the president receive them because
they would bring "important communications."[32]

A sergeant took Ord's message from the War Department telegraph office to the White House shortly after nine-thirty Friday
evening. Lincoln had already gone out. The staff were idling away the
time in gossip. With them was S. P. Hanscom, the editor of the *National Republican*. Hanscom had antagonized his press colleagues by
insinuating himself into Lincoln's favor to the point that he often
walked into the president's office without an appointment. He offered
to take the sealed cable to Lincoln. He walked down to Tenth Street
and delivered the message to the president in his box at Ford's Theatre
about intermission time. It was probably the last dispatch Abraham
Lincoln read.

CHAPTER 18

THE ORDER OF THE DAY

Saturday, April 15, and After

O Captain! My Captain! our fearful trip is done.
—Walt Whitman

With his field hospital, Daniel Nelson followed Grant's army toward Appomattox Court House, through a countryside "strewed with burnt wagons, dead horses, mules & the debris of War." He swore that the wounded Confederates he treated after the surrender looked as fierce as cannibals and accused them of an arrogant sense of entitlement for expecting their captors to take care of them. No thoughts of reconciliation yet glimmered in the mind of this callow Yankee doctor. On the way back to Richmond, the stench of bloated animal carcasses by the hundred marred the glory of woodland springtime. Nelson's cryptic diary entries showed that even though war had ended in Virginia, legal killing had not: "Bad hills & dead horses. Paroled prisoners violate their parole & are hung."[1]

IN SMALL GROUPS, still under the command of their officers as stipulated by the surrender terms, Confederate soldiers left Appomattox for the trek home. They went to all points of the compass, some to North Carolina and destinations farther south, some to the Valley of

Virginia and other parts of the state, but the largest number headed for Richmond, either because it was home or because it was the best point for finding transportation to more distant destinations. By horse, ambulance, and wagon, and mostly on tired, ill-shod feet, they converged on the city.

On Saturday, April 15, Lee returned, too. His ragged entourage arrived in the driving rain, without fanfare, at the south end of the string of pontoons that replaced Mayo's burned toll bridge. People had been expecting him, and word spread quickly.

On hand was Thomas Chester, the only African American journalist to record Lee's arrival. It had been a triumphant two weeks for Chester, marching in with the victorious army as he did on the day of the fire and then presiding over a jubilant gathering of freedmen at the African Baptist Church three days later. Now it was given to him to see the South's hero return in defeat. Along the route, the first efforts to cheer Lee failed. People contented themselves with quietly waving their hands and hats, a melancholy pantomime amid the ruins. But then, Chester had to admit, as Lee neared his destination, the crowd grew and cheers rose from the throats of the depressed white residents, echoing the hoarse tribute of his men at Appomattox: beaten, defiant, downcast, proud.

As he approached his house on Franklin Street, threatened by fire but not touched nearly two weeks earlier, more people spilled out onto the sidewalks. When the general dismounted, Chester wrote, "he immediately uncovered his head, thinly covered with silver hairs, as he had done in acknowledgment of the veneration of the people along the streets. There was a general rush of the small crowd to shake hands with him. During these manifestations not a word was spoken, and when the ceremony was through, the General bowed and ascended his steps. The silence was then broken by a few voices calling for a speech, to which he paid no attention."[2]

For the rest of the afternoon, from all outward appearances, no sign of life stirred in the house. Occasionally friends of the family walked up to the door, but most of them were turned away. Edward Crapsey, another Philadelphia journalist, reported much the same things as his

African American colleague. Like Chester, he loathed Confederates, but despite his desire to lord it over the defeated southerners, he conceded a measure of dignity in the general's demeanor and in the response of the crowd. Lee's presence moved them, Crapsey said. "It was their blasted hopes, their thwarted ambition, as well as their military idol, that rode through the streets of Richmond today, and it is no wonder the people wept."[3]

No wonder, too, that the journalist called Lee's return "the great sensation of the day, in fact, the only one."[4] He was only half right. Though the spectators lining the pathways through the rubble did not yet know it, at the same instant they were uncovering their heads out of respect for Lee, shocking news from Washington flashed down the military telegraph lines. When their operator deciphered the encrypted Morse tappings, Federal officers had no time to think about the defeated Confederate commander. There was, indeed, another sensation of that day.

General Ord had already received the first coded warning in the early hours of Saturday: President Lincoln had been shot "and cannot live." Ord tried to suppress the news as long as possible, at least until the army could put its forces on full alert. Still keeping silent, that afternoon he went to the Spotswood suite of a visiting Pennsylvania publisher, one of the tourists come to gawk at the ruins. Other guests included John Mulford, the Federal prisoner exchange commissioner, and his Confederate counterpart, Robert Ould, who had been captured but released on parole. Urbane, ambitious, and shrewd, Ould was making the most of his wartime contacts with the other side. Such was Mulford's trust that he allowed Ould and his staff to continue their work closing out files and returning prisoners' money and belongings entrusted to them. When a messenger arrived confirming that Lincoln had died, everyone present reacted with shock and dismay. The one southerner in the group denounced the news most vehemently. "That is the worst blow the confederacy has yet had," cried Ould, blustering with anger. "Lee's surrender is nothing to it."[5]

Provost Marshal General Marsena Patrick brought in soldiers from outlying posts to form a reserve in case of trouble.[6] Though civilians noticed the unusual troop movements that night, they did not yet know the reason. Many were preoccupied trying to learn the fate of their loved ones with the southern army. As if to mock the mothers and wives who implored returning soldiers for news, the local thespians revived their inane entertainments. Acted out against the backdrop of a cheerless and occupied city, these frivolities seemed even more incongruous than they did during the last days of the Confederacy. D'Orsay Ogden's New Richmond Theatre celebrated the weekend with a hodgepodge of ballads, while Buckley & Budd's minstrels packed their hall for a rollicking Saturday night.

Robert Ould apparently kept the confidence inadvertently shared with him at the Spotswood, but by midday on Sunday, the shocking truth leaked out well beyond army headquarters. Like the sudden word of evacuation two Sundays before, the thunderbolt from Ford's Theatre smote residents of the abandoned southern capital just as church services concluded. By evening, all the flags in the city flew at half-mast.[7]

In Washington, Grant and Stanton worried about the safety of the government. The conspirators had also wounded Secretary of State William Seward. Perhaps there were other plots still in the works. The presence of so many paroled southern officers in the Federal capital troubled the secretary of war. What mischief might even greater numbers of them cause in Richmond? Grant ordered his commanders to arrest Mayo, Campbell, and any city councillor who had not taken the oath of allegiance. The same applied to all paroled officers, even army doctors caring for the wounded at Chimborazo Hospital. Throw them into Libby Prison, Grant barked. With an outburst of emotion at odds with his usual flat, laconic cables, he vowed they would need to take extraordinary measures "whilst assassination remains the order of the day with the rebels."[8]

As commander in Richmond, Ord took it upon himself to dispute the order. Lee and his staff were in town, asserted the general. If he arrested them, "I think the rebellion here would be reopened—I will risk my life that the present paroles will be kept." By the time he received Ord's plea, Grant calmed down and left his subordinate to act as local conditions dictated. Ord could not believe the Booth conspiracy originated with the Richmond Confederates. Campbell and Hunter would not likely have shown up at his office on Friday morning asking permission to see Lincoln if they had known about the assassination plot. Besides, he said rather naively, "they are [old, nearly helpless] and I think incapable of harm."[9]

"IT STRUCK ME like death. It did everybody," wrote Capt. John Prescott of the 12th New Hampshire Volunteers that Sunday. Two weeks before, he and his men had exhausted themselves battling the fire and thought the locals were grateful. Now this horrible news was too much for some of them to comprehend, and it triggered instant suspicion and renewed sectional hatred. A northerner who left town on Sunday by boat said he felt as if he had spent the whole day in a morgue. Every vessel his ship passed in the narrow channel below the city flew its flag at half-mast. As his steamer drew alongside a troopship coming upriver, the soldiers on deck silently held up a great placard bearing three words: "President Lincoln Assassinated."[10]

Ever since men of the disbanded Army of Northern Virginia began to straggle back into town, Confederate gray had blended with Union blue on the city streets. Though they knew most southern soldiers did not own any civilian clothes, some northern journalists professed to be enraged by the sight of gray uniforms. Not even utter defeat, fumed Edward Crapsey, "has whipped out of them the impudence that is an essential element of Southern character." He could not fathom "this spirit of bravado amid the ruin and desolation of Richmond."[11] Even before the assassination, the *Philadelphia Inquirer*'s man demanded that the army hang some southerners—he did not care which ones—as an example to the others; otherwise they would view treason "as a fashionable amusement instead of a capital crime."[12]

A more levelheaded Yankee than the volatile Crapsey doubted the Confederates were planning insurrection. Such an act, he wrote, "would be the work not only of demons but of idiots."[13] The threat of violence came from quite another quarter. Paroled southern officers who were in Richmond en route home to other places and took their meals at the Spotswood Hotel understood that very well. On Sunday morning at least as many gray uniforms as blue occupied the Spotswood's crowded breakfast tables, but after word of the assassination spread, few Confederate officers showed themselves in public.[14]

The private jottings and letters of northerners justified Confederate caution. Their feelings were too deep for words, wrote Henry Spaulding, a Yankee soldier stationed in Virginia. "Others were for making one universal sweep over the whole South. . . . Let the army loose, & let every man go in & kill & slay."[15] James Hane, a twice-wounded twenty-two-year-old corporal in Richmond with the 81st New York, condemned "traitors who deserve no better fate than be hung between Heaven and earth for foul birds to pick their bones."[16] He was eager to exact punishment and not especially concerned to discriminate between innocent and guilty. Another private wrote his parents that the army should have accepted Lee's surrender and then butchered the prisoners: "We ought to Hang every Damn Rebel in the Southern Confederacy."[17]

The fugitive Confederate government did not orchestrate the assassination, as many in the North believed. But the private reaction of some southerners, if publicly known, would have stoked the fears of Yankees inclined to paranoia.[18] Lucy Fletcher, who confided to her diary her disgust at the apotheosis of the dead president in the North, typified this quietly unrepentant southern hostility. "While I could not but experience a thrill of horror on hearing of his miserable end . . . ," she sneered, "it was a just retribution for the thousands of murders which must be heavy on his soul."[19] When Judith McGuire learned of the assassination, her first reaction was to worry about Yankee retaliation and to blame Lincoln for shedding so much southern blood.[20] The few imprudent Confederates who expressed such sentiments publicly, such as a paroled officer at the Ballard House Hotel and another at City Point, were beaten and nearly lynched by Union soldiers.[21]

The army draped Richmond in funerary black as best it could. There cannot have been a great supply of appropriate fabric, but soldiers found enough to decorate Davis's mansion, the Custom House, and other important public buildings. Black cloth draped the doors to the Capitol and the railing around Houdon's statue of Washington. All commissioned officers wore black crepe on their left arms. On the day of the funeral, the army suspended nonessential work. At noon warships in the river fired twenty-one guns. The crash of artillery once more reverberated through the cobblestone streets.[22]

Once again as well, the Virginia capital earned a sad distinction, for no crowds gathered to express collective grief as they did in cities in the North. It was not for want of trying. Some residents asked permission to hold meetings, but nervous Federal commanders turned down their requests. With its citizens denied the chance to express their sorrow publicly, Richmond after the assassination was a doubly morose place. Thomas Chester, however, doubted the sincerity of the would-be mourners and interpreted another silence as proof of the true feelings of white Virginians. He was in Petersburg on the day of the funeral and noted with scorn that only two of six churches with bells caused them to toll for Lincoln.[23]

Some work had to go on. The army assigned rooms at the governor's mansion to members of Lee's small headquarters staff who came with him to Richmond. While their general closeted himself with his family at the house on Franklin Street, the aides spread out their muster rolls and order books at the mansion on Capitol Square and attended to the final sorting out of the affairs of the Confederate army.[24] With minute guns firing their salutes in the background throughout the day of Lincoln's funeral, Lee's gray-clad adjutants presided over the quieter, bureaucratic obsequies of the Army of Northern Virginia.

THE INFLUX OF soldiers and displaced civilians of all kinds continued unabated. Provost Marshal Patrick fretted about his ability to control them. "Richmond," he wrote Stanton's assistant, Charles Dana, "is full of non-residents, paroled prisoners, refugees, followers of the army, and colored people. Every boat brings from the North persons on business of various kinds, often very indiscreet in their conduct."[25] For weeks after the surrender, the city overflowed with Confederate soldiers unable to reach their homes. The prison warehouses bulged with men in dirty homespun gray. A Federal commander summed up their predicament—and his disdain—with the terse, dismissive order to "allow the prisoners prayer books & tobacco."[26]

There was some initial apprehension among the occupiers that unrepentant Confederates might resort to guerrilla warfare. This specious prospect appealed to more credulous commentators in later years than to southern military men at the time. It was an exaggerated fear all along. Even so, the victors wanted to get word to as many Confederates still under arms as quickly as possible. In Richmond, Grant's aide Adam Badeau, who had the unfortunate distinction of being a Booth family friend, announced one such order in the *Whig*. It extended terms given at Appomattox to "soldiers of the Army of Northern Virginia, who were not present at the surrender."[27] A few weeks later, as fears of irregular warfare dissipated, the army was less apprehensive, and less generous. Henceforth, said General Order No. 6 of the Military Division of the James, any Confederates found bearing arms in opposition to the authority of the United States government "will be treated as robbers and outlaws."[28]

Along with the wave of southern civilians and soldiers, northern tourists in search of souvenirs continued for weeks to fill the streets of downtown Richmond. The speaker's gavel from the Confederate House of Representatives found its way into the hands of Schuyler Colfax, the speaker in Washington. The army appropriated a large flag that flew when the Confederate Congress was in session, and sent it to Washington. Indiscriminate thieves even filched Weitzel's personal property during the week and a half he occupied the Davis mansion.[29]

Clever scavengers picked over the trash and squirreled away historic items to sell to discriminating latecomers, who found a thriving trade in Confederate and Virginia documents. One dealer offered Chicago minister William Patton some Jefferson Davis autographs and a survey plat drawn by the young George Washington.[30] With little effort, he was able to fill his pockets with Confederate mementoes for a charity raffle back home. A few visitors knew how to sift wheat from chaff, foremost among them the great narrative historian Francis Parkman. During his brief sojourn in Richmond, and with a bankroll of only $500, he founded the Boston Athenaeum's vast collection of Confederate imprints, including a perfect run of the *Richmond Examiner*.[31]

When the secondary market began to dry up, the archival remains of the Confederacy fared poorly. Street vendors hawked fat wads of documents that people increasingly eyed as a source of cheap wrapping paper rather than historical curios. Daybooks and ledgers from the auditor's and treasurer's offices that still had blank pages found new employment in the revived countinghouses of Richmond. The Confederate army's payrolls, even those half-burned, were bundled up and sent to the paper mills for recycling.

Like the Confederate illuminati who preceded them, visiting Yankee dignitaries put up at the Spotswood Hotel. From its windows, many now lacking glass, they could peer out over the Burned District. It may have been the grandest Richmond hotel, but the demand forced some guests to settle for makeshift accommodations in the hallways. One counted himself lucky to find a room despite obscenities scrawled on the walls and filthy beds.[32] A visiting clergyman complained that the only things plentiful in the hotels were "servants, dirt and unmentionable nocturnal company."[33]

George Templeton Strong, who had caused the bells of New York City's Trinity Church to ring out for joy when Richmond fell, visited the great den of rebel iniquity at the end of April for the Sanitary Commission. Union regiments still paraded through the city, and white southerners still watched with the same sullen hostility as on the first day of occupation. An urbane man and an unselfish, diligent charity worker in New York, Templeton shared the stern view of the South expressed by many northern visitors. On Capitol Square, he observed a young man of about eighteen in a Confederate captain's uniform unhappily watching a grand review of his conquerors march past: "He would give us a furtive side glance, such as a subjugated wildcat gives a spectator whom it would bite if it dared," wrote Strong. "It was a look of malice and of curiosity."[34]

Strong could not resist likening southerners to animals. They resented northern charity, he said, "much as a hungry, sulky, ill-conditioned hound accepts a bone—uncertain whether to gnaw the donation or to bite the fingers of the donor." He described women receiving free food as sour and arrogant but then admitted that "there were poor little children with wan faces and pitiful stories of sick mothers and of privation and misery endured for months."[35] He overcame this momentary pang of compassion and ordered their free rations stopped because, to his way of thinking, it only encouraged them to imagine they were superior to Yankees.

Other northern visitors like Strong were eager to write home their impressions of what they had seen. One wrote of seeing "crowds of melancholy, lazy men, both white and black . . . lounging about the streets," without considering that the fire had thrown thousands out of work.[36] Visitors often irritated the soldiers assigned to Richmond duty. The more self-important tourists pestered the army for free transportation to nearby battlefields. An officer who had entered the city on the day of the fire—and was not above making disparaging remarks of his own about southerners—heartily despised these uninvited guests from the North. They would come back from their day trips out to the deserted fortifications around the city like gleeful children clutching fragments of shells, minié balls, and even human remains. "Robbing a battle-field of its bones," wrote William Kreutzer, colonel of the 98th New York Volunteers, "is a species of Vandalism not hitherto witnessed in this country."[37]

If Kreutzer held his fellow Yankee tourists in poor regard, the natives found their presence oppressive. Worst of all were northerners who went to Richmond to look up antebellum acquaintances. An unrepentant southerner said he bitterly resented their offers of forgiveness because he never had done anything wrong.[38]

New York artilleryman William Nichols sent home his thoughts about Richmond and Richmonders. He wandered through Hollywood Cemetery on the hills to the west overlooking the falls of the James and giving a vantage point that let him look back over the city. The Tredegar ironworks, spared from the fire, lay idle down below the bluff. Just beyond, the ruined business district stretched out along the waterfront. At Hollywood no one had raised a single marble tombstone since the war began, though the gravediggers had buried thousands of soldiers there. Former president John Tyler, a Virginian who sided with the Confederacy, died in 1862, but no stone yet marked his grave. A simple board with J. E. B. Stuart's name painted on it in white was all that marked the final resting place of that Confederate hero.

While Nichols was there, he witnessed the reinterment of a Confederate lieutenant who had fallen at the end of the campaign. The family had just recovered the remains and was burying them next to the grave of a brother who had died defending Richmond in 1862. Watching the weeping relatives who gathered for this private ceremony, Nichols admitted it was an affecting scene. Then he went a little farther to the edge of the cemetery on the bluff overlooking the James and saw Belle Isle, the open-air prison camp in the middle of the river where so many Union men had died. Their graves, rudely marked with barrel staves, had already begun to wash away. Looking back at the grieving family, Nichols said, "I felt my heart grow hard towards them."[39]

CHAPTER 19

THE SORRY SILENCE OF A CONQUERED PEOPLE

April into May

In deep mourning . . . the broken-hearted daughters of the Capital moved like shadows of the past.
—T. C. DeLeon[1]

Alexander Gardner missed a historic opportunity while he was in Richmond, one that fell into the lap of his rival and onetime boss, the flamboyant entrepreneur with the camera, Mathew Brady. Gardner's men finished their photographic series on the wet morning of Saturday, April 15. They were glad to pack up after days of tromping through the ruins. Brady had arrived in the capital after Gardner, or else he, too, might have finished by then. His delay meant that it was he and not Gardner who was in the city on the afternoon that Lee returned from Appomattox. As soon as he heard the news, Brady put out feelers. He approached Robert Ould, who had used his own good relations with the occupiers to retain his freedom, at least for the time being. Ould agreed to act as go-between and enabled the photographer to make contact with the general.

Brady's overture bore fruit on the following Thursday afternoon in the form of six large glass-plate negatives. Two portrayed the general flanked by his son, Custis Lee, and his aide, Walter Herron Taylor, who had kept his promise to rejoin Lee after his evacuation-night wedding. Four focused on Lee alone.[2] By the time the celebrated photographer captured his image, Lee, like everyone else in the city, knew about the assassination and wondered what it would mean for the prostrated South. That apprehension added one more burden to his shoulders, one more reason among many for his solemn, careworn appearance in the Brady plates, destined to be reproduced over and over again, from that day forward.

The family set up a roster of gatekeepers to shield the general from unwanted visitors, who appeared outside the Franklin Street town house with alarming frequency. For exercise, he took walks under cover of darkness late at night. It did not take many days of being the uncomfortable object of curiosity for Lee, a shy man, to decide to leave Richmond.[3] It had never been his real home. Home was Arlington House, his wife's inherited mansion on the Potomac overlooking the city of Washington. He could never return there, however, now that the house was forfeit and the grounds a Union military cemetery. He was resigned to the war's outcome and turned to the needs of his family and of the South for rebuilding.

Lee clung to the belief that the parole he had signed at Appomattox shielded him from prosecution. But the assassination killed talk of leniency, and the North was hot to inflict punishment. For a time, a few exemplary hangings seemed likely. When he was shocked to learn that a vindictive Federal grand jury had indicted him for treason, Lee appealed to his former adversary for help. Grant agreed that the men who surrendered at Appomattox could not be tried for treason as long as they kept the terms of their parole. But it took a threat by Grant to resign to squelch the indictment.[4]

LIKE LEE, the other residents of Richmond had to come to terms with the new order. At first, diehard Confederates refused to acknowledge the reality of Union occupation and shunned Lee's example of accepting defeat. After the assassination, though, few of these intransigents dared entertain hopes as extravagant as those expressed by Thomas

Munford. Unlike his commanding general, Colonel Munford refused to surrender his cavalry at Appomattox and eluded Grant's army.[5] Munford would not give up, even though his command melted away each mile they trotted to the west, as men singly and in small groups recognized the futility of resistance and rode off to their homes. Nearly two weeks later, Munford appealed to his soldiers with a special printed order to continue fighting. It ended with a plea that was at the same time insane, romantic, and irresponsible: "We have still a country, a flag, an army, a Government. Then to horse!"[6] The printer in whatever town set this broadside in type cannot have had much hope of collecting payment in a currency that would do him any good.

It was true that at that point Joseph Johnston had not yet surrendered his army in North Carolina, and more than a hundred thousand Confederate soldiers still were under arms. But they were scattered across the South, mostly small clusters of garrison troops, and represented no serious threat of a continuation of the fighting. It would only be a matter of time before they gave themselves up or simply went home.

At the opposite end of the spectrum from Munford was Mary West, who, seated at her window, could see the United States flag waving over Richmond. She prayed it would remain there "until time shall be no more." A native Virginian, she shared the Unionist sympathies of her New Hampshire–born husband. Frank West's job as a newspaper typesetter had exempted him from the Confederate draft for a time. He was eventually conscripted, but Mary pulled strings and got him released. Her father offered a home away from the capital for her and her children, but she said her duty was there.

She hid her own despair because she knew Frank was weak and needed constant support. "So, Mrs. McCawber like," she wrote, wistfully recalling the wife of the improvident Dickens character, "I have stayed with my husband waiting for 'something to turn up.'" She grieved for a sister whose son had died in Confederate service. By the end of the war, she had sold all her jewelry and clothes for food, all save two dresses. Happily for the Wests, on the day of occupation

Frank found work as a compositor at the transformed, Unionist *Evening Whig*. For the first time in years, he earned enough hard money to feed both his family and his frail self-esteem.[7]

Mary West and her joyful welcome of Federal rule, however, represented a decidedly minority sentiment among the white women of Richmond. More typical was Susan Hoge, who cherished the southern cause even as she accepted occupation and continued in defeat as in war to be an example for the Confederate faithful. During the war, while her husband, Moses, preached to the troops and ran the blockade to buy them Bibles abroad, Susan had maintained their large, chaotic household with her accustomed efficiency. It cannot have been easy. In 1863 a guest who repaid her hospitality by spying for the North was unmasked just when one of the Hoge children sickened and died.[8]

Two weeks after Appomattox—and two days after Tom Munford issued his plea to renew the fighting—Hoge fumed at a sermon she heard on the assassination.[9] The remarks were made by the Rev. Dr. Thomas Moore, minister of First Presbyterian Church. During the war, the scholarly Pennsylvania native had extended his pastoral care to sick Union prisoners. When he learned of the assassination, he wrote that if Davis had been shot it would not have caused a fraction of the grief expressed in Richmond on the death of Lincoln.[10] That sentiment must have crept into the sermon that so offended Hoge.

Moore knew he had made an unpopular statement. Provost Marshal Patrick, who had known the preacher before the war, said Moore came to him a few hours after giving the sermon and lamented that "the women are all after him."[11] Patrick reassured him it was not so, but the provost marshal did not have access to Susan Hoge's private expressions of Confederate loyalty.

Nor did he know the feelings of another minister's wife, Lucy Fletcher. Her burdens increased as her husband, unable to provide for his family, headed for a mental breakdown. Her reduced circumstances, at times depending on charity, embittered her toward former slaves, even the children. The sight of them playing on the previously forbidden green of Capitol Square seemed to her an unbearable punishment for the white people of Richmond: "Hundreds of ragged & dirty negro boys are rolling over the beautiful grass. . . . At intervals throughout the grounds, dirty tents are placed for the sale of cakes & pies, & this is Yankee *civilization!* I hope they enjoy each other's society."[12] A northern visitor had women like Hoge and Fletcher in mind, thousands of them, when he wrote that they were "gloomy, sullen, subjugated, in despair of the Confederacy yet hating the Union."[13]

The painful divisions that had troubled families throughout the war continued. Mary West sided with her husband against her blood relatives. Political differences alienated Lucy Fletcher from a sister in the North. More poignant still were the circumstances of the Palmer family, even when there was a measure of reconciliation.

Charles Palmer, an elderly, prosperous import-export merchant, lived and worked in a building at the corner of Cary and Virginia streets, an intersection at the center of the Burned District. He lost everything in the fire but was grateful for northern victory, for he was a staunch Unionist. He had shared prison with his friends John Minor Botts and Franklin Stearns, given money to needy Union families, and provided some of the military intelligence Elizabeth Van Lew passed along to the Yankee army. The merchant's son, Dr. William Price Palmer, was as equally ardent a Confederate. He saw action with the Richmond Howitzers and, after his health failed, served as surgeon for returning prisoners of war at a camp west of town. After the war the homeless Unionist father moved in with the proud Confederate son, though neither man recanted his political allegiance.[14]

With each day that passed, even devout Confederates decided to sign the pledge of allegiance to the hated United States. Some of them did so with sincerity, observed a northern traveler, and some "with words of hypocrisy on their lips." It was a simple oath, but it included a passage inserted especially to remind southerners of one outcome of the war. Each person who subscribed to the pledge agreed to support all of the president's proclamations regarding slaves.[15]

It was a matter of practicalities. Lincoln and Weitzel may have agreed with Campbell and Myers that the oath should not be compulsory, but no one could conduct business without taking the pledge.

People realized that they must take the oath or see their families go hungry. Even women from prominent families, according to Confederate diarist John Beauchamp Jones, made cakes and pies to sell to Yankee soldiers, black and white, to obtain the greenbacks they needed to sustain their households.[16]

One at a time, the owners of businesses resumed operations. Powhatan Weisiger managed to save from the fire a few of those Parisian hats he had advertised the week before the evacuation. He announced his plan to open shop, for the time being in the basement of his residence a block down Franklin Street from the Lee house. Tom Griffin, the black restaurateur who had supplied the visiting member of Parliament Thomas Conolly with one of the last feasts of Confederate Richmond, lost both of his saloons in the fire. He resolved to rebuild and converted a large iron-front store on Governor Street into an eatery in the hope that the Federal military authorities would give him permission to open for business.

The Crenshaw family survived with the source of their wealth intact: the Haxall-Crenshaw mills somehow escaped the fire. Even before Appomattox, the firm obtained Federal permission to remove personal property from the mill, especially food for family consumption. And the international aspect to the firm's business allowed the Crenshaws to be Confederate patriots and to bank their gold in London without reproach.[17]

Schools began to reopen, including Turner's Classic and English School and Squire's Classical School, both of which announced they would begin taking pupils for instruction on the Monday after the fire. Sallie and Mary Partington, who sang for the theater under the Stars and Bars and were friends of John Wilkes Booth, announced the reopening of their dancing academy. There were many new schools, too, as northern teachers came to Richmond to educate the freed slaves, whose thirst for learning astonished all the whites.

If they had to take the pledge to keep body and soul together, the Confederate people of Richmond did not have to embrace their conquerors. It galled some of them to see how northern forbearance eroded Confederate resolve. "The Yankees are pretending to great kindness now," wrote one Virginian, "but they dont deceive me, the time will come when we shall not be able to say our souls are Gods without asking their permission. And the people of Virginia will submit & kiss the rod & praise their dear Masters."[18]

Others were grateful for the leniency and for the fact that Godfrey Weitzel's successor in Richmond was the impetuous Gen. Edward Ord. "He is still Crazy Ord. Goes off half cocked," said a colleague.[19] Predisposed by sentiment and his southern wife, Mary, to forgive the Confederates, he made his first decision as Richmond commander before he arrived. With Grant's blessing, he ordered black units of the occupation army to leave the capital. One of Mary Ord's cousins who lived in the capital wrote a friend that her personal troubles paled next to the fate of the South. It was a consolation, though, that Cousin Mary had influence with her husband and used it to encourage his leniency toward former enemies.[20]

For three weeks the stubborn Episcopal churches kept their doors shut. They remained closed on Easter Sunday, when the North mourned the murdered president. But Richmonders tired of the tug-of-war between the clerics and the Federal army. On April 29, the rectors of three Episcopal churches—Grace, St. James's, and Monumental—wrote to Ord's replacement as army commander, Henry Halleck. (Ord, like Weitzel, did not last long in the Richmond command.) They told the general they would no longer wait for word from their bishop but would take the responsibility of restoring the prayer for the president of the United States of America.[21] Halleck made too much of their acquiescence when he cabled Grant the same day that "the rebel feeling in Virginia is utterly dead."[22]

"LAST NIGHT ON ringing the bell for Millie, she was nowhere to be found." With this tardy epiphany granted to her on the fifth day of Union rule, Fannie Taylor Dickinson belatedly began to comprehend the greatest change wrought by the occupation—the end of slavery. Living with her parents, her young preacher husband, and her children in a house that was now next to a Federal army camp, she should have seen it coming but was blind until it did.[23] A week after Millie failed to answer the bell, the Taylor and Dickinson families lost all their former slaves. "Today," wrote Fannie, "our servants have all left. Father offered them higher wages but they preferred to set up for themselves. This is indeed the unkindest cut of all. I cannot write about it."[24] For her as for every resident of the former Confederate capital, black and white, the death of slavery heralded a revolution in labor and in race relations that would profoundly affect daily life.

Some tried to dismiss or minimize the changes. "Poor deluded creatures," one woman said of the free people, "they will soon be tired of their freedom."[25] Lelian Cook, the girl who lived with Susan and Moses Hoge and shared their Confederate loyalties, noted with approval that the army put thousands of black men to work cleaning streets, repairing bridges, and digging coal. She said, "I expect a great many of them think freedom isn't as sweet as they thought it would be."[26]

In private opinions expressed at the time and in recollections long afterward, white Richmonders poured out their disdain for black men in Union blue and for the beneficiaries of emancipation. Lucy Fletcher, whose brother had died in Confederate service, observed the USCTs with fear and scorn. To her, the regiments of black soldiers looked "like an army of savages & cannibals just imported from Africa."[27] Anne Hobson's lament after a week's occupation, and her realization of the changes wrought by the forcible end to slavery, was typical: "The results of years might not have changed life as much as these six days have done. My God! What have I suffered, what do I not still suffer."[28]

The long view taken by one Confederate suggested the unhappy course that postwar race relations would take. Col. Christopher Tompkins, a West Point graduate, had fought in western Virginia, where he operated coal mines before the war. By 1865 he was supervising the Dover coal pits in Goochland County fifteen miles upriver from Richmond. It was he who had given Extra Billy Smith whiskey and breakfast when the fleeing governor turned up wet from being dunked in the canal by his unsteady horse. After the city fell, Tompkins watched the labor system crumble, quietly, without fanfare, but quickly.

Though only a handful of the slaves who worked the pits left on the Monday of the fire, by the next evening "every soul who had legs to walk was running to Richmond." Tompkins feared for the future of Virginia but thought that some good might come of emancipation. What he defined as "good," however, included the prediction that with the end of slavery, African Americans were fated for extermination like the Indians.[29]

White ministers of black churches did not last many Sundays after the occupation. On Palm Sunday, before news of Appomattox reached the city, Robert Ryland dared to warn his flock at the African Baptist Church against the USCT recruiting officers. On hearing his inflammatory remarks, black soldiers in the congregation tried to arrest Ryland when the service ended. Some parishioners pleaded with them to spare the old man that indignity.[30] Like so many whites who thought they understood black Richmonders, Ryland could not fathom the loathing of people for their enslavement and their exaltation at its demise.

As much was clear from a conversation he had with the Rev. Peter Randolph some weeks later. Born a slave in Prince George County, Virginia, but freed by his owner before the war, Randolph moved to the North. He returned to be the postwar pastor of Ebenezer Baptist Church in Richmond. Not realizing Randolph was a Virginian, Ryland tried to tell him that slavery in the Old Dominion had been an exceedingly mild institution. Randolph later remembered that he replied, with a long sigh, "If Hell was any worse than slavery in Virginia, I did not want to go there."[31]

Emancipation was a fact, but the hopes of the freed people were in some ways almost as unrealistic, and certainly as unrealized, as those of their Confederate neighbors for Lee's army in the week before Appomattox. But disappointment was far from their minds on the day of their liberation, when Weitzel's army entered Richmond and the joy of black residents knew no bounds.

Even the cynical Thomas Chester allowed his hopes to get the better of his judgment at first. After talking to his fellow African Americans, he was captivated by their joy and even thought white

Virginians would accept them as equal citizens of a restored Union. On the fourth day of occupation, he wrote that "nothing can exceed the courtesy and politeness which the whites everywhere manifest to the negroes . . . even masters are addressing their slaves as 'Mr. Johnson,' 'Mrs. Brown,' and 'Miss Smith.' A cordial shake of the hand and a gentle inclination of the body, approaching respectful consideration, are evident in the greetings which now take place between the oppressed and the oppressor."[32]

He may have been emboldened in this optimism by what happened to him two days before, when he wrote his first Richmond dispatch seated in the speaker's chair at the Capitol. The chair dated from the time when the state capital moved from Williamsburg and originally had borne the coat of arms of the British crown. It was now just a discarded relic of another overthrown regime, but the symbolism of sitting in it was not lost on Chester. While he composed his impressions of the Union entrance into the city, a paroled Confederate officer saw him and took offense. He resented the presumption of an African American daring to sit in that chair, and demanded that Chester leave. When the reporter stood his ground, the Virginian grabbed him and tried to evict him. Chester, a muscular thirty-year-old, hit the man hard enough to knock him down and give him a black eye. Defeated, the man sulked away and left Chester triumphant.[33]

The incident may have persuaded Chester, flushed with the joy of victory, that it would take little effort to usher in the New Jerusalem in race relations. Maybe, after all, southern whites would easily be cowed like the bully in the Capitol or meekly learn to treat blacks with respect, like those he professed to hear addressing their former slaves as equals. In a few weeks he repented of this optimism. He would have done so sooner if he could have heard the private thoughts of white Virginians like Fannie Dickinson, Lucy Fletcher, and Christopher Tompkins.

The portents for racial harmony were not good. Black citizens were grateful for the chance to have Union rations in exchange for work, but some of them resented the disparity in treatment: white Richmonders could receive free food by petitioning the Union army but without having to work for it. There were occasional outright threats of racial violence. Daniel Nelson, the Union army surgeon who had little sympathy for his former enemies, witnessed two instances. He said the army was called out to protect white families whose former slaves threatened to evict them from their houses.[34] Later that summer, treatment at the hands of the Union army of occupation would appear so hostile to black Richmonders that they would send a delegation to Washington to protest.

CRIME DID NOT take a holiday just because one flag replaced another on Capitol Square. With so many soldiers, blue and gray, and with hundreds of impoverished rural Virginians drifting into town in search of work, the tally of crimes continued unabated. Richmonders believed with some cause that their city was increasingly unpleasant and even dangerous for law-abiding citizens. Certainly the number of petty infractions rose with so many idle young men in uniform. "There is rich pillaging hereabouts," wrote an indulgent white officer with the all-black XXV Corps, "and the old soldiers understand it & live on the inhabitants while their chickens & turkeys last."[35] Castle Thunder, a jail for political prisoners of the Confederacy, now housed Union soldiers convicted of the same offenses they were there to protect the public against. In the month of April, the range of charges included "throwing stones in windows," "arrested for stabbing a woman," "assaulting a citizen," "rape," "horse stealing," "murderer," and "scoundrel."[36]

Official violence continued as well. The army of occupation enforced discipline with the harshest of time-honored penalties. For threatening the life of his superior officer and inciting mutiny, Samuel Mapp of the 10th USCT, a unit recruited from the black men of Maryland, paid with his life. The army made it a grand affair—to punish, to impress, and to warn. A crowd assembled to watch the procession arrive at the place of execution. First came the band of the 16th New York Regiment, then the first firing party, then the coffin borne by four soldiers, then the condemned man, and finally a second firing party of twelve more soldiers.

Mapp leaned for support on the arm of Garland White, chaplain of the 28th USCT, who only a few weeks before had preached freedom to the liberated black people of Richmond. Now he consoled a fellow African American soldier who had helped eradicate slavery in the Confederate capital only to be shot to death for disobeying a white officer of his own army. A quick prayer by White, a good-bye from Mapp, and the crash of a well-aimed volley ended the proceedings. "It was," wrote the chaplain, "the saddest spectacle I ever witnessed."[37]

FRANCIS PIERPONT, governor of the tiny, ignored loyalist Virginia government based in Alexandria, finally saw Richmond, but not until nearly two months after the fire. He arrived at the Rocketts wharf at the end of May on board the *Diamond*, a former blockade runner. The governor's family, aides, and assorted northern military officers and politicians accompanied him. The *Diamond*'s captain was in no hurry to make the passage. He feared that unexploded mines and other obstructions still hid in the narrow channel of the James and declined to make the run up to the capital at night. Unlike the Union sailors on April 4, he did not have Abraham Lincoln to spur him on, heedless of the threat.

And unlike Lincoln on his arrival, Pierpont was met at the wharf by a reception committee. The chairman who greeted the governor was Charles Palmer, the elderly Virginian and Unionist merchant who had moved in with his Confederate son after the fire dispossessed him of home and business. Palmer's welcome was heartfelt in its enthusiasm. Pierpont responded briefly and then rode by carriage to the governor's mansion past a line of Massachusetts soldiers, rigid at attention, with the thunder of an artillery salute crashing in his ears. Along the way, no one raised a flag or cheered, except a party of visiting northern women watching from the windows of the Spotswood Hotel. A few African American civilians turned out, but most of the people in the streets wore blue uniforms. At Capitol Square a large, curious crowd appeared, "but no demonstration of any kind, except that of silence."[38] It was, echoed another northerner, "the sorry silence of a conquered people."[39]

EPILOGUE

Blunt and Withered Laurels

The people that walked in darkness have seen a great light.
—Isaiah 9:2

At least since the turn of the twentieth century, when many Americans looked back at the end of the Civil War, they professed to see the beginnings of this country's rise to world power. Words that appeared in a Chicago newspaper only one day after the fall of the Confederate capital seemed prophetic. "The golden age of America," the editor proclaimed, "will date from the 3d of April, 1865, when the flag of the Union was restored upon the battlements of Richmond. . . . The future henceforth is full of the promise of greatness to America and freedom to the World."[1]

Perhaps the northern writer was right, but defeated southerners could hardly have shared that expansive vision. For a long and bitter time, they would embrace the bilious malediction pronounced by the *Richmond Daily Dispatch* on the eve of its destruction in the fire. "After what has occurred for four long years," the *Dispatch's* editor spat, "the future unity of America is a dream of maniacs."[2] It would take a prodigious amount of selective forgetting and remembering on both sides before that unity would be realized.

In the meantime, people far beyond Virginia would come to know Richmond's gaunt ruins through the eyes of the photographers who swarmed over the city while the rubble still smoldered. And they would recognize the stricken city through Currier and Ives's popular fanciful print showing Confederates fleeing across Mayo's bridge ahead of the flames. These views were stamped into national memory, and for a long time to come Richmond in ashes signified irretrievable loss to the South and the fruits of failed rebellion to the North.

By summer 1865, though, the sounds of Richmond's future began to ring out from the hammers and saws of carpenters and the chipping and tapping of masons laying course upon course of recycled James River brick as they erected bigger and better warehouses, stores, and factories. Laborers and craftsmen, black and white, they set about the task of the physical rebuilding of their city. With wild optimism, one resident declared that "the debris of the ruins are fast being cleared away and nearly every one [is] preparing to rebuild. This city is destined to be within a few years the second New York."[3] The reconstruction of Richmond had begun.

More significant, some people remembered signs as early as the first full day of occupation that hinted at the reconciliation to come. LaSalle Pickett, wife of the Confederate general, remembered that on that day, while the smoke rose thick and menacing above the Virginia capital, she tremulously answered a knock at the door. A sad-faced man, tall and gaunt and dressed in ill-fitting clothes, asked if he had found George Pickett's house. Abraham Lincoln himself had come to inquire about the family of an old acquaintance he had known before the war. Overwhelmed by the president's sympathy and his simple humanity, the astonished woman could only admit that she was Pickett's wife and hold out her infant for Lincoln to cradle.[4]

Thomas Thatcher Graves, aide-de-camp to Maj. Gen. Godfrey Weitzel, recalled a scene of similar pathos two weeks later. When the Union army learned that Robert E. Lee had returned, with his nephew Fitzhugh Lee and others, Weitzel called his aide into a room at headquarters in the former Confederate White House for a private talk. He pulled out a wallet stuffed with greenbacks and handed it to Graves.

"Go to General Lee's house," the Federal commander ordered, "find Fitzhugh Lee, and say that his old West Point chum Godfrey Weitzel wishes to know if he needs anything."[5]

When Graves knocked on the door of the house on Franklin Street, Fitzhugh Lee answered, still dressed in his Confederate uniform. Upon hearing the purpose of Graves's visit, he was overcome by the generosity. For a moment, he walked over to the other side of the parlor to compose himself, and then he went to an adjoining room. Through a half-opened door, the Union aide saw him speak to Robert E. Lee, seated in a chair with a worn, tired expression on his face. Fitzhugh Lee knelt down beside his uncle, placing a hand on his knee as he did, and explained why the visitor was there. He returned to the front parlor and, in Graves's words, "in a most dignified and courteous manner sent his love to Godfrey Weitzel, and assured him that he did not require any loan of money."[6]

Several weeks later, after the Episcopal churches had reopened, Robert E. Lee was in attendance at St. Paul's when an extraordinary thing happened. As parishioners prepared to kneel at the chancel rail to take communion, a tall black man with a military bearing came forward to kneel as well. Nothing like that had ever happened under slavery. The white communicants were stunned. Lee took the lead, walked up to the rail, and knelt reverently beside the man.

These accounts—Lincoln's solicitude for Pickett's family, Weitzel's generous offer to his West Point classmate, and Lee's Christian response to the man who tested a racial barrier—are filled with a spirit of reconciliation and of hope for the future of the broken country, reunited by force of arms and facing an uncertain road ahead. But the three stories also share the likelihood of being outright fiction.

LaSalle Pickett was a notorious plagiarizer and forger. She made a career of publishing letters she claimed were written to her during the war by her husband but in fact were postwar concoctions of her own mind. Her account of Lincoln was of the same cloth.

Two days before Fitzhugh Lee and his uncle returned to Richmond, General Ord replaced General Weitzel, who promptly left town under a cloud and in ill humor.[7] Weitzel could have expressed a generous spirit toward an old friend from West Point. But he could not have done it in Richmond in the manner Graves described.

The source for the touching scene at St. Paul's stems from a misinterpretation of a 1905 newspaper story. Later readers have inferred from that account by an aging Confederate veteran that Lee took the lead in a novel situation and set an example of proper Christian conduct. In fact, the veteran meant to show how Lee set an example of a different kind for the rest of the congregation, and by implication, for all white southerners "under the most trying and offensive circumstances." He meant for Lee's action to show how to deal with the impudence of a black man who dared cross the racial line at Holy Communion—not by accepting him as an equal but by ignoring him as if he did not exist.[8] Whatever happened at St. Paul's, all we know for certain is the singularly unchristian perspective intended by the 1905 newspaper account, written by someone who could not have divined what was in Lee's mind as he knelt to take communion.

If taken at face value, the stories told by Pickett and Graves are as affecting today as they were more than a century ago, as is the uplifting modern misinterpretation of the account of Lee at St. Paul's. But fabrications and distortions do not help us determine what really happened or what people really felt. To understand the minds of Richmonders and other Americans at the end of the war, we must look directly at the fierce, unforgiving opinions written down then, not those written long after.

Just five days after the fire was lit—and before the ruins had stopped smoking or Lee had surrendered at Appomattox—some unnamed Virginia Unionists proposed to erect a monument in the Burned District. It would commemorate for all time "the infamy of those who sought to destroy, by treachery, a city they could not hold by force of arms."[9] Expensive inlaid tablets in this imagined granite structure would solemnly instruct future generations about Richmond's place in the concluding chapter of the failed rebellion against the United States of America.

The editor of the *Evening Whig*, though sympathetic with the politics of the memorialists, thought their effort unnecessary. The awful scenes of destruction that he could see out his office window, just across the street and stretching for blocks down to the river, convinced him that for years to come the ruins themselves would constitute a fitting remembrance to the perfidy of the Confederates.[10] He was wrong about that. The ruins would not last long, and eventually there would be monuments in Richmond. But grand and numerous as they would be, none would be of the kind envisioned by these Unionists of April 1865, flush with the victor's triumphalist condescension, for they would be dedicated to the memory of Confederate, not Union, heroes.

In the bustle of rebuilding, the mutter of distant cannon fire that had been a minatory accompaniment to the sound of the James River rapids quickly faded in memory. But passions did not die so quickly, and participants in Richmond's four-year ordeal began to write about the experience—to make sense of it and to instruct others how to interpret what had happened to their city and their country. Two stand out as early exponents of radically different memories, John Minor Botts and Edward Pollard.

Few Virginia Unionists remained more consistent to their principles under conditions of great personal adversity than the bombastic former U.S. congressman John Minor Botts. A gargantuan man, nicknamed "Bison," he was aggressive in his speeches and his opinions, as intolerant of the fools he thought opposed him as they were of him. Though he owned slaves, Botts excoriated the secessionists and paid the price. For his opinions, he spent two months on the second floor of Lumpkin's slave jail with a view through its barred windows of factories in Shockoe Bottom that would not survive the fire.[11] Botts knew in his bones that the bad blood engendered by civil war would last for generations. He dedicated his account to General Grant for delivering the South from "the most oppressive, grinding, and detestable military despotism," words not unlike those the would-be memorialists wanted to carve on their monument to the fire.

In *The Great Rebellion*, as he called his book, Botts passed judgment throughout his text, nowhere more thunderously than in his concluding paragraph. It was, in fact, not a paragraph but a single long, fulminating sentence of no fewer than 208 words that burned with the white-hot anger of one who knew what had been lost. In that sentence, Botts condemned in rolling cadences those who had attempted to sunder the Union and in the process wrought death and destruction on an unimagined, colossal scale. He knew in his heart that "the party that is responsible for the loss of the dead, the sufferings of the living . . . to say nothing of the infuriate, incarnate feeling that has been engendered between the different sections of the country and between citizens of the same states and neighborhoods, will, as I firmly believe, have to answer hereafter, both in this world and in the world to come, for the most atrocious and stupendous crime that has been committed since the crucifixion of our Lord and Savior Jesus Christ."[12]

Edward Pollard would have none of it. Not the dedication to Grant, not the cause of disunion, not the blame for war and destruction, and certainly not the prospect of divine damnation. The former *Examiner* editor had remained behind to witness the occupation. His presence in the Spotswood dining room enraged northern reporters who knew his views, and the army expelled him from the city for refusing to stifle his seditious opinions.

Pollard got his revenge with a book that appeared, like Botts's, the year after Appomattox. In it and in other works, he scorned what he called the Davis government's indecent haste to evacuate. Richmond, he sneered, "yet cherishes its blunt and withered laurels as capital of the Southern Confederacy."[13] With scathing words, he held Jefferson Davis accountable for frittering away the assets at his disposal. These included, in Pollard's brutal enumeration, "a servile Congress, a Cabinet of dummies, and a people devoted to his person."[14] It was an unfair judgment, but it reflected Davis's widespread unpopularity at that time, a disdain that did not diminish until the North, through a spiteful, impolitic imprisonment, endeared the frail but unbending Confederate leader to white southerners with an intensity he never inspired as president.

Where Botts dedicated his book to Grant, Pollard used his to casti-
gate the Union general. He mocked Grant for taking a year to crush
Richmond, and at a cost in killed and wounded greater than the numbers arrayed against him. It is the general who defeats a larger army
with a smaller one, and by stratagem, not brute force, who deserves
high honors, argued the aggrieved editor. He therefore hailed Lee a
greater commander in his defeat than Grant in his victory over Richmond. To him, the preponderance of generalship, chivalry, and humanity rested on the Confederate side, and to him that would be the
judgment of history.

The editor voiced sentiments that Confederate civilians were already thinking as they watched Godfrey Weitzel's men march into
their burning city on April 3, 1865. Before the fires were out, the
southern rationale for defeat was born, and within a year Pollard gave
it both literary expression and a name. He called his book *The Lost
Cause*.

About the time Botts and Pollard were writing, another story reflected the feelings in Richmond in the early years after the fire. Richmonders of African descent had their own notion of what the war
meant, and they planned to celebrate the first anniversary of the occupation with a grand march. An organization called the Colored League
led the effort that eventually involved every black church and organization in the city. White Richmond, appalled, tried to prevent the celebration. Some employers threatened to fire any worker known to
participate in the festivities. The newspapers encouraged landlords to
evict tenants doing the same. The army feared trouble on the appointed day, and the local Federal commander joined the governor in
urging African American citizens to stay home.

Leaders of the march acknowledged the anxiety of their white
neighbors and sought to allay their fears with a broadside posted
around the city. They claimed they did not "Intend to Celebrate The
Failure of The Southern Confederacy, As it has been stated in the papers of this City, but simply as the day which GOD was pleased to Liberate their long-oppressed race." It was a futile effort, and anyway the
two results of the war—defeat of the Confederacy and liberation of

the slaves—could not be separated. Despite the threats, two thousand men and women marched in the parade, and perhaps fifteen thousand came out to watch.[15]

White Richmonders could not completely ignore an event on this scale, as Lee was said to ignore the black man at Holy Communion. Nor could they accept emancipation as the focus for commemorating the war. The hurt and the loss were too strong for them to do other than honor the sacrifice of the Lost Cause, the cause that lost. And the implications for relations among the races were not happy ones. For generations, the former Confederate capital would be, in the words of a later historian, "a city in thralldom to its past."[16]

In time, by the early twentieth century, Americans North and South achieved the unity that defeated Confederates in April 1865 believed could never happen. They did it by remembering and honoring the fallen on both sides. But that was not enough. They also did it by denying or forgetting the part that slavery played in the coming of the war and by thwarting the promise of emancipation at its end.[17]

In more recent times, as some of that denying and forgetting has been called into question, differences in the way Americans view the Civil War have increased. For some they are as stark as the issues that separated Botts and Pollard, as spiteful as those that divided black and white Richmonders on the first anniversary of Appomattox. They are differences that cannot be masked by the warm sepia glow cast over our great national trauma by popular books and documentary films.

Because guilt and virtue are both part of that story, both should be acknowledged. Yet some would flaunt the first and reject the second, while others deny the first and embrace the second. The pity is that such extremes should continue after so many years and after what this country has endured, reunited now for nearly a century and a half.

In any event, one intransigent historical outcome from that past cannot be denied. In the words of Edward Pollard's angry lament, in Richmond, Virginia, on April 3, 1865, "all the hopes of the Southern Confederacy were to be consumed in one day as a scroll in the fire!"[18]

ACKNOWLEDGMENTS

My house sits on a hill high above the south bank of the James River, several miles west of downtown Richmond. From the front porch you can hear the rush of water cascading through the rapids. Usually by early April the buds have begun to thicken with the approach of spring, and the hardwoods in the ravine down below the house have come back to life. Before the trees fully leaf out, however, you can see the river's surface shimmering through their stark branches. Below the house, at the foot of the hill, you can also see the railroad as it snakes along the riverbank. Because of twists and turns in the roadbed, the wheels of the occasional freight trains that use the line squeal like fingernails drawn across a chalkboard. The railroad, in fact, generally follows the same tight curves defined by the river as it did in 1865. I imagine the wheels squealed when Jefferson Davis's presidential coach crawled along this same stretch of track in the last hour of April 2 that year. Since beginning this book, when I hear a train from home, I often wonder what went through the minds of the unhappy passengers that night as they passed below my hill.

My curiosity about that event and others that happened 137 years ago led to this book. I can only hope that my version of Richmond burning brings that dramatic part of our national story alive for readers. To tell the story of the city that those passengers on the Richmond & Danville line abandoned to fire and conquest has put me in the debt of many people and institutions. To begin at the beginning, I thank all those writers of the past who have been intrigued by this often-told tale. The best account was Rembert Patrick's *The Fall of Richmond*, written more than four decades ago. More recently we have Pat Furgurson's excellent *Ashes of Glory*, but it covers the whole four years of war.

The senior archivist at the Virginia Historical Society, my colleague

E. Lee Shepard, has kept me apprised of newly acquired manuscripts that touch on the fall of Richmond, some of which have not yet been consulted by historians. Charles F. Bryan, Jr., director of the VHS and my coeditor on other Civil War books, offered his continuing support and advice. Many other colleagues at the VHS have helped in many different ways during the four years I have worked on this book: Jon Bremer, Toni Carter, Ann de Witt, Graham T. Dozier, Bryan Green, Tom Illmensee, Susan King, Crista LaPrade, Paul A. Levengood, Michelle McClintick, Frances Pollard, AnnMarie Price, Paulette Schwarting, Janet Schwarz, Greg Stoner, and David Ward. Many institutions beyond the VHS, mentioned at the beginning of the bibliography, hold collections that were invaluable to my research, and I thank the staff of each of them.

Friends and colleagues at other institutions who gave advice and suggested sources include Lynn Bayliss, Sara B. Bearss, Julie Campbell, Cliff Dickinson, William R. Erwin, Jr., Noel Harrison, Ervin L. Jordan, Gregg Kimball, Robert E. L. Krick, Candace McKinniss, Mike Musick, J. Tracy Power, Theresa Roane, Emily Todd, Minor Weisiger, and Steven L. Wright.

I thank my agents, Julian Bach, Carolyn Krupp, and Susan Reed at IMG Literary, for their guidance throughout the project. At Viking, my editor, Wendy Wolf, gave excellent advice and encouragement. I am grateful to her and her colleagues, including Clifford Corcoran, Bruce Giffords, and Ted Johnson. George Skoch's classic maps added the right touch, as did Martin White's index.

I give my most heartfelt thanks to those friends who read some version of the manuscript and made invaluable suggestions for improving it. Those readers were Terry Alford, Steve Ash, Charles F. Bryan, Jr., Michael B. Chesson, John Coski, Gary W. Gallagher, Dale Sorenson, Carole Summers, Marie Tyler-McGraw, and Rich Ugland. My wife, Judy, was, as always, a keen critic and for her pains got to read more than one version. The faults that remain—things done and left undone—are my own.

I dedicate *Richmond Burning* to my godson, Harrison Strickler, and his sisters, Olivia and Maggie. Fortunately, their Richmond is a far different place.

—*Nelson Lankford*
Richmond, Virginia

ABBREVIATIONS

ANB   *American National Biography*

B&L   R. U. Johnson and C. C. Buel, eds. *Battles and Leaders of the Civil War. Being for the Most Part Contributions by Union and Confederate Officers. Based Upon "The Century War Series."* 4 vols. New York: Century, 1884–88.

CHS   Chicago Historical Society, Chicago, Illinois

CV   *Confederate Veteran*

DAB   *Dictionary of American Biography*

DU   Rare Book, Manuscript & Special Collections Library, Duke University, Durham, North Carolina

ISHL   Illinois State Historical Library, Springfield, Illinois

JSH   *Journal of Southern History*

LC   Library of Congress, Washington, D.C.

LVA   Archives Research Services, Library of Virginia, Richmond, Virginia

MOC   Eleanor S. Brockenbrough Library, Museum of the Confederacy, Richmond, Virginia

NA   National Archives, Washington, D.C.

NHHS   New Hampshire Historical Society, Concord, New Hampshire

OR   U.S. War Department, *The War of the Rebellion: A Compilation of the Official Records of the Union and Confederate Armies*

ORN   U.S. Naval War Records Office, *Official Records of the Union and Confederate Navies in the War of the Rebellion*

RNBP   Richmond National Battlefield Park, Richmond, Virginia

SHC   Southern Historical Collection, Wilson Library, University of North Carolina, Chapel Hill, North Carolina

SHSP   Southern Historical Society, *Southern Historical Society Papers*

USAMHI   United States Army Military History Institute, Carlisle Barracks, Pennsylvania

UVA   The Albert and Shirley Small Special Collections Library, University of Virginia Library, Charlottesville, Virginia

VC   *Virginia Cavalcade*

VHS   Virginia Historical Society, Richmond, Virginia

VMHB   *Virginia Magazine of History and Biography*

NOTES

All dates are in 1865 unless another year is specified.

Prologue

1. Hatcher, *Along the Trail*, pp. 118–19.
2. Pollard, *Lost Cause*, p. 697.
3. Statement of Apr. 23, 1861, quoted in Freeman, *Lee*, 1:468.
4. Fitzhugh Lee, *General Lee*, p. 398 n.
5. Entry for Apr. 16, McGuire, *Diary of a Southern Refugee*, p. 356.
6. Taylor, *General Lee*, p. 297.
7. Dispatch of Apr. 16, in Blackett, ed., *Chester*, p. 308.
8. Bruce, *Capture and Occupation*, p. 38.
9. Pollard, *Lost Cause*, p. 698.
10. Entry for Apr. 16, McGuire, *Diary of a Southern Refugee*, p. 356.
11. Undated entry between Apr. 14 and Apr. 22, Alice Fitzhugh Dixon Payne diary, VHS.
12. Constance Cary to mother and brother, Apr. 4, quoted in Harrison, *Recollections*, p. 216.

Chapter 1: Citadel

1. Entry for Mar. 9, in Lankford, ed., *Irishman in Dixie*, p. 39.
2. Crofts, "Late Antebellum Virginia Reconsidered," p. 253.
3. Wyatt-Brown, *The Shaping of Southern Culture*, p. 202.
4. Tyler-McGraw, *At the Falls*, p. 139.
5. Entry for Mar. 1864, in Woodward, ed., *Mary Chesnut's Civil War*, p. 585.
6. O'Brien, "Factory, Church, and Community," p. 527.
7. Weis, "Negotiating Freedom," pp. 51–64, 80, 162.
8. Barber, "Sisters of the Capital," p. 32.
9. Quoted in Furgurson, *Ashes*, p. 52.
10. *Southern Literary Messenger* 16 (1850): 172.

11. Maddex, *Reconstruction*, pp. 4–5.
12. Neely, *Southern Rights*, p. 3.
13. Ryan, ed., *A Yankee Spy in Richmond*, p. 11.
14. Stuart, "Colonel Ulric Dahlgren," p. 180 n. 63, p. 202.
15. Chesson, *Richmond After the War*, pp. 25–38.
16. Takagi, *"Rearing Wolves,"* pp. 127–38.
17. Entry for Jan. 29, in Chesson and Roberts, eds., *Exile in Richmond*, p. 298.
18. Quoted in Donald Pfanz's sketch in *ANB*.
19. Abstract from trimonthly return, Dept. of Richmond, Mar. 20, in *OR*, ser. I, vol. 46, iii, 1331.
20. Longacre, *Army of Amateurs*, p. 321; Pfanz, *Ewell*, p. 409 (quotation).
21. Kemper to S. Cooper, Mar. 30, in *OR*, ser. IV, vol. 3, 1158–59.
22. *Richmond Whig*, Apr. 1.

Chapter 2: Daily Bread

1. *Richmond Daily Examiner*, Mar. 29.
2. *Richmond Daily Dispatch*, Apr. 1.
3. Ibid., Mar. 31.
4. Entries for Mar. 8 and Mar. 25 (quotation), in Lankford, ed., *Irishman in Dixie*, pp. 38, 66.
5. Ibid., p. 79 n. 58.
6. *Richmond Daily Dispatch*, Mar. 31.
7. Ibid., Apr. 1.
8. Ibid., Mar. 31 and Apr. 1.
9. Ibid., Apr. 1.
10. Weis, "Negotiating Freedom," pp. 133–35, 166; *Richmond Daily Dispatch*, Apr. 1 (quotation).
11. *Richmond Daily Dispatch*, Mar. 31 and Apr. 1.
12. *Richmond Daily Examiner*, Mar. 29.
13. Ibid.; Mrs. William A. Simmons to husband, Mar. 23 (quotation), in Jones, ed., *Ladies of Richmond*, p. 265.
14. *Richmond Daily Examiner*, Mar. 29 and 30.
15. Hustings Court Minutes, no. 29, Mar. 15, Richmond City Courthouse, 1863–1866, reel 97, LVA.
16. *Richmond Daily Dispatch*, Mar. 31 and Apr. 1.
17. Ord to Weitzel, Mar. 27, in *OR*, ser. I, vol. 46, iii, 212.
18. George H. Sharpe to Edward Ord, Mar. 24, in *OR*, ser. I, vol. 46, iii, 101–2.
19. *Richmond Daily Examiner*, Mar. 27, quoted in Preisser, "Virginia Decision," p. 112.
20. George H. Sharpe to Edward Ord, Mar. 24 (quotation), in *OR*, ser. I, vol. 46, iii, 101; dispatch of Mar. 26, in Blackett, ed., *Chester*, p. 283.
21. *New York Herald*, Apr. 7 (first quotation); entry for Mar. 22 (second quotation), in Owen, *In Camp*, p. 366.

22. *Richmond Daily Dispatch*, Mar. 31; *Richmond Daily Examiner*, Mar. 15, 18, and 20, quoted in Furgurson, *Ashes*, p. 309.

23. Lee to Davis, Mar. 24 (first quotation), in *OR*, ser. I, vol. 46, iii, 1339; Davis to John Forsyth, Feb. 21 (second quotation), quoted in Cooper, *Jefferson Davis, American*, p. 518; Lee to Breckinridge, Mar. 27, in *OR*, ser. I, vol. 46, iii, 1356–57.

24. Durden, *Gray and Black*, pp. 271, 275.

25. Turner to S. R. Shinn, Apr. 2 (quotation), in *OR*, ser. IV, vol. 3, 1194; entry for Mar. 22, in Richard Maury diary, VHS.

26. Marion Fitzpatrick to Amanda Fitzpatrick, Mar. 27, in Lowe and Hodges, eds., *Letters to Amanda*, pp. 205–6.

Chapter 3: Waiting

1. *Richmond Daily Dispatch*, Mar. 31.

2. Entry for Feb. 10, in Younger, ed., *Inside the Confederate Government*, p. 201.

3. Entry for Feb. 18, ibid., p. 201.

4. Entry for Mar. 6, in Wiggins, ed., *Gorgas Journals*, p. 155.

5. Entry for Mar. 23, in Younger, ed., *Inside the Confederate Government*, p. 204.

6. Lee to Breckinridge, Mar. 9, in *OR*, ser. I, vol. 46, ii, 1295.

7. Longstreet to W. H. Taylor, Mar. 30, in *OR*, ser. I, vol. 46, iii, 1367; Lee to Breckinridge, Mar. 27 (quotation), ibid., p. 1353.

8. Entry for Mar. 31 (first quotation), in McGuire, *Diary of a Southern Refugee*, p. 342; Brown to Ann (Murphy) Brown, Mar. 27 (second quotation), in Alexander Gustavus Brown papers, VHS.

9. The characterization is from Jones's editor, Howard Swiggett, in Swiggett, ed., *Rebel War Clerk's Diary*, 1:6; entry for Apr. 1, ibid., 2:464.

10. Faust, ed., *Encyclopedia*, p. 165; Samuel Cooper to Sarah Cooper, Apr. 1 (quotation), in Page, *Letters of a War Correspondent*, pp. 341–42.

11. Stuart, "Samuel Ruth," pp. 81–82; Stuart, "Colonel Ulric Dahlgren," pp. 165, 182–84.

12. Entries for Feb. 18 (first quotation) and Apr. 1 (second quotation), in Chesson and Roberts, eds., *Exile in Richmond*, pp. 322, 365.

13. James Thomas Wickham slave and employee account book, Woodside plantation, Wickham family papers, Valentine Richmond History Center.

14. Scharf, *History*, p. 777; Harris, "Gold," *SHSP* 32 (1904): 157–59.

15. Parker, *Recollections*, pp. 346–47; Scharf, *History*, p. 745 (quotation).

16. Semmes to Frank Tremlett, Mar. 6, Semmes papers, VHS.

17. Alexander to wife, Mar. 24 (first quotation), photocopy typescript, vol. 94, RNBP, original at SHC; Alexander to wife, Apr. 1 (second quotation), in E. P. Alexander papers, #7, SHC.

18. Basinger to mother, Feb. 23, typescript, in William Starr Basinger papers, #1266, SHC.

19. Marion Fitzpatrick to Amanda Fitzpatrick, Mar. 27 and 28, in Lowe and Hodges, eds., *Letters to Amanda*, pp. 204–7.
20. Weitzel to chief of staff, Feb. 27, in RG 108 (M 504 roll 429), NA.
21. Rumrill to his mother, Apr. 1, photocopy typescript at RNBP, original in Rumrill family papers, USAMHI.
22. John Gibbon to Ord, Mar. 21 (quotation), in RG 393, entry 5071, pt. 1, NA; Brig. Gen. Commanding, HQ, 3rd Div., XXIV AC, to T. Read, AAG, Dept. of Va., AJ, Mar. 26, RG 393, pt. 2, entries 6977, 7000, NA; entry dated Mar. 26 at back of volume, John Mottram diary (no. 10988), UVA.
23. Dispatch of Mar. 26, in Blackett, ed., *Chester*, pp. 281–83.
24. White to William Seward, May 18, 1864, in Berlin et al., eds., *Freedom*, ser. 2, *Black Military Experience*, p. 349.
25. Redkey, "Black Chaplains," pp. 332, 336–37.
26. White to Edwin Stanton, May 7, 1862, in Berlin et al., eds., *Freedom*, ser. 2, *Black Military Experience*, p. 83.
27. Entry for Mar. 28 (first quotation), photocopy typescript diary, in Daniel T. Nelson papers, VHS; Daniel Nelson to Sarah Nelson, Mar. 25 (second quotation), photocopy typescript, ibid.
28. The character sketch derives from James McPherson's entry for Grant in *ANB*.
29. Grant to Jesse Root Grant, Mar. 1, in Simon et al., eds., *Grant Papers*, 14:186.
30. Grant, *Personal Memoirs*, 1:250, quoted in McPherson sketch in *ANB*.
31. Pierpont to Grant, Mar. 7, in *OR*, ser. I, vol. 46, ii, 885.

Chapter 4: A Day for Fools

1. Entry for Apr. 1, in Owen, *In Camp*, p. 369.
2. Quoted in Thomas, *Lee*, p. 354.
3. Dabney, *Pistols*, p. 38 (quotation); Pollard, *Lost Cause*, p. 693.
4. *Richmond Daily Examiner*, Mar. 31.
5. *Richmond Daily Dispatch*, Apr. 1.
6. *Richmond Whig*, Apr. 1.
7. Minutes of city council meeting of Apr. 1, in Manarin, ed., *Richmond at War*, pp. 589–91.
8. Entry for Apr. 1, in Chesson and Roberts, eds., *Exile in Richmond*, p. 365.
9. *Richmond Daily Dispatch*, Apr. 1.
10. Ibid., Mar. 31 (first quotation); *Richmond Whig*, Apr. 1 (second quotation).
11. Jordan, comp., *North Carolina Troops*, 11:122; Hollywood Memorial Association, *Register of the Confederate Dead*, p. 65.
12. *Richmond Daily Dispatch*, Apr. 1.
13. Marvel, *Appomattox*, p. 198.
14. Gordon, *General George E. Pickett*, pp. 146–50; Marvel, *Appomattox*, pp. 198–201.
15. Quoted in Gordon, *General George E. Pickett*, p. 154.

16. Entry for Apr. 1, in Owen, *In Camp*, p. 369.
17. Davis, *Breckinridge*, p. 503; entry for Apr. 30, in Wiggins, ed., *Gorgas Journals*, p. 159.
18. John W. Riely to Ewell, 7:30 p.m., Apr. 1, in *OR*, ser. I, vol. 46, iii, 1375; Ewell to Longstreet, Apr. 1 (quotation), in Lee headquarters papers, VHS.
19. Wood, "More of the Last Defense of Richmond," *CV* 16 (1908): 397.
20. Pfanz, *Ewell*, pp. 426–27.
21. Howard, "Closing Scenes," *SHSP* 31 (1903): 129.
22. Lee to Breckinridge, Apr. 2, in *OR*, ser. I, vol. 46, iii, 1379.
23. Quoted in Duke and Jordan, eds., *A Richmond Reader*, p. 80.
24. *Richmond Daily Dispatch*, Apr. 1.
25. Set in type and printed on Sunday, Apr. 2, but dated Apr. 3, this notice was carried by the *Richmond Examiner* in its last issue before it was consumed by the fire.

Chapter 5: Sabbath Rest

1. Entry for Apr. 2, in Margaret Brown Wight diary, Wight family papers, VHS.
2. Mary Burrows Fontaine to Marie Burrows Sayre, Apr. 30 (quotation), typescript, MOC; Pollard, *Lost Cause*, p. 693.
3. Camp to "Nony" [Emma Blow Camp], Apr. 6, photocopy, MOC.
4. Bruce, *Capture and Occupation*, p. 6.
5. Smith, *Lee and Grant*, p. 248.
6. Entry for Mar. 13, in Lankford, ed., *Irishman in Dixie*, p. 48.
7. Davis, *Jefferson Davis*, pp. 598–600; Cooper, *Jefferson Davis, American*, pp. 514–20; Paul Escott, "Jefferson Davis," *ANB*.
8. "Agnes" to Mrs. Roger A. Pryor, Apr. 5, in Pryor, *Reminiscences*, p. 354.
9. Pollard, *Lost Cause*, p. 693.
10. C. E. L. Stuart, in *New York Herald*, July 4, cited in Ballard, *A Long Shadow*, p. 37.
11. Entry for Apr. 2, in Kate Mason Rowland diary, typescript, MOC.
12. Irons, "And All These Things," pp. 27–32.
13. Entry for Apr. 2 (first quotation), in Swiggett, ed., *Rebel War Clerk's Diary*, 2:466; *New York Herald*, July 4 (second quotation).
14. Letter of Apr. 9 (first quotation), in Fisk, *Anti-Rebel*, p. 321; entry for Apr. 2 (second quotation), in Sparks, ed., *Inside Lincoln's Army*, pp. 486–87.
15. Grant to Weitzel, Apr. 2, 10:45 a.m., in Simon et al., eds., *Grant Papers*, 14:323.
16. Parker, *Recollections*, pp. 349–50.
17. Handy, "Fall of Richmond," p. 9.
18. Frank Potts to John Potts, Apr. [25], in Freeman, ed., *Death of the Confederacy*, pp. 6–7.
19. Entry for Apr. 2, in Chesson and Roberts, eds., *Exile in Richmond*, p. 366.

20. Entry for Apr. 1 and 2, in John C. Rutherfoord diary, Rutherfoord papers, VHS.
21. John Gottfried Lange, "The Changed Name, or the Shoemaker of the Old and New World . . . ," p. 196, memoir, c. 1870–80, trans. by Ida Windmueller, VHS.
22. Bell, *Memoirs of Governor William Smith*, p. 62.
23. Entry for Apr. 4, in Fannie E. Taylor Dickinson diary, VHS.

Chapter 6: A Fugitive Government

1. Entry for Apr. 2, in Margaret Brown Wight diary, Wight family papers, VHS.
2. Inaugural address, Feb. 22, 1862, in Rowland, ed., *Jefferson Davis*, 5:202.
3. Lee to Breckinridge, Apr. 2, received 10:40 a.m., in *OR*, ser. I, vol. 46, iii, 1378.
4. Davis to Lee, Apr. 2, ibid.
5. Lee to Davis, 3 p.m., Apr. 2, Lee headquarters papers, VHS.
6. Pfanz, *Ewell*, pp. 426–27.
7. Memoir of Mann S. Quarles, Apr. 2, 1901, MOC (quotation); Treasury warrant number 3504, Apr. 1, in Confederate Treasury Department papers, DU.
8. Entry for Apr. 2, in Swiggett, ed., *Rebel War Clerk's Diary*, 2:466; Jones, ed., *Ladies of Richmond*, p. 276 (quotation).
9. Irvine, "Fate of Confederate Archives," pp. 828–29.
10. *Richmond Daily Examiner*, Mar. 29.
11. Heite, "Judge Robert Ould," pp. 10–18; Davis, *Breckinridge*, p. 491; Grant to Col. Theodore S. Bowers, Apr. 2, and Bowers to Grant, Apr. 2, in Simon et al., eds., *Grant Papers*, 14:328–30.
12. Report from Fortress Monroe, Apr. 3, in *Boston Daily Evening Transcript*, Apr. 4.
13. Mallory to Semmes, Apr. 2, in *ORN*, ser. I, vol. 12, 191.
14. Entry for Mar. 25, in Lankford, ed., *Irishman in Dixie*, p. 66.
15. Semmes, *Service Afloat*, p. 810.
16. Recollections of "Carter," a Confederate soldier or sailor on the flag-of-truce steamer *William Allison*, in *Richmond Dispatch*, Feb. 7, 1888.
17. Pollard, *Lost Cause*, p. 694.
18. Richmond city council records no. 15, 1862–1866, minutes, Apr. 2, in reel 106, LVA.
19. Davis, *Rise and Fall*, 2:667–68.
20. Cooper, *Jefferson Davis, American*, p. 522; Davis, *Jefferson Davis*, p. 601 (quotation).
21. Pollard, *Lost Cause*, p. 685.
22. Lee to Davis, 3 p.m., Apr. 2, Lee headquarters papers, VHS.
23. Irvine, "Fate of Confederate Archives," p. 823; Davis to Mrs. O'Melia, Apr. 2, MOC; Davis, *Jefferson Davis*, p. 605.
24. Quoted in Cooper, *Jefferson Davis, American*, p. 523.
25. "Agnes" to Mrs. Roger A. Pryor, Apr. 5, in Pryor, *Reminiscences*, p. 355; entry for Apr. 2, in Swiggett, ed., *Rebel War Clerk's Diary*, 2:466.

26. Alfred Paul to Drouyn de Lhuys, Apr. 11 (first quotation), in Spencer, "A French View," p. 183; Connor, *John Archibald Campbell*, p. 257 (second quotation).
27. Campbell to Breckinridge, Mar. 5, quoted in Davis, *Breckinridge*, p. 495.
28. Campbell to B. R. Curtis, July 20, in *Century Magazine* 38:6 (Oct. 1889): 952.

Chapter 7: Flitting Shadows

1. Eggleston, *A Rebel's Recollections*, p. 243.
2. *Richmond Daily Examiner*, Apr. 3.
3. Carrington to Robert Lancaster [?], Mar. 15 (first quotation), in Carrington papers, DU; R. P. Archer to Carrington (for Ewell), Apr. 2 (second quotation), in *OR*, ser. I, vol. 46, iii, 1381.
4. Hill, "First Burial," *SHSP* 19 (1891): 183–86; Robertson, *General A. P. Hill*, pp. 320–21.
5. Dispatch of Apr. 5, in *Philadelphia Inquirer*, Apr. 10.
6. Samuel T. Bayly to Turner, Apr. 2, in *OR*, ser. II, vol. 8, 463.
7. Peter Helms Mayo, "Episodes of a Busy Life," memoir, c. 1900, #1858, SHC.
8. Susan Hoge to Moses Drury Hoge, Apr. 4, in Hoge papers, VHS.
9. Entry for Apr. 3, in Handy, "Fall of Richmond," p. 10.
10. Gallagher, ed., *Fighting for the Confederacy*, p. 518.
11. Alexander to wife, Apr. 3 (first quotation), in Edward Porter Alexander papers, #7, SHC; entry for Apr. 30 (second quotation), in Josiah Gorgas journal, #279-z, SHC.
12. Towner, ed., *Lee's Adjutant*, p. 22.
13. Thomas, *Lee*, p. 355.
14. Wiley, ed., *Southern Woman's Story*, p. 137.
15. Statements of W. A. Irving and Samuel H. Freeman, June 10, in Flournoy, ed., *Calendar of Virginia State Papers*, p. 436.
16. Hale to D. H. Wood, Apr. 2, in captured letterbook of George Trenholm, printed in *Chicago Tribune*, Apr. 10.
17. Account of Midshipman R. H. Fielding, in Harris, "Gold," *SHSP* 32 (1904): 159–60; Parker, *Recollections*, p. 351.
18. Parker, *Recollections*, p. 352.
19. Coffin, *Freedom Triumphant*, p. 422.
20. Parker, *Recollections*, p. 352.
21. Entry for Apr. 2, in Anna Holmes Trenholm diary, #1402-z, SHC; Jones, ed., *Ladies of Richmond*, p. 266; Mallory, "Last Days," p. 104 (quotation).
22. Mallory, "Last Days," p. 102 (first quotation); Bruce, "Some Reminiscences," *SHSP* 9 (1881): 209 (second quotation).
23. Wise, *End of an Era*, p. 415.
24. Entry for Apr. 2, in Cornelius Walker diary, MOC.
25. Entry for Apr. 30, in Wiggins, ed., *Gorgas Journals*, p. 159.
26. Entry for Apr. 2, in John Coles Rutherfoord diary, Rutherfoord papers, VHS; Hettle, " 'The Self-Analysis' of John C. Rutherfoord," pp. 103–7.

27. William Smith, order, Apr. 2, with explanation written later by D. B. Stuart, MOC.
28. Statement of D. B. Stewart, c. 1910, MOC.
29. Bell, *Memoirs of Governor William Smith*, p. 61; entry for Apr. 3, in Swiggett, ed., *Rebel War Clerk's Diary*, 2:467.
30. Bell, *Memoirs of Governor William Smith*, p. 61.
31. Campbell, *Recollections*, p. 4; Harrison, *Recollections*, p. 208 (quotation).

Chapter 8: Mad Revelry of Confusion

1. Pollard, *Lost Cause*, p. 695.
2. Entry for Apr. 2, in Handy, "Fall of Richmond," p. 14 (first quotation); Camp to "Nony" [Emma Blow Camp], Apr. 6, photocopy, MOC (second quotation).
3. *Philadelphia Inquirer*, Apr. 5.
4. Semmes, *Service Afloat*, p. 812.
5. Dispatch of Apr. 3, 5:00 a.m., in *New York Herald*, Apr. 5.
6. Entry for Apr. 3, abstract log of USS *Malvern*, in *ORN*, ser. I, vol. 12, 176.
7. Semmes, *Service Afloat*, p. 812.
8. Susan Hoge to Moses Drury Hoge, Apr. 4, Hoge family papers, VHS.
9. Dispatch of Apr. 4, in Blackett, ed., *Chester*, p. 292.
10. Entry for Apr. 4, in Fannie E. Taylor Dickinson diary, VHS.
11. Alexander to wife, Apr. 3, in Edward Porter Alexander papers, #7, SHC.
12. John R. Moss to editor, Apr. 26, in *Richmond Times*, Apr. 28; *Richmond Evening Whig*, Apr. 6.
13. *Richmond Evening Whig*, Apr. 6.
14. Dew, *Ironmaker*, pp. 285–86; dispatch of Apr. 10, in *New York Times*, Apr. 17; report on Tredegar, Apr. 28, in *OR*, ser. I, vol. 46, iii,1007–10.
15. *Richmond Evening Whig*, Apr. 5 and 6; Alexander to wife, Apr. 3, in Edward Porter Alexander papers, #7, SHC.
16. *Richmond Whig*, Apr. 27.
17. George Washington Camp, Jr., to "Nony" [Emma Blow Camp], Apr. 6, photocopy, MOC; M. K. Ellis to Powhatan Ellis, May 1, in Munford-Ellis family papers, DU.
18. *New York Herald*, July 4; Beverley Randolph Wellford diary, in White, Wellford, Taliaferro, and Marshall family papers, #1300, SHC.
19. *Danville Register*, Apr. 5, quoted in *Richmond Whig*, Apr. 19.
20. *New York Herald*, July 4.
21. Entry for Apr. 3, in John Coles Rutherfoord diary, Rutherfoord papers, VHS.
22. Entry for Apr. 6, Christopher Tompkins, memorandum of events, in Rachal, ed., "Occupation of Richmond," pp. 190–91.
23. Mitchel, "Journal: Being a Continuation of 'Jail Journal,'" *The Irish Citizen*, July 9, 1870. Thanks to Dr. Lynn Bayliss for this citation.
24. Swiggett, ed., *Rebel War Clerk's Diary*, 2:467 n. 2.
25. Woods, "Last Scenes," *CV* 27 (1919): 140–41.

26. Pollard, *Lost Cause*, p. 696 (first quotation); Putnam, *Richmond During the War*, p. 368 (second quotation).
27. Perry, *A Bohemian Brigade*, pp. 185–87, 210–12.
28. Entry for Apr. 3, in Cornelius Hart Carlton diary, typescript, VHS.
29. Sulivane, "The Fall of Richmond," p. 726.
30. Ibid.
31. W. L. Timberlake, "The Last Days in Front of Richmond," *CV* 22 (1914): 303.
32. Howard, "Brig. Gen. Walter H. Stevens," *CV* 30 (1922): 249.
33. Handy, "Fall of Richmond," p. 17.
34. The difference between Breckinridge and Davis over whether and how to bring the Confederate government to an end is the theme of William Davis's *Honorable Defeat*.
35. Marvel, *Appomattox*, p. 88.
36. Gallagher, ed., *Fighting for the Confederacy*, p. 519.

Chapter 9: Cruel Cataclysm

1. Thomas Barker, 12th N.H. Regt., Apr. 3, in Bartlett, *History*, p. 269.
2. AAG, XXIV AC HQ to E. H. Ripley, Mar. 27, RG 363, pt. 2 entry 6977–7000, NA; W. L. Goodrich, special order 85, Mar. 27, in *OR*, ser. I, vol. 46, iii, 213.
3. William Merriman's dispatch of Apr. 2, in *New York Herald*, Apr. 5.
4. Weitzel to Devens, Apr. 2, RG 108 (M 504 roll 429) NA.
5. Weitzel to Grant, Apr. 2, RG 108 (M 504 roll 429) NA; Weitzel to Grant, Apr. 2 (quotation), in Simon et al., eds., *Grant Papers*, 14:323n.
6. Report of George A. Bruce, Apr. 4, in *OR*, ser. I, vol. 46, i, 1212–13.
7. Weitzel to Grant, Apr. 3, 4:30 a.m. and 5:25 a.m. (quotation), in *OR*, ser. I, vol. 46, iii, 533.
8. Charles Washburn to family, Apr. 3 (quotation), photocopy typescript, vol. 76, RNBP, original at Hancock Historical Society, Hancock, N.H.; report of Weitzel, Apr. 17, in *OR*, ser. I, vol. 46, i, 1227–28; report of Charles Devens, Apr. 3, ibid., p. 1211.
9. Ripley, *Capture and Occupation of Richmond*, p. 6.
10. Chesson memoir, photocopy typescript at RNBP, original at USAMHI.
11. Marshall to "Dear Folks at home," Apr. 3, in Henry Grimes Marshall papers, Clements Library, Ann Arbor, Mich.
12. Letter of Sergeant Clarke, Apr. 3, in Bartlett, *History*, p. 270.
13. Johns and Johns, "Chimborazo," p. 200; Gildersleeve, "History of Chimborazo," pp. 92–93.
14. William Merriam's dispatch of Apr. 3, in *New York Herald*, Apr. 6.
15. Mary Burrows Fontaine to Marie Burrows Sayre, Apr. 30, typescript, MOC.
16. Joseph Mayo, surrender note, Apr. 3, MOC.
17. Quoted in Ryan, ed., *A Yankee Spy in Richmond*, p. 106.
18. Quoted ibid., p. 6.
19. Entry for Jan. 24, 1864, Van Lew journal, ibid.

20. Stuart, "Colonel Ulric Dahlgren," p. 160.
21. Quoted in Furgurson, *Ashes of Glory*, p. 295.
22. Annie Randolph Van Lew to Aunt Anna, Apr. 3, in Van Liew, *Van Liew-Lieu-Lew*, p. 77.
23. Quoted in Ryan, ed., *A Yankee Spy in Richmond*, p. 105.
24. James Hane to mother and father, Apr. 4 (first quotation), photocopy typescript, vol. 80, RNBP; Charles Washburn to "Dear Folks at Home," Apr. 3 (second quotation), photocopy typescript, vol. 76, RNBP, original at Hancock Historical Society, Hancock, N.H.
25. Foner and Mahoney, *America's Reconstruction*, plate after p. 62.
26. Stuart, "Colonel Ulric Dahlgren," p. 165 n. 32, p. 177.
27. Morrell to brother, Apr. 13 (quotation), LC; Adams to his father, Apr. 10, in Ford, ed., *Cycle of Adams Papers*, 2:262.
28. Edwin Ware to "My Dear Folks," Apr. 4, photocopy typescript, vol. 76, RNBP, original at Hancock Historical Society, Hancock, N.H.
29. Linus Sherman to Alva Sherman, Apr. 4, photocopy typescript, vol. 90, RNBP.

Chapter 10: Requiem for Buried Hopes

1. Entry for Apr. 3, in Chesson and Roberts, eds., *Exile in Richmond*, p. 368.
2. Cooke, *Mohun*, p. 355.
3. Entry for Apr. 6, in McGuire, *Diary of a Southern Refugee*, p. 350.
4. Mary Burrows Fontaine to Marie Burrows Sayre, Apr. 30, typescript, MOC.
5. Entry for Apr. 3, in Kate Mason Rowland diary, typescript, MOC.
6. Entry for Apr. 3, in Chesson and Roberts, eds., *Exile in Richmond*, pp. 367–68.
7. Entry for Apr. 4, in Fannie E. Taylor Dickinson diary, VHS.
8. Entry for Apr. 5, ibid.; entry for Apr. 3 (quotation), in McGuire, *Diary of a Southern Refugee*, p. 345.
9. Dispatch of Apr. 4, in Blackett, ed., *Chester*, p. 289.
10. Fragment of undated letter of April, probably written by Julia P. Reed, Reed family papers, VHS.
11. Entry for Apr. 3, in McGuire, *Diary of a Southern Refugee*, p. 347.
12. The quotation comes from a letter purportedly written on Apr. 4, 1865, but Cary edited it much later when she published it in her memoir (Harrison, *Recollections*, p. 212).
13. DeLeon, *Four Years in Rebel Capitals*, p. 363.
14. Entry for Apr. 3, Kate Mason Rowland diary, typescript, MOC.
15. Leyburn, "Fall of Richmond," p. 96.
16. Entry for Apr. 4, in Fannie E. Taylor Dickinson diary, VHS.
17. Leyburn, "Fall of Richmond," p. 95.
18. Dispatches of Apr. 4 (first quotation) and 6 (second quotation), in Blackett, ed., *Chester*, pp. 290, 296.
19. Dispatch of Apr. 4, ibid., p. 293; quotation in Litwack, *Been in the Storm So Long*, p. 169.

20. Dispatch of May 9, in Blackett, ed., *Chester*, p. 339.
21. White to editor, Apr. 12, in *Christian Recorder*, Apr. 22.
22. Ibid.
23. Semmes, *Service Afloat*, pp. 813–16.
24. Mary Burrows Fontaine to Marie Burrows Sayre, Apr. 30, typescript, MOC.
25. Guzman-Stokes, "A Flag & a Family," pp. 54–56.
26. Grant to David W. Young, July 22, in *OR*, ser. I, vol. 46, i, 1262.
27. Putnam, *Richmond During the War*, p. 367.
28. R. F. Andrews to editor, in *Richmond Whig*, Apr. 10; dispatch of Apr. 10, in Blackett, ed., *Chester*, p. 303; Kautz to Mrs. Savage, Apr. 3 (quotation), in August V. Kautz papers, ISHL.
29. Dispatch of Apr. 3, dateline, Washington, D.C., in *New York Herald*, Apr. 4; report of Charles Devens, Apr. 3, in *OR*, ser. I, vol. 46, i, 1211.
30. Report of Weitzel, Apr. 17, in *OR*, ser. I, vol. 46, i, 1228.
31. R. F. Andrews to editor, in *Richmond Whig*, Apr. 10; dispatch of Apr. 10 (quotation), in Blackett, ed., *Chester*, p. 303.
32. Bossuot to sister, Apr. 5, photocopy typescript at RNBP, original at Pierpont Morgan Library, New York.
33. *New York Times*, Apr. 9.
34. Entry for Apr. 3, in Cornelius Walker diary, MOC.
35. Receipt, Apr. 3, Ruffin family papers, VHS.
36. Report of Weitzel, Apr. 17, in *OR*, ser. I, vol. 46, i, 1227–28.
37. This is the wording from Weitzel's handwritten message sent by mounted orderly to XXIV Corps HQ at Fort Harrison. There, W. B. Wood, one of the military telegraph operators, passed it along electronically to Washington while keeping as a personal souvenir the original signed by Weitzel (copy at MOC). Wood's message was also forwarded, with slightly different wording, from City Point in Bowers to Stanton, 10:30 a.m., Apr. 3; in Simon et al., eds., *Grant Papers*, 14:340–41 n.
38. Dispatch of William Merriam, Apr. 3, in *New York Herald*, Apr. 6.

Chapter 11: Burning

1. Mary Burrows Fontaine to Marie Burrows Sayre, Apr. 30, typescript, MOC.
2. Bruce, *Capture and Occupation*, p. 18.
3. Pollard, *Lost Cause*, p. 697.
4. Pollard, *Life of Jefferson Davis*, p. 497.
5. *Richmond Whig*, Apr. 22.
6. Gache to the Rev. Philip de Carriere, July 18, in Buckley, trans., *A Frenchman*, p. 220.
7. Dade, "The Fall of Richmond," p. 102.
8. Mary Burrows Fontaine to Marie Burrows Sayre, Apr. 30, typescript, MOC.
9. Quoted in *SHSP* 32 (1904): 73.
10. William Merriam's dispatch of Apr. 3, in *New York Herald*, Apr. 6.

11. Ibid.; *Richmond Evening Whig,* Apr. 5; Edwin Ware to "My Dear Folks," Apr. 4, vol. 76, photocopy typescript at RNBP, original at Hancock Historical Society, Hancock, N.H.
12. Entry for Apr. 5, in Swiggett, ed., *Rebel War Clerk's Diary,* 2:471.
13. *Richmond Evening Whig,* Apr. 7; Scott and Stanard, *The Capitol of Virginia,* p. 7.
14. *Richmond Evening Whig,* Apr. 5; Morrell to brother, Apr. 13 (quotation), LC.
15. *Richmond Daily Examiner,* Apr. 3.
16. Pollard, *Lost Cause,* p. 696.
17. *Richmond Evening Whig,* Apr. 5.
18. Ibid., Apr. 7; *Richmond Whig,* Apr. 12 and 29.
19. Stuart, "Samuel Ruth," p. 90; *Richmond Whig,* Apr. 11 and 19.
20. *Richmond Evening Whig,* Apr. 4.
21. Warren to Louisa Jane Warren Mitchell, Apr. 23, William E. Warren papers, 1846–1865 (accession 31052), LVA.
22. *Richmond Evening Whig,* Apr. 4.
23. Weitzel, "Entry of the United States Forces into Richmond," Mss qW436 RMV, vol. 1, p. 662, Cincinnati Historical Society Library (printed in Manarin, ed., *Richmond Occupied,* p. 62); entry for Apr. 3, Kate Mason Rowland diary, typescript, MOC.
24. Flournoy, ed., *Calendar of Virginia State Papers,* p. 436.
25. Dispatch of Apr. 8, in *Chicago Tribune,* Apr. 11.
26. Blanton, *The Making of a Downtown Church,* p. 109; Susan Hoge to Moses D. Hoge, Apr. 4, in Hoge family papers, VHS; entry for Apr. 3, in Lelian Cook diary, printed in *Richmond News Leader,* Apr. 3, 1935.
27. Testimony of Dr. F. Davidson, deposed in insurance case, 1879, quoted in *Richmond Daily Dispatch,* Apr. 1, 1883.
28. *Richmond Evening Whig,* Apr. 4.
29. Entry for Apr. 3–4, diary, box 1, folder 2, in John H. Prescott papers, NHHS.
30. Susan Hoge to Moses D. Hoge, Apr. 4, in Hoge family papers, VHS.
31. Camp to "Nony" [Emma Blow Camp], Apr. 6, photocopy, MOC.
32. John West to his mother, Apr. 6, VHS.
33. *Richmond Whig,* Apr. 10.
34. Anna Deane to her sister Sallie, Apr. 12, photocopy transcript at RNBP, original in Mary E. (Fleming) Schoole papers, DU.

Chapter 12: Let It Burn

1. *Richmond Whig,* Apr. 21.
2. Entry for Apr. 3, photocopy typescript diary, in Daniel T. Nelson papers, VHS.
3. Riggs, *Embattled Shrine,* pp. 98–99.
4. Bates, *Lincoln in the Telegraph Office,* pp. 359–60.
5. At 5:15 p.m. on Monday, City Point headquarters telegraphed Grant that it

had not heard from Weitzel since receiving his first dispatch of his taking of Richmond that morning (Simon et al., eds., *Grant Papers*, 14:341 n.).

6. *New York Herald*, Apr. 4.
7. *New York Tribune*, Apr. 4.
8. Donald, *Lincoln*, p. 565.
9. Johnson, "Remarks on the Fall of Richmond," Apr. 3, in Graf et al., eds., *Johnson Papers*, 7:544.
10. Sommers, *Richmond Redeemed*, p. 20; dispatch of Apr. 3, in *New York Herald*, Apr. 4 (quotation).
11. Washington, D.C., *Daily National Intelligencer*, Apr. 5; Thomas and Hyman, *Stanton*, p. 352; *New York Herald*, Apr. 4 and 5.
12. Entry for Apr. 3, in Nevins and Thomas, eds., *Strong Diary*, 3:575.
13. *New York Herald*, Apr. 4.
14. *New York Times*, Apr. 4.
15. *New York Herald*, Apr. 4 (first quotation); *New York Times*, Apr. 4 (second quotation); excerpt from *New York Independent* in *Chicago Tribune*, Apr. 11 (third quotation).
16. *Philadelphia Inquirer*, Apr. 4; excerpt from *Baltimore American*, Apr. 3 (first quotation), in *Richmond Evening Whig*, Apr. 7; "Union Victory!" 1865 broadside, VHS (second quotation).
17. *Chicago Tribune*, Apr. 4.
18. Entry for Apr. 3, in Davis and Swentor, eds., *Bluegrass Confederate*, p. 675.
19. Entries for Apr. 3 through 7, William Nalle diary, VHS.
20. Entry for Apr. 3, in Scarborough, ed., *Diary of Edmund Ruffin*, 3:829.
21. Entry for Apr. 6, in Crabtree and Patton, eds., *Journal of a Secesh Lady*, p. 689.
22. Entries for Apr. 8, 15, and 23, in James Grant Wilson, ed., "John R. Thompson and His London Diary, 1864–5, First Paper," printed in *The Criterion*, an unidentified periodical, VHS.
23. DeLeon, *Four Years in Rebel Capitals*, p. 363.
24. Dispatch of Apr. 6, in Blackett, ed., *Chester*, p. 298.
25. Emma Mordecai to Edward Cohen, Apr. 5, in 1943 photocopy typescript of Emma Mordecai diary, VHS.
26. "Hdq'rs Military Governor of Richmond, Richmond, Va., April 3, 1865," in *Richmond Evening Whig*, Apr. 4.
27. Kreutzer, *Notes and Observations*, p. 316.
28. Ripley, *Capture and Occupation of Richmond*, p. 19.
29. Barber, "Sisters of the Capital," p. 436; entry for Apr. 3 (quotation), Sabbath book, in Lucy Muse Walton Fletcher papers, DU.
30. Dispatch of Apr. 4, in Blackett, ed., *Chester*, p. 292.
31. Wiley, ed., *Southern Woman's Story*, pp. 139–41.
32. Bruce, *Capture and Occupation*, p. 21.
33. Pollard, *Lost Cause*, p. 698.

Chapter 13: Upon the Wings of Lightning

1. Quoted in Porter, *Incidents*, p. 294.
2. Perry, *A Bohemian Brigade*, pp. 41, 81; Griffis, *Coffin*, pp. 14–15, 185–87.
3. A northern reporter on the steamer *William Allison* departed the Rocketts landing at two o'clock and encountered Lincoln in Porter's barge two miles below the city. See report of "our James River Correspondent, Steamer William Allison," Apr. 4, *New York Herald*, Apr. 8.
4. Donald, *Lincoln*, pp. 568–73.
5. Lincoln to Stanton, Apr. 2, 11 a.m., in Basler et al., eds., *Lincoln Collected Works*, 8:382.
6. Stanton to Lincoln, Apr. 3, 10:30 a.m., in *OR*, ser. I, vol. 46, iii, 509; Lincoln to Stanton, Apr. 3, 5 p.m. (quotation), ibid.
7. Quoted in Porter, *Incidents*, p. 294.
8. Quoted in Gallagher, ed., *Fighting for the Confederacy*, p. 517.
9. Entry for Apr. 3, in George H. Hearne diary, photocopy typescript, p. 10, RNBP; K. R. Breese, USS *Malvern*, to William Ronckendorff, USS *Onondago*, Apr. 3, in *ORN*, ser. I, vol. 12, 97; report of R. Chandler, USS *Sangamon*, May 24, in *ORN*, ser. I, vol. 12, 98.
10. Entry for Apr. 3, in George H. Hearne diary, photocopy typescript, p. 10, RNBP.
11. Frank M. Ramsay, USS *Unadilla*, to D. D. Porter, Apr. 6, in *ORN*, ser. I, vol. 12, 104.
12. *New York Times*, Apr. 10.
13. Private journal, number 2, p. 12, David Dixon Porter papers, LC.
14. Dispatch of Apr. 6, in Blackett, ed., *Chester*, p. 294.
15. Coffin to Thomas Nast, July 19, 1866, in Coffin, "Lincoln's Visit," pp. 27–29.
16. *Richmond Evening Whig*, Apr. 5.
17. Dispatch of Apr. 6 (first quotation), in Blackett, ed., *Chester*, p. 297; Bartlett, *History*, p. 272 (second quotation).
18. Dispatch of Apr. 6, in Blackett, ed., *Chester*, p. 294; Manarin, ed., *Richmond Occupied*, p. 55.
19. Dispatch of Apr. 6, in Blackett, ed., *Chester*, p. 296.
20. Entry for Apr. 6 (first quotation), in Kate Mason Rowland diary, typescript, MOC; letter of Apr. 4 (second quotation), in Harrison, *Recollections*, p. 216.
21. Dispatch of Apr. 6, in Blackett, ed., *Chester*, p. 295.
22. Dispatch of Apr. 5, in *New York Tribune*, Apr. 6; dispatch of Apr. 8, evening, in *Chicago Tribune*, Apr. 11; L. L. Crounse's dispatch of Apr. 7, in *New York Times*, Apr. 11.
23. Grattan, "Under the Blue Pennant," p. 227, in John W. Grattan papers, LC.
24. Dispatch of Apr. 8, in *New York Times*, Apr. 9.
25. William Merriam's dispatch of Apr. 4, in *New York Herald*, Apr. 7.
26. Entry for Apr. 4 (first quotation), in Chesson and Roberts, eds., *Exile in Richmond*, p. 370; dispatch of Apr. 6, in Blackett, ed., *Chester*, p. 295; Samuel H. Roberts to "My Dear Son," Apr. 5 (second quotation), Sotheby's *Fine Books and Manuscripts*, catalog for auction, sale 7394, Dec. 7, 1999, p. 30.

27. Dispatch of Apr. 6, in Blackett, ed., *Chester*, p. 295; dispatch of Apr. 4, in *New York World*, Apr. 7; William Merriman's dispatch of Apr. 4, in *New York Herald*, Apr. 7.
28. Porter, *Incidents*, pp. 295–98, quoted in O'Brien, "Reconstruction," p. 262.
29. Entry for Apr. 4, Lelian Cook diary, printed in *Richmond News Leader*, Apr. 3, 1935.
30. Dispatch of Apr. 8, evening, in *Chicago Tribune*, Apr. 11.
31. Dana to Stanton, Apr. 10, 4 p.m. (first quotation), in *OR*, ser. I, vol. 46, iii, 684; Weitzel to Lincoln, Apr. 12, noon (second quotation), ibid., 724; Manarin, ed., *Richmond Occupied*, p. 56 (third quotation).
32. Entry for Apr. 4, abstract log of USS *Malvern*, in *ORN*, ser. I, vol. 12, 176; dispatch of Apr. 6, in Blackett, ed., *Chester*, p. 297; entry for Apr. 5, in August V. Kautz diary, LC.
33. John Hill Hewitt autobiography, in Hewitt papers, Emory University Library, quoted in Harwell, *Brief Candle*, p. 45.
34. Quoted in Harwell, *Brief Candle*, p. 87.
35. Charles A. Page's dispatch of Apr. 6, in *New York Tribune*, Apr. 8; *Richmond Evening Whig*, Apr. 5; entry for Apr. 5, in August V. Kautz diary, LC.

Chapter 14: A Week in April

1. Weitzel to T. S. Bowers, Apr. 4, in *OR*, ser. I, vol. 46, iii, 566.
2. Ord to Weitzel, Apr. 4, in Manarin, ed., *Richmond Occupied*, p. 55.
3. AAG HQ, 3rd Div., XXIV Corps, to Angel, chief of artillery, Apr. 5, RG 393, pt. 2, entries 6977, 7000, NA.
4. Ripley to D. H. Wheeler, Apr. 7, Letters Received, XXIV AC, RG 393, pt. 2, entry 6983, NA.
5. *Richmond Whig*, Apr. 11.
6. *Richmond Evening Whig*, Apr. 6; *Richmond Whig*, Apr. 11.
7. Report of Peter S. Michie, chief engineer, May 12, in *OR*, ser. I, vol. 46, i, 1165; entry for Apr. 25, photocopy typescript diary, in Daniel T. Nelson papers, VHS; *Richmond Times*, Apr. 25.
8. Construction corps journal, Apr. 6, RG 92 (entry 1640), NA (thanks to Susan Williams for this citation); report of J. J. Moore to D. C. McCallum, July 1, in *OR*, ser. III, vol. 5, 73–75.
9. J. B. Howard to T. Read, Apr. 8, RG 393, entry 5063, pt. 1, NA; Theodore C. Wilson's dispatch of Apr. 10, in *New York Herald*, Apr. 13.
10. *New York Herald*, Apr. 12.
11. Entry for Mar. 23 (first quotation), in Younger, ed., *Inside the Confederate Government*, p. 204; Theodore C. Wilson's dispatch of Apr. 10 (second quotation), in *New York Herald*, Apr. 13; *New York Tribune*, Apr. 8 (third quotation).
12. Entries for Apr. 5 (quotation) and Apr. 7, in Chesson and Roberts, eds., *Exile in Richmond*, pp. 371, 373–74.
13. Entry for Apr. 2, in Margaret Brown Wight diary, in Wight family papers, VHS.

14. Dispatch of Apr. 6, in Blackett, ed., *Chester*, p. 296; Weitzel to Dana, Apr. 8, in *OR*, ser. I, vol. 46, iii, 658.
15. *Richmond Whig*, Apr. 20.
16. E. F. Williams to Weitzel, undated, ca. Apr. 7, in Manarin, ed., *Richmond Occupied*, pp. 64–65.
17. *Richmond Whig*, Apr. 11.
18. Entry for Apr. 4 (first quotation), anonymous diary kept by soldier of 21st Conn. Regt., published in *Willimantic Journal*, Apr. 13, and quoted in Connecticut Infantry, *Story of the Twenty-first*, p. 420; undated letter of April–May, probably written by Julia P. Reed, Reed family papers, VHS; dispatch of Apr. 24 (second quotation), in Blackett, ed., *Chester*, p. 320.
19. Dispatch of Apr. 9, in *Philadelphia Inquirer*, Apr. 11.
20. Dispatch of Apr. 9, in *New York Times*, Apr. 14.
21. *Richmond Evening Whig*, Apr. 4.
22. Ibid., Apr. 5.
23. F. A. Macartney to Cresswell, Apr. 11, LC.
24. *Richmond Evening Whig*, Apr. 4.
25. Norton Folsom to William A. Conover, Apr. 6, RG 393, pt. 1, entry 5063, NA.
26. *Richmond Whig*, Apr. 18; Margaret Wolfe, paper given at the Southern Historical Association, November 1998, quoted in Wyatt-Brown, *The Shaping of Southern Culture*, p. 249.
27. *Richmond Evening Whig*, Apr. 5.
28. Entry for Apr. 5, diary, box 1, folder 2, in John H. Prescott papers, NHHS.
29. *New York Times*, Apr. 14.
30. *Richmond Evening Whig*, Apr. 7.

Chapter 15: A Whirlwind Sweeping

1. Margaret Keeling Ellis to Powhatan Ellis, May 1, in Munford-Ellis papers, DU.
2. Statements of W. A. Irving and Samuel H. Freeman, June 10, in Flournoy, ed., *Calendar of Virginia State Papers*, 11:436–38.
3. Entry for Apr. 7, in Lelian Cook diary, printed in *Richmond News Leader*, Apr. 3, 1935.
4. Robert Warren Powers memoir, 1905, VHS.
5. According to *Cincinnati Daily Gazette*, June 13, Lewellen became a partner with Walker, Daniel's heir, in publishing a new paper called the *Republic*; Lewellen to John P. Packer, Apr. 5 (quotation), in Lewellen family papers, VHS.
6. Stuart, "Colonel Ulric Dahlgren," p. 178 n. 57, p. 180 n. 63.
7. Barber, "Sisters of the Capital," pp. 94–95, 119.
8. Fields to Amanda Fitzpatrick, June 8, in Lowe and Hodges, eds., *Letters to Amanda*, p. 209.
9. Entry for Apr. 4, in Kate Mason Rowland diary, typescript, MOC.
10. Entry for Apr. 4, Frances Caldern de la Barca Hunt diary, photocopy typescript, RNBP, original at USAMHI.

11. *Richmond Evening Whig*, Apr. 7.
12. Dispatch of Apr. 7, in *New York Times*, Apr. 10.
13. *Richmond Whig*, Apr. 10, quoted in *New York Herald*, Apr. 12.
14. Ibid.
15. Charles Carleton Coffin's dispatch of Apr. 8, in Page, *Letters of a War Correspondent*, p. 344.
16. Stuart, "Samuel Ruth," p. 99; Stuart, "Colonel Ulric Dahlgren," pp. 159, 182 n. 69.
17. *Richmond Evening Whig*, Apr. 5.
18. Hall, "Virginia Historical Society," p. 46.
19. Dana, *Recollections*, p. 263.
20. Steele, *The Sun Shines for All*, pp. 35, 42–43, 54–59.
21. L. L. Crounse's dispatch of Apr. 5, in *New York Times*, Apr. 10; entry for Apr. 5, in Sparks, ed., *Inside Lincoln's Army*, p. 488.
22. *Richmond Whig*, Apr. 11.
23. Joseph Mayo, surrender note, Apr. 3, and attached account of its provenance with notarized, undated signature of Emma A. Doane, MOC.
24. Page, *Letters of a War Correspondent*, p. 313.
25. Whitelaw Reid's dispatch of Apr. 4, in Smart, ed., *A Radical View*, 2:195.
26. Dispatch of Apr. 8, in *New York Times*, Apr. 14.
27. Dispatch of Apr. 4, in *New York World*, Apr. 7.
28. *Richmond Evening Whig*, Apr. 7.
29. Frassanito, *Grant and Lee*, p. 379.
30. *Richmond Evening Whig*, Apr. 7.
31. *Richmond Whig*, Apr. 11.
32. Whitelaw Reid's dispatch of Apr. 5, in Smart, ed., *A Radical View*, 2:199.
33. Wells and Dalton, *Virginia Architects*, p. 136; Brumbaugh, "Evolution of Crawford's 'Washington,'" pp. 11–12.
34. *Richmond Evening Whig*, Apr. 8.
35. James Thomas Wickham slave and employee account book, Woodside plantation, Wickham family papers, Valentine Richmond History Center.
36. *New York Herald*, Apr. 5 and 6; L. L. Crounse's dispatch of Apr. 7, in *New York Times*, Apr. 10.
37. Quoted in Edwin Ware to father, Apr. 7, photocopy typescript, vol. 76, RNBP, original at Hancock Historical Society, Hancock, N.H.
38. Dispatch of Apr. 9, in Blackett, ed., *Chester*, p. 299.
39. Dispatch of Apr. 7, in *New York Times*, Apr. 11.
40. Dispatch of Apr. 9, in Blackett, ed., *Chester*, p. 299.
41. Grant to Weitzel, Apr. 4, in Simon et al., eds., *Grant Papers*, 14:345.
42. Dispatch of Apr. 6, in *New York Tribune*, Apr. 8 (quotation); dispatch of Apr. 8, in *New York World*, Apr. 12.
43. *New York Times*, Apr. 9.

Chapter 16: Prayers for the President

1. Harrison, *Recollections*, p. 215.
2. Pollard, *Lost Cause*, p. 700.
3. Entry for Apr. 3, Kate Mason Rowland diary, typescript, MOC.
4. Entry for Apr. 5, in Lelian Cook diary, printed in *Richmond News Leader*, Apr. 3, 1935.
5. McCabe to Mary Early, Apr. 7, in Early family papers, VHS, quoted in Gallagher, *Confederate War*, p. 107.
6. Jefferson Davis, "To the People of the Confederate States of America," in *OR*, ser. I, vol. 46, iii, 1383.
7. Cary to mother and brother, Apr. 4, in Harrison, *Recollections*, p. 215.
8. Ripley, *Capture and Occupation of Richmond*, p. 26.
9. Quoted in Cooper, *Jefferson Davis, American*, p. 388.
10. Townsend, *Campaigns*, pp. 346–47.
11. Minnigerode to Ripley, Apr. 7, in *OR*, ser. I, vol. 51, i, 1212–15.
12. Dispatch of Apr. 9, in *Philadelphia Inquirer*, Apr. 12.
13. Entry for Apr. 9, in Lelian Cook diary, printed in *Richmond News Leader*, Apr. 3, 1935.
14. Townsend, *Campaigns*, p. 347 (first and second quotations); Uriah H. Painter's dispatch of Apr. 10 (third quotation), in *Philadelphia Inquirer*, Apr. 12.
15. *Richmond Evening Whig*, Apr. 10.
16. Entry for Apr. 10, in McGuire, *Diary of a Southern Refugee*, p. 351.
17. Dispatch of Apr. 10, in Blackett, ed., *Chester*, p. 301.
18. Quoted in "Scenes in and around Richmond, Va.," p. 22, sermon preached by William Patton on Apr. 23, First Congregational Church, Chicago, William Weston Patton papers, CHS.
19. L. L. Crounse's dispatch of evening, Apr. 9, in *New York Times*, Apr. 12.
20. Stanton to Weitzel, Apr. 9, in *OR*, ser. I, vol. 46, iii, 678.
21. Weitzel to Stanton, Apr. 10, and Weitzel to J. A. Hardie, Apr. 11, in Manarin, ed., *Richmond Occupied*, pp. 58–59.
22. Lincoln to Weitzel, Apr. 12, in Basler et al., eds., *Lincoln Collected Works*, 8:405.
23. Stanton to Grant, Apr. 5, in *OR*, ser. I, vol. 46, iii, 573.
24. *Richmond Whig*, Apr. 15.
25. Entry for Apr. 14, in McGuire, *Diary of a Southern Refugee*, p. 355.
26. William H. Merriam's dispatch of Apr. 5, evening, in *New York Herald*, Apr. 9.
27. Connor, *John Archibald Campbell*, pp. 146–47.
28. Clipping from *New York Evening Post*, May 17, 1861, in Campbell family papers, #135, SHC.
29. Connor, *John Archibald Campbell*, p. 257.
30. Donald, *Lincoln*, p. 573.
31. Campbell, *Recollections*, pp. 5–9.
32. Charles Page's dispatch of Apr. 9, in *New York Tribune*, Apr. 10; Page, *Letters*, p. 329.
33. Gustavus Adolphus Myers, "Memoranda," Apr. [5], VHS.

34. John W. Grattan, "Under the Blue Pennant," p. 230, in John W. Grattan papers, LC.
35. Campbell to Lincoln, Apr. 5, in John A. Campbell papers, ISHL; Gustavus Adolphus Myers, "Memoranda," Apr. [5], VHS.
36. Campbell, *Recollections*, p. 12.
37. Entry for Apr. 5, in Sparks, ed., *Inside Lincoln's Army*, p. 488.
38. Dana to Stanton, 4 p.m., Apr. 5, in *OR*, ser. I, vol. 46, iii, 575.
39. Donald, *Lincoln*, pp. 578–79.
40. Quoted ibid., p. 399.
41. Weitzel testimony, May 18, U.S. Congress, *Report of the Joint Committee on the Conduct of the War*, p. 521; Boritt, ed., *The Historian's Lincoln*, p. 156; Lincoln to Weitzel, Apr. 6 (quotation), in Basler et al., eds., *Lincoln Collected Works*, 8:389.
42. Weitzel testimony, May 18, U.S. Congress, *Report of the Joint Committee on the Conduct of the War*, p. 522.
43. Campbell to Joseph Reid Anderson and others, Apr. 7, in Campbell, *Recollections*, pp. 23–24.
44. Campbell to Weitzel, Apr. 7, in John A. Campbell papers, ISHL.
45. Lincoln to Grant, 12 m., Apr. 6, in *OR*, ser. I, vol. 46, iii, 593.
46. Lincoln to Grant, Apr. 7, in Basler et al., eds., *Lincoln Collected Works*, 8:392.
47. Donald, *Lincoln*, p. 580.
48. *Richmond Evening Whig*, Apr. 8.
49. U. H. Painter's dispatch of Apr. 9, in *Philadelphia Inquirer*, Apr. 11.
50. Dispatch of Apr. 8, *New York Times*, Apr. 12.
51. U. H. Painter's dispatch of Apr. 9, in *Philadelphia Inquirer*, Apr. 11.

Chapter 17: Important Communications

1. George Alfred Townsend's dispatch of Apr. 9, *New York World*, Apr. 12.
2. John W. Grattan, "Under the Blue Pennant," pp. 231–32, in John W. Grattan papers, LC.
3. Uriah Painter's dispatch of Apr. 9, in *Philadelphia Inquirer*, Apr. 12.
4. Entry for Apr. 9, in Cornelius Walker diary, MOC.
5. Entry between Apr. 2 and Apr. 9, in Alice Fitzhugh Dixon Payne diary, VHS.
6. Entry for Apr. 9, in Chesson and Roberts, eds., *Exile in Richmond*, p. 375.
7. Dispatch of Apr. 10, in Blackett, ed., *Chester*, p. 300.
8. *Richmond Whig*, Apr. 11.
9. Quoted in Wyatt-Brown, *The Shaping of Southern Culture*, p. 242.
10. Basinger to mother, Mar. 28, typescript, in William Starr Basinger papers, #1266, SHC.
11. Basinger to mother, Apr. 14, typescript, ibid.
12. *Richmond Whig*, Apr. 29.
13. Entry for Apr. 12, Margaret Brown Wight diary, in Wight family papers, VHS.

14. Fanny Churchill Braxton Young to "dearest Mother & sisters," Apr. 11, in Young family papers, VHS.
15. *New York Herald*, Apr. 12.
16. *New York Times*, Apr. 11.
17. *Richmond Whig*, Apr. 12.
18. Longacre, *Army of Amateurs*, p. 314.
19. Weitzel to Butler, Apr. 26, in Butler, *Private and Official Correspondence*, 5:585–86.
20. Entries for Apr. 6, 12, and 14, in John Coles Rutherfoord diary, Rutherfoord papers, VHS.
21. *New York Herald*, Apr. 12 and 14.
22. Smart, *A Radical View*, 1:1; quotation from Reid's dispatch begun in Richmond but completed in Cincinnati, in Cortissoz, *Life of Whitelaw Reid*, p. 115.
23. Thomas and Hyman, *Stanton*, p. 355.
24. Lincoln to Pierpont, Apr. 10, in *OR*, ser. I, vol. 46, iii, 703.
25. Ambler, *Pierpont*, pp. 255–59; Donald, *Lincoln*, p. 590.
26. Lincoln to Weitzel, 9 a.m., Apr. 12, in Basler et al., eds., *Lincoln Collected Works*, 8:405.
27. Thomas and Hyman, *Stanton*, p. 356.
28. Bates, *Lincoln in the Telegraph Office*, pp. 362–63; Lincoln to Weitzel, cipher cable, Apr. 12 (quotation), in Abraham Lincoln papers, CHS.
29. Ord to Lincoln, 5:45 p.m., Apr. 13, in John A. Campbell papers, ISHL; Grant to Ord, 6:15 p.m., Apr. 13, in Simon et al., eds., *Grant Papers*, 14:388.
30. Undated manuscript signed by Lincoln, probably written on Apr. 14, in Basler et al., eds., *Lincoln Collected Works*, 8:410.
31. Marvel, *Appomattox*, p. 240.
32. Ord to Lincoln, Apr. 14, 11 a.m., received 9:30 p.m., in *OR*, ser. I, vol. 46, iii, 748.

Chapter 18: The Order of the Day

1. Daniel Nelson to Sarah Nelson, Apr. 13, photocopy typescript (first quotation), in Daniel T. Nelson papers, VHS; entries for Apr. 12, 18, and 19 (second quotation), photocopy typescript diary, ibid.
2. Dispatch of Apr. 16, in Blackett, ed., *Chester*, pp. 308–9.
3. Edward Crapsey's dispatch of Apr. 15, 11 p.m., in *Philadelphia Inquirer*, Apr. 18.
4. Ibid.
5. Thomas T. Eckert to Grant, Apr. 14, midnight (first quotation), in Simon et al., eds., *Grant Papers*, 14:390 n.; Heite, "Judge Robert Ould," pp. 12–13; dispatch of Apr. 15, midnight (second quotation), in *New York World*, Apr. 18.
6. Entry for Apr. 16, in Sparks, ed., *Inside Lincoln's Army*, p. 496.
7. *Richmond Whig*, Apr. 18.

8. Grant to Ord, Apr. 15, 4 p.m., in Simon et al., eds., *Grant Papers*, 14:391.
9. Ord to Grant, Apr. 15, 7:30 p.m., ibid., 14:391–92.
10. Entry for Apr. 16 (first quotation), diary, box 1, folder 2, John H. Prescott papers, NHHS; dispatch of Apr. 16, afternoon (second quotation), in *New York World*, Apr. 18.
11. Edward Crapsey's dispatch of Apr. 14, in *Philadelphia Inquirer*, Apr. 19.
12. Ibid., Apr. 18.
13. Dispatch of Apr. 16, 10 p.m., in *New York Times*, Apr. 21.
14. Ibid.
15. Entry for Apr. 23, diary, in Henry S. Spaulding papers (no. 38-156), UVA.
16. Hane to father and mother, Apr. 20, vol. 80, photocopy typescript, RNBP.
17. Quoted in Marvel, *Appomattox*, p. 269.
18. Turner, "Beware the People Weeping," in Boritt, ed., *Historian's Lincoln*, p. 346.
19. Entry in diary book beginning Apr. 27, in Lucy Muse Walton Fletcher papers, DU.
20. Entry for Apr. 16, in McGuire, *Diary of a Southern Refugee*, p. 356.
21. *Richmond Times*, Apr. 24.
22. *Richmond Times*, Apr. 28; *Richmond Whig*, Apr. 18 and 20.
23. Dispatch of Apr. 19, in Blackett, ed., *Chester*, p. 318.
24. *Philadelphia Inquirer*, Apr. 21.
25. Patrick to Dana, Apr. 19, in *OR*, ser. I, vol. 46, iii, 836–37.
26. H. W. Halleck to N. A. Miles, May 24, RG 393, pt. 1, entry 5071, NA.
27. *Richmond Whig*, Apr. 15.
28. J. C. Kelton, Gen. Order No. 6, HQ, Military Div. of the James, May 5, *OR*, ser. I, vol. 46, iii, 1091.
29. *Richmond Whig*, Apr. 28.
30. Patton, "Scenes in and around Richmond, Va.," p. 20, sermon delivered at First Congregational Church, Chicago, Apr. 23, in William Weston Patton papers, CHS.
31. Crandall, *Confederate Imprints*, 1:xii–xiv.
32. Stevens, *A Trip to Richmond*, p. 8.
33. Patton, "Scenes in and around Richmond, Va.," p. 14, sermon delivered at First Congregational Church, Chicago, Apr. 23, in William Weston Patton papers, CHS.
34. Entry for Apr. 25, in Nevins and Thomas, eds., *Strong Diary*, 3:594.
35. Entry for Apr. 24, ibid., 3:592.
36. Stevens, *A Trip to Richmond*, p. 7.
37. Kreutzer, *Notes and Observations*, p. 350.
38. DeLeon, *Four Years in Rebel Capitals*, p. 369.
39. William H. Nichols to "Dear Friends," Apr. 30, photocopy typescript, vol. 38, RNBP, original in CW Misc. Coll., USAMHI.

Chapter 19: The Sorry Silence of a Conquered People

1. DeLeon, *Four Years*, p. 363.
2. The *Richmond Whig* of April 21 announced that Brady had photographed Lee the day before; Frassanito, *Grant and Lee*, pp. 417–18.
3. Thomas, *Lee*, p. 369.
4. Lee to Grant, June 13, cited in Grant to Lee, June 20, in Simon et al., eds., *Grant Papers*, 15:210–11; Thomas, *Lee*, pp. 370–71.
5. Marvel, *Appomattox*, p. 243.
6. Special Orders, No. 6, Munford to soldiers of Munford's Cavalry Brigade, Apr. 21, in *OR*, ser. I, vol. 46, iii, 1395.
7. Mary Andrews West to Clara, Apr. 12, VHS.
8. Blanton, *The Making of a Downtown Church*, p. 112.
9. Susan Hoge to Moses D. Hoge, Apr. 24, in Hoge family papers, VHS.
10. Thomas V. Moore to Phineas D. Gurley, Apr. 17, ISHL.
11. Entries for Apr. 13 and 23 (quotation), in Sparks, ed., *Inside Lincoln's Army*, pp. 495, 499.
12. Entry dated Apr. 25, "Little Red Book," in Lucy Muse Walton Fletcher papers, DU, quoted in Barber, "Sisters of the Capital," pp. 236, 436–39 (quotation on p. 236).
13. William Weston Patton, "Scenes in and around Richmond, Va.," p. 13, sermon delivered at First Congregational Church, Chicago, Apr. 23, in William Weston Patton papers, CHS.
14. Stuart, "Colonel Ulric Dahlgren," pp. 188–89.
15. Stevens, *A Trip to Richmond*, p. 10 (quotation); *Richmond Whig*, Apr. 13.
16. M. K. Ellis to Powhatan Ellis, May 1, in Munford–Ellis family papers, DU; entry for Apr. 13, in Swiggett, ed., *Rebel War Clerk's Diary*, 2:476.
17. Haxall & Crenshaw to Gen. G. F. Shepl[e]y, Apr. 8, in Crenshaw family papers, VHS.
18. George W. Munford to Elizabeth T. Munford, Apr. 28, in Munford–Ellis family papers, DU.
19. Entry for Apr. 16, in Marsena Patrick diary, LC.
20. Cresap, *Appomattox Commander*, chap. 14; unidentified cousin of Mary Mercer Thompson Ord to Anna Rives Heath Lassiter, Apr. 19, Anna Rives Heath Lassiter collection (no. 10590), UVA (quotation).
21. *New York Times*, Apr. 21; F. M. Baker, J. Peterkin, and George Woodbridge to Halleck, Apr. 29, in *OR*, ser. I, vol. 46, iii, 1010.
22. Halleck to Grant, Apr. 29, in *OR*, ser. I, vol. 46, iii, 1005–6.
23. Entry for Apr. 8, in Fannie E. Taylor Dickinson diary, VHS.
24. Entry for Apr. 17, ibid.
25. Entry for Apr. 19, unidentified diary, probably kept by Julia Reed, in Reed family papers, VHS.
26. Entry for Apr. 11, Lelian Cook diary, printed in *Richmond News Leader*, Apr. 3, 1935.
27. Entry for early April, Sabbath book, in Lucy Muse Walton Fletcher papers, DU.

28. Entry for Apr. 9, in Anne Jennings Wise Hobson diary, VHS.
29. Entries for Apr. 7 and 8, in Christopher Tompkins, memorandum of events, in Rachal, ed., "Occupation of Richmond," pp. 192–94.
30. Dispatch of Apr. 10, in Blackett, ed., *Chester*, p. 302.
31. Randolph, *From Slave Cabin to the Pulpit*, pp. 76–77.
32. Dispatch of Apr. 6, in Blackett, ed., *Chester*, p. 295.
33. Dispatch of Apr. 4, ibid., p. 288; *Richmond Whig*, Apr. 19; Charles Page's dispatch of Apr. 6, in *New York Tribune*, Apr. 8.
34. Daniel Nelson to Sarah Nelson, May 11, photocopy typescript, in Daniel T. Nelson papers, VHS.
35. Henry Grimes Marshall to "Dear Folks at home," Apr. 5, in Henry Grimes Marshall papers, Clements Library, Ann Arbor, Mich.
36. Charges filed against prisoners in Castle Thunder in month of April, RG 393, pt. 4, entry 2075, NA.
37. Dispatch of Apr. 24, in Blackett, ed., *Chester*, pp. 321–22; Redkey, "Black Chaplains," p. 342 (quotation).
38. Isaac C. Richardson to Esther Richardson, May 26, #3033-z, SHC; dispatch of May 27, in *Cincinnati Daily Gazette*, June 2. Richardson gave the date as May 26; the *Gazette* said it was May 27.
39. Stevens, *A Trip to Richmond*, p. 8.

Epilogue

1. *Chicago Tribune*, Apr. 4.
2. *Richmond Daily Dispatch*, Apr. 1.
3. R. E. Macomber to Mr. Hall, May 8, in John W. Hall papers, 1863–1903 (accession 36206), miscellaneous reel 305, LVA.
4. Pickett, *What Happened to Me*, pp. 167–69, quotation on p. 167.
5. Thomas Thatcher Graves, "The Fall of Richmond. II. The Occupation," *B&L*, 4:728. Graves contributed his account, appropriately, to *Century* magazine's phenomenally successful *Battles and Leaders* series, the leading reconciliationist compilation of the 1880s. See Blight, *Race and Reunion*, pp. 173–79.
6. Thomas Thatcher Graves, "The Fall of Richmond. II. The Occupation," *B&L*, 4:728.
7. Dana to Stanton, transcript of telegram, Apr. 12, LC.
8. Recollection of Maj. Thomas Broun, printed in *Richmond Times-Dispatch*, Apr. 16, 1905, and reprinted in *CV* 13 (1905): 360. Thanks to Dr. Philip J. Schwarz, Virginia Commonwealth University, for the citation, used in his presentation at the Stratford Hall Plantation Seminar on Slavery, Aug. 4, 2000.
9. *Richmond Evening Whig*, Apr. 8.
10. Ibid.
11. Simpson, *Good Southerner*, p. 127; Stuart, "Colonel Ulric Dahlgren," pp. 180–81, n. 63.
12. Botts, *The Great Rebellion*, p. 226.

13. Pollard, *Life of Davis*, p. 494.
14. Ibid., p. vii.
15. Brown, "Uncle Ned's Children," pp. 20–22.
16. Chesson, *Richmond After the War*, p. 3.
17. See Blight, *Race and Reunion*, p. 2.
18. Pollard, *Lost Cause*, p. 693.

BIBLIOGRAPHY

Primary sources about the fall of Richmond are legion. Many participants in this dramatic episode at the conclusion of the Civil War wrote about their experiences. But most of them did so only much later when the tricks of age and memory render such accounts suspect or at least less reliable than accounts written at the time. Even so, memoirs can be revealing, and they take their place among the sources for this book. Accounts written close to the events, though less numerous, are still plentiful if not quite legion. As a rule, they receive more credence in this retelling of the story than do memoirs or other accounts written much after the fact.

The wealth of unpublished primary source materials on the fall of Richmond is spread across the country in many repositories. The richest for private letters, diaries, and other similar accounts is the Virginia Historical Society in Richmond. The other main libraries holding such documents are the Rare Book, Manuscript, and Special Collections Library of Duke University in Durham, North Carolina; the Eleanor S. Brockenbrough Library of the Museum of the Confederacy in Richmond; the Southern Historical Collection of the Wilson Library at the University of North Carolina in Chapel Hill, North Carolina; and the Hargrett Rare Book and Manuscript Library, University of Georgia, Athens, Georgia. The headquarters of the Richmond National Battlefield Park in Richmond has made a valuable photocopy collection of unpublished sources on wartime Richmond at other repositories, with special emphasis on those found at the United States Army Military History Institute at Carlisle Barracks, Pennsylvania.

Essential holdings of public documents, and some private ones as well, are mainly to be found at the Library of Virginia in Richmond and at the National Archives and Library of Congress in Washington, D.C.

Other repositories whose primary sources have informed this work include the Chicago Historical Society in Chicago, Illinois; the Cincinnati Historical Society Library at the Cincinnati Museum Center in Cincinnati, Ohio; the William L. Clements Library of the University of Michigan in Ann Arbor, Michigan; the Illinois State Historical Library in Springfield, Illinois; the New Hampshire Historical Society in Concord, New Hampshire; the Valentine Richmond History Center in Richmond; and the Special Collections Department of the Alderman Library at the University of Virginia in Charlottesville, Virginia.

Newspapers offer valuable insights of a distinctive kind. The major northern metropolitan papers sent reporters to be with Grant's armies in central Virginia. Some of these journalists marched into Richmond on the day of the fire. Others reached the city a day or so later. They sent lengthy descriptive accounts by telegraph and express steamer back to their papers in New York, Philadelphia, Boston, and Washington, D.C. In some cases, firsthand reports from occupied Richmond appeared in these northern papers only a day or so after they were written on the spot. Of special value is the fact that the reporters often gave a dateline and byline, allowing us to fix to the hour the state of knowledge on the ground about affairs in Richmond. This information is especially useful for the twilight period between the Union army's occupation of the city on Monday, April 3, and Lincoln's assassination on Friday, April 14.

Published Primary Sources

Adams, Charles Francis. *Charles Francis Adams, 1835–1915: An Autobiography*. Boston and New York: Houghton Mifflin, 1916.

Alford, Terry, ed. *John Wilkes Booth: A Sister's Memoir by Asia Booth Clarke*. Jackson, Miss.: University of Mississippi Press, 1996.

"An Alleged Proclamation of President Lincoln." *SHSP* 7 (1879): 95–98.

Arnold, William B. "The Fourth Massachusetts Cavalry: In the Closing Scenes of the War for the Maintenance of the Union, From Richmond to Appomattox." Unidentified printed clipping. MOC.

Avary, Myrta Lockett. *A Virginia Girl in the Civil War, 1861–1865* . . . New York: D. Appleton, 1903.

Averill, J. H. "Richmond, Virginia: The Evacuation of the City and the Days Preceding It." *SHSP* 25 (1897): 267–73.

Bagby, the Rev. Alfred. *King and Queen County, Virginia*. New York and Washington: Neale, 1908.

Barnes, John S. "With Lincoln from Washington to Richmond in 1865." *Appleton's Magazine* 9:5 (May 1907): 515–24; 9:6 (June 1907): 742–51.

Basler, Roy P., et al., eds. *The Collected Works of Abraham Lincoln*. Vol. 8. New Brunswick, N.J.: Rutgers University Press, 1953–55.

Bates, David Home. *Lincoln in the Telegraph Office: Recollections of the United States Military Telegraph Corps During the Civil War*. New York: Century, 1907.

Beach, William H. *The First New York (Lincoln) Cavalry: From April 19, 1861, to July 7, 1865*. New York: Lincoln Cavalry Association, 1902.

Beale, Howard K., and Alan W. Brownsword, eds. *Diary of Gideon Welles: Secretary of the Navy Under Lincoln and Johnson*. 3 vols. New York: W. W. Norton, 1960.

Beecher, Herbert W. *History of the First Light Battery Connecticut Volunteers, 1861–1865* . . . New York: A. T. De La Mare, 1901.

Berlin, Ira, et al., eds. *Freedom: A Documentary History of Emancipation, 1861–1867 . . .* Ser. 2, *The Black Military Experience*. Cambridge: Cambridge University Press, 1982.

Blackett, R. J. M., ed. *Thomas Morris Chester, Black Civil War Correspondent: His Dispatches from the Virginia Front*. Baton Rouge and London: Louisiana State University Press, 1989.

Blackford, Susan Leigh, comp. *Letters from Lee's Army . . .* New York: Charles Scribner's Sons, 1947.

Blake, Thomas B. "Artillery Brigade at Sailor's Creek." *CV* 28 (1920): 213.

Botts, John Minor. *The Great Rebellion: Its Secret History, Rise, Progress, and Disastrous Failure*. New York: Harper & Brothers, 1866.

[Boykin, Edward M.]. *The Falling Flag: Evacuation of Richmond, Retreat and Surrender at Appomattox, by an Officer of the Rear-Guard*. New York: E. J. Hale & Son, 1874.

Broun, William Le Roy. "The Red Artillery." *SHSP* 26 (1898): 365–76.

Brown, Philip F. "Reminiscences of the War, 1861–1865." N.p., n.d.

Bruce, George A. *The Capture and Occupation of Richmond*. N.p. [1918?].

Bruce, H. W. "Some Reminiscences of the Second of April, 1865." *SHSP* 9 (1881): 206–11.

Buckley, Cornelius M., S. J., trans. *A Frenchman, a Chaplain, a Rebel: The War Letters of Père Louis-Hippolyte Gache, S. J.* Chicago: Loyola University Press, 1981.

Burnett, Mrs. Theodore L. "Reminiscences of the Confederacy." *CV* 15 (1907): 173–74.

Butler, Benjamin F. *Private and Official Correspondence of Gen. Benjamin F. Butler*. 5 vols. N.p.: privately issued, 1917.

Campbell, John A. "Evacuation Echoes: Assistant-Secretary of War Campbell's Interview with Mr. Lincoln." *SHSP* 24 (1896): 351–53.

———. "Papers of Hon. John A. Campbell." *SHSP* 42 (1987): 61–75.

———. *Recollections of the Evacuation of Richmond, April 2d, 1865*. Baltimore: John Murphy, 1880.

Cary, Constance. See Mrs. Burton Harrison.

Chambrun, Adolphe de. *Impressions of Lincoln and the Civil War: A Foreigner's Account*. Trans. by Aldebert de Chambrun. New York: Random House, 1952.

Chesson, Michael Bedout, and Leslie Jean Roberts, eds. *Exile in Richmond: The Confederate Journal of Henri Garidel*. Charlottesville and London: University Press of Virginia, 2001.

Christian, George L. *Confederate Memories and Experiences*. Richmond: privately printed, 1915.

"City Battalion. Richmond, Va. Roster of Officers of the Twenty-fifth Battalion of Infantry." (Reprinted from *Richmond Times-Dispatch*), *SHSP* 31 (1903): 323–25.

Coffin, Charles Carleton. *The Boys of '61: Four Years of Fighting. Personal Observations with the Army and Navy. From the First Battle of Bull Run to the Fall of Richmond*. Boston: Estes & Lauriat, 1888.

———. *Four Years of Fighting: A Volume of Personal Observation with the Army and Navy, from the First Battle of Bull Run to the Fall of Richmond.* Boston: Ticknor & Fields, 1866.

———. *Freedom Triumphant: The Fourth Period of the War of the Rebellion from September, 1864, to Its Close.* New York: Harper & Brothers, 1891.

Coffin, Charles Carleton, to Thomas Nast, July 19, 1866. Printed in "Lincoln's Visit to Richmond, April 4, 1865." *Moorsfield Antiquarian* 1 (May 1937): 27–29.

Cole, Donald B., and John J. McDonough. *Benjamin Brown French, Witness to the Young Republic: A Yankee's Journal, 1828–1870.* Hanover, N.H., and London: University Press of New England, 1989.

Collier, Charles F., to George S. Bernard, May 24, 1894. Printed in *SHSP* 22 (1894): 69–73.

Collis, Septima M. *A Woman's War Record, 1861–1865.* New York and London: G. P. Putnam's Sons, 1889.

Connecticut Infantry, 21st Regiment. *The Story of the Twenty-first Regiment, Connecticut Volunteer Infantry, During the Civil War, 1861–1865, by Members of the Regiment.* Middletown, Conn.: Stewart Printing Co., 1900.

Cook, Lelian M. Diary. Printed in *Richmond News Leader*, Apr. 3, 1935.

Cooke, John Esten. *Mohun: or, The Last Days of Lee and His Paladins.* [A novel.] Originally published in 1869. Charlottesville: Historical Publishing Co., 1936.

Crabtree, Beth G., and James W. Patton, eds. *"Journal of a Secesh Lady": The Diary of Catherine Ann Devereux Edmondston, 1860–1866.* First edition 1979. Raleigh: Division of Archives and History, 1995.

Cunningham, John L. *Three Years with the Adirondack Regiment, 118th New York Volunteers Infantry.* N.p.: Privately printed, 1920.

Dade, Virginia E. "The Fall of Richmond." In *"Our Women in the War": The Lives They Lived; The Deaths They Died. . . .* Charleston, S.C.: The News and Courier Book Presses, 1885.

Dana, Charles A. *Recollections of the Civil War: With the Leaders at Washington and in the Field in the Sixties.* New York: D. Appleton, 1902.

Danforth, John B., and Herbert A. Claiborne. *Historical Sketch of the Mutual Assurance Society of Virginia, Richmond, Va., from Its Organization in 1794 to 1879.* Richmond: Wm. Ellis Jones, 1879.

Daniel, Frederick S. *The Richmond Examiner During the War; or, The Writings of John M. Daniel, with a Memoir of His Life, by His Brother.* New York: printed for the author, 1868.

Davis, Jefferson. *The Rise and Fall of the Confederate Government.* New York: D. Appleton, 1912.

Davis, Varina. *Jefferson Davis: Ex-President of the Confederate States of America. A Memoir.* 2 vols. New York: Belford, 1898.

Davis, William C., and Meredith L. Swentor, eds. *Bluegrass Confederate: The Headquarters Diary of Edward O. Guerrant.* Baton Rouge: Louisiana State University Press, 1999.

DeLeon, T. C. *Four Years in Rebel Capitals* . . . Mobile, Ala.: Gossip Printing Company, 1892.

Dennett, John Richard. *The South As It Is: 1865–1866*. Ed. by Henry M. Christman. New York: Viking, 1965.

Dowdey, Clifford, and Louis H. Manarin, eds. *The Wartime Papers of R. E. Lee*. Boston: Little, Brown, 1961.

Doyle, J. H. "When Richmond Was Evacuated." *CV* 39 (1931): 205–6.

Dudley, George T. "Lincoln in Richmond." *Washington, D.C., National Tribune*, Oct. 1, 1896, pp. 1–2.

Duke, Maurice, and Daniel P. Jordan, eds. *A Richmond Reader, 1733–1983*. Chapel Hill and London: University of North Carolina Press, 1983.

Duke, R. T. W. "Burning of Richmond." *SHSP* 25 (1897): 134–38.

———. "With the Confederate Reserves." *CV* 26 (1918): 486–87.

Eggleston, George Cary. *A Rebel's Recollections*. New York: G. P. Putnam's Sons, 1878.

Eisenschiml, Otto, ed. *Vermont General: The Unusual War Experiences of Edward Hastings Ripley, 1862–1865*. New York: Devin-Adair, 1960.

Ewell, R. S. "Evacuation of Richmond: Report of General R. S. Ewell." *SHSP* 13 (1885): 247–52.

"The First Federal to Enter Richmond." Reprinted from the *Richmond Dispatch*, Feb. 10, 1893. *SHSP* 30 (1902): 152–53.

Fisk, Wilbur. *Anti-Rebel: The Civil War Letters of Wilbur Fisk*. Croton-on-Hudson, N.Y.: Emil Rosenblatt, 1983.

Flanders, Alan B., and Neale O. Westfall, eds. *Memoirs of E. A. Jack, Steam Engineer, CSS Virginia*. White Stone, Va.: Brandyland Publishers, 1998.

Flournoy, H. W., ed. *Calendar of Virginia State Papers and Other Manuscripts from January 1, 1836, to April 15, 1869; Preserved in the Capitol at Richmond*. Vol. 11. Richmond: n.p., 1893. Reprint edition.

Ford, Worthington Chauncey, ed. *A Cycle of Adams Letters, 1861–1865*. London: Constable, 1921.

Freeman, Douglas Southall, ed. *The Death of the Confederacy: The Last Week of the Army of Northern Virginia as Set Forth in a Letter of April, 1865*. Richmond: privately printed, 1928.

Gallagher, Gary W., ed. *Fighting for the Confederacy: The Personal Recollections of General Edward Porter Alexander*. Chapel Hill and London: University of North Carolina Press, 1989.

Gerald, S. A. "Last Soldiers to Leave Richmond." *CV* 18 (1910): 432.

Gerry, Margarita Spalding, comp. and ed. *Through Five Administrations: Reminiscences of Colonel William H. Crook, Body-Guard to President Lincoln*. New York: Harper & Brothers, 1910.

Gildersleeve, J. R. "History of Chimborazo Hospital, C.S.A." *SHSP* 36 (1908): 86–94.

Gilliam, Robert. "Last of the Confederate Treasury Department." *CV* 37 (1929): 423–25.

Gordon, George H. *A War Diary of Events in the War of the Great Rebellion, 1863–1865*. Boston: James R. Osgood, 1882.

Gorgas, Amelia. "As I Saw It: One Woman's Account of the Fall of Richmond." *Civil War Times Illustrated* 25:3 (May 1986): 40–43.

———. "The Evacuation of Richmond." *CV* 25 (1917): 110–11.

Graf, Leroy P., et al., eds. *The Papers of Andrew Johnson*. Vol. 7, *1864–1865*. Knoxville, Tenn.: University of Tennessee Press, 1986.

Handy, Moses Purnell. "The Fall of Richmond in 1865." *American Magazine and Historical Chronicle* 1:2 (Autumn–Winter 1985–86): 2–21.

Harris, John W. "The Gold of the Confederate States Treasury." *SHSP* 32 (1904): 157–59.

Harrison, Mrs. Burton [Constance Cary]. *The Carlyles: A Story of the Fall of the Confederacy*. [A novel.] New York: D. Appleton, 1905.

———. *Recollections Grave and Gay*. London: Smith, Elder, 1912.

Harvie, Lewis E., to General I. M. St. John, Jan. 1, 1876. *SHSP* 3 (1877): 109–11.

Hatcher, William E. *Along the Trail of the Friendly Years*. New York: Fleming H. Revell, 1910.

Haw, Joseph R. "The Last of C. S. Ordnance Department." *CV* 34 (1926): 450–52; 35 (1927): 15–16.

Haynes, Martin A. *A History of the Second Regiment, New Hampshire Volunteer Infantry, in the War of the Rebellion*. Lakeport, N.H.: n.p., 1896.

Hill, G. Powell. "First Burial of General Hill's Remains." *SHSP* 19 (1891): 183–86.

Hoge, Moses Drury. *Life and Letters*. Ed. Peyton Harrison Hoge. Richmond: Presbyterian Committee of Publication, 1899.

Hollywood Memorial Association. *Register of the Confederate Dead, Interred in Hollywood Cemetery*. Richmond: Gary, Clemmitt & Jones, 1869.

Howard, James McH. "Brig. Gen. Walter H. Stevens." *CV* 30 (1922): 249–50.

Howard, John. "The Evacuation of Richmond, April 3, 1865." Reprinted from the *Richmond Dispatch*, Nov. 24, 1895. *SHSP* 23 (1895): 175–80.

———. *Graeme's Executor vs. Mutual Ass. So. of Va. Argument of John Howard of Counsel for Plaintiff. Liability of Insurers for Losses by the Fire of April 3d, 1865*. . . . N.p., n.d. VHS.

Howard, McHenry. "Closing Scenes of the War About Richmond." Reprinted from the *New Orleans Picayune*, Oct. 4–11, 1903. *SHSP* 31 (1903): 129–45.

———. *Recollections of a Maryland Confederate Soldier Under Johnston, Jackson and Lee*. Introduction by James I. Robertson, Jr. Dayton, Ohio: Morningside, 1975.

Hughes, Robert W. *"Editors of the Past": Lecture of Judge Robert W. Hughes, Delivered before the Virginia Press Association*. Richmond: Wm. Ellis Jones, Book and Job Printer, 1897.

———. "John Moncure Daniel." *The Baltimorean*, January 10, 1885.

Jones, Katharine M. *Ladies of Richmond, Confederate Capital*. Indianapolis: Bobbs-Merrill, 1962.

Jones, Terry L., ed. *Campbell Brown's Civil War: With Ewell and the Army of Northern Virginia*. Baton Rouge: Louisiana State University Press, 2001.

Kean, R. G. H., to Jubal A. Early, Nov. 15, 1873. *SHSP* 2 (1876): 56–57.

Keckley, Elizabeth. *Behind the Scenes.* New York: G. W. Carleton, 1868.

Kershaw, J. B. "Report of General J. B. Kershaw." *SHSP* 13 (1885): 252–54.

Kimball, William J., ed. *Richmond in Time of War.* Boston: Houghton Mifflin, 1960.

Kreutzer, William. *Notes and Observations Made During Four Years of Service with the Ninety-eighth N.Y. Volunteers in the War of 1861.* Philadelphia: Grant, Faires & Rodgers, 1878.

Langdon, Loomis L. "The Stars and Stripes in Richmond." *Century Magazine* 40:2 (June 1890): 307–8.

Lankford, Nelson D., ed. *An Irishman in Dixie: Thomas Conolly's Diary of the Fall of the Confederacy.* Columbia: University of South Carolina Press, 1988.

"Last Days of the Southern Confederacy." Reprinted from the *New York Herald,* Mar. 13, 1891. *SHSP* 19 (1891): 329–33.

Leavenworth, Abel E. "Vermont at Richmond." *Proceedings of the Rutland County Historical Society* 2:24–29.

Lee, Fitzhugh. *General Lee.* Introduction by Gary Gallagher. Originally published 1894. Wilmington, N.C.: Broadfoot, 1989.

Lee, G. W. C. "Report of General G. W. C. Lee, from the 2d to the 6th of April, 1865." *SHSP* 13 (1885): 255–59.

[Leyburn, John.] "The Fall of Richmond." *Harper's New Monthly Magazine* 33:193 (June 1866): 92–96.

Lightfoot, Mrs. William B. [Emmeline Allmond Crump Lightfoot]. "The Evacuation of Richmond." *VMHB* 41 (1933): 215–22.

Long, E. B., ed. *Personal Memoirs of U. S. Grant.* New York: Da Capo, 1886.

Lowe, Jeffrey C., and Sam Hodges, eds. *Letters to Amanda: The Civil War Letters of Marion Hill Fitzpatrick, Army of Northern Virginia.* Macon, Ga.: Mercer University Press, 1998.

McDonald, Cornelia. *A Diary with Reminiscences of the War and Refugee Life in the Shenandoah Valley, 1860–1865.* Nashville: Cullom & Ghertner, 1934.

McGuire, Judith W. *Diary of a Southern Refugee During the War by a Lady of Virginia.* Introduction by Jean V. Berlin. Originally published in 1867. Lincoln and London: University of Nebraska Press, 1995.

McNeilly, J. S. "A Mississippi Brigade in the Last Days of the Confederacy." *Publications of the Mississippi Historical Society* 7. Oxford, Miss.: printed for the Society, 1903.

Mallory, Stephen R. "Last Days of the Confederate Government." *McClure's Magazine* 16:2 (December 1900): 99–107.

Manarin, Louis H., ed. *Richmond at War: The Minutes of the City Council, 1861–1865.* Chapel Hill: University of North Carolina Press, 1966.

———. ed. *Richmond Occupied: Entry of the United States Forces into Richmond, Va., April 3, 1865; Calling Together of the Virginia Legislature and Revocation of the Same.* [Account of Godfrey Weitzel first published in 1881.] Richmond: Richmond Civil War Centennial Commission, 1965.

Maynard, Lizzie Green, to Helen Dodge Edwards, July 20, 1865. Printed in James T. Hickey, ed., "A Family Divided." *Journal of the Illinois State Historical Society* 70:1 (February 1977): 22–26.

Miller, Mrs. Fannie Walker. "The Fall of Richmond." *CV* 13 (1905): 305.

Mitchel, John. "Journal. Being a Continuation of 'Jail Journal.'" *The Irish Citizen* 3:143 (week ending July 9, 1870).

Moore, Edward A. *The Story of a Cannoneer Under Stonewall Jackson: In Which Is Told the Part Taken by the Rockbridge Artillery of the Army of Northern Virginia.* New York: Neale, 1907.

Myers, Gustavus A. "Memoranda." *VMHB* 41 (1933): 318–22.

Nevins, Allan, and Milton Halsey Thomas, eds. *The Diary of George Templeton Strong.* Vol. 3. *The Civil War, 1860–1865.* New York: Macmillan, 1952.

Newton, A. H. *Out of the Briars: An Autobiography and Sketch of the Twenty-ninth Regiment Connecticut Volunteers.* Philadelphia: A.M.E. Book Concern, 1910.

Nolan, B. P., to General I. M. St. John, Apr. 16, 1874. *SHSP* 3 (1877): 107–8.

Owen, William Miller. *In Camp and Battle with the Washington Artillery of New Orleans.* Baton Rouge: Louisiana State University Press, 1999.

Page, Charles A. *Letters of a War Correspondent.* Ed. by James R. Gilmore. Boston: L. C. Page, 1899.

Parker, David B. *A Chautauqua Boy in '61 and Afterwards: Reminiscences.* Boston: Small, Maynard, 1912.

Parker, William Harwar. "The Gold and Silver in the Confederate States Treasury: What Became of It." Reprinted from the *Richmond Dispatch*, July 16, 1893. *SHSP* 21 (1893): 304–13.

———. *Recollections of a Naval Officer, 1841–1865.* New York: Charles Scribner's Sons, 1883.

[Penrose, Charles H.] "Lincoln's Visit to Richmond." *Century Magazine* 40:2 (June 1890): 307.

Perdue, Charles L., Jr., Thomas E. Barden, and Robert K. Phillips, eds. *Weevils in the Wheat: Interviews with Virginia Ex-Slaves.* Charlottesville: University Press of Virginia, 1976.

Pickett, LaSalle Corbell. *What Happened to Me.* New York: Brentano's, 1917.

Pollard, Edward A. *Life of Jefferson Davis, with a Secret History of the Southern Confederacy Gathered "Behind the Scenes in Richmond"* . . . Philadelphia: National Publishing, 1869.

———. *The Lost Cause; A New Southern History of the War of the Confederates.* New York: E. B. Treat, 1866.

———. *Southern History of the War.* New York: Charles B. Richardson, 1866.

Porter, Admiral [David D.]. *Incidents and Anecdotes of the Civil War.* New York: D. Appleton, 1885.

Porter, Horace. *Campaigning with Grant.* New York: Century, 1897.

Pryor, Mrs. Roger A. *Reminiscences of Peace and War.* New York: Macmillan, 1905.

Putnam, Sallie Brock. *Richmond During the War: Four Years of Personal Observation*. Introduction by Virginia Scharff. First published in 1867. Lincoln and London: University of Nebraska Press, 1996.

Rachal, William M. E., ed. "The Occupation of Richmond, April 1865: The Memorandum of Events of Colonel Christopher Q. Tompkins." *VMHB* 73 (1965): 189–98.

Randolph, Peter. *From Slave Cabin to the Pulpit*. Boston: James H. Earle, 1893.

Reagan, John H. *Memoirs with Special Reference to Secession and the Civil War*. New York and Washington: Neale, 1906.

Reed, William Howell. *Hospital Life in the Army of the Potomac*. Boston: William V. Spencer, 1866.

Reese, George H., ed. *Proceedings of the Virginia State Convention of 1861*. 4 vols. Richmond: Virginia State Library, 1965.

Reid, Whitelaw. *After the War: A Southern Tour. May 1, 1865, to May 1, 1866*. London: Sampson Law, Son, & Marston, 1866.

Ripley, Edward H. "The Burning of Richmond, April 3, 1865." Reprinted from the *Richmond Times-Dispatch* [no date given]. *SHSP* 32 (1904): 73–76.

———. *The Capture and Occupation of Richmond, April 3rd, 1865*. New York: G. P. Putnam's Sons, 1907.

Roberts, Samuel H., to "My Dear Son," Apr. 5, 1865. Sotheby's *Fine Books and Manuscripts . . .* , catalog for auction, Dec. 7, 1999.

Robertson, James I., Jr., ed. "English Views of the Civil War: A Unique Excursion to Virginia, April 2–8, 1865." [Account of Edward Moseley.] *VMHB* 77 (1969): 201–12.

Robinson, W. F. "Last Battle Before Surrender." *CV* 32 (1924): 470–71.

Rowland, Dunbar, ed. *Jefferson Davis, Constitutionalist: His Letters, Papers, and Speeches*. Jackson: Mississippi Department of Archives and History, 1923.

Ryan, David D., ed. *A Yankee Spy in Richmond: The Civil War Diary of "Crazy Bet" Van Lew*. Mechanicsburg, Pa.: Stackpole Books, 1996.

St. John, I. M. "Resources of the Confederacy in 1865—Report of General I. M. St. John, Commissary General." *SHSP* 3 (1877): 97–111.

Scarborough, William Kauffman, ed. *The Diary of Edmund Ruffin*. Vol. 3, *A Dream Shattered: June, 1863–June, 1865*. Baton Rouge and London: Louisiana State University Press, 1989.

Scharf, J. Thomas. *History of the Confederate States Navy . . .* New York: Fairfax Press, 1977.

Semmes, Raphael. *Service Afloat; or, The Remarkable Career of the Confederate Cruisers "Sumter" and "Alabama" During the War Between the States*. Baltimore: Baltimore Publishing Company, 1887.

Shepley, George F. "Incidents of the Capture of Richmond." *Atlantic Monthly*, July 1880, pp. 18–28.

Simon, John Y., ed. *The Papers of Ulysses S. Grant*. 24 vols. Carbondale and Edwardsville, Ill.: Southern Illinois University Press, 1967–2000.

———. The Personal Memoirs of Julia Dent Grant [Mrs. Ulysses S. Grant]. Carbondale and Edwardsville, Ill.: Southern Illinois University Press, 1975.

"A Sketch of the Life of General Josiah Gorgas, Chief of Ordnance of the Confederate States." SHSP 13 (1885): 216–28.

Smart, James G., ed. A Radical View: The "Agate" Dispatches of Whitelaw Reid, 1861–1865. Memphis: Memphis State University Press, 1976.

Southall, John R. "Recollections of the Evacuation of Richmond." CV 37 (1929): 45–59.

Sparks, David S., ed. Inside Lincoln's Army: The Diary of Marsena Rudolph Patrick, Provost Marshal General, Army of the Potomac. New York and London: Thomas Yoseloff, 1964.

Spencer, Warren F., ed. "A French View of the Fall of Richmond: Alfred Paul's Report to Drouyn de Lhuys, April 11, 1865." VMHB 73 (1965): 178–88.

Stevens, S. W. A Trip to Richmond: or Notes by the Way. Lowell, Mass.: Stone & Huse, 1865.

Sturgis, H. H. "About the Burning of Richmond." CV 17 (1909): 374.

Sulivane, Clement. "The Fall of Richmond." B&L 4, pt. 2, pp. 725–76.

———. "Last Soldiers to Leave Richmond." CV 17 (1909): 602.

———. "Who Was the Last Soldier to Leave Burning City." SHSP 37 (1909): 317–18.

Summers, Festus F., ed. [William Lyne Wilson.] A Borderland Confederate. Pittsburgh: University of Pittsburgh Press, 1962.

Swallow, W. H. "Retreat of the Confederate Government." Magazine of American History 15 (June 1886): 596–608.

Swiggett, Howard, ed. A Rebel War Clerk's Diary: At the Confederate States Capital. [By John Beauchamp Jones.] 2 vols. New York: Old Hickory Bookshop, 1935.

Swint, Henry L., ed. Dear Ones at Home: Letters from Contraband Camps. Nashville: Vanderbilt University Press, 1966.

Taylor, Walter H. General Lee, His Campaigns in Virginia, 1861–1865, with Personal Reminiscences. Norfolk: Nusbaum Book and News Company, 1906.

Thatcher, Thomas Graves. "The Fall of Richmond: The Occupation." B&L 4, pt. 2, pp. 726–28.

Thompson, S. Millett. Thirteenth Regiment of New Hampshire Volunteer Infantry in the War of the Rebellion, 1861–1865. A Diary Covering Three Years and a Day. Boston and New York: Houghton Mifflin, 1888.

Timberlake, W. L. "In the Siege of Richmond and After." CV 29 (1921): 412–14.

———. "The Last Days in Front of Richmond." CV 22 (1914): 303.

———. "The Last Days in Front of Richmond, 1864–65." CV 20 (1912): 119.

Tower, Lockwood, ed., with John S. Belmont. Lee's Adjutant: The Wartime Letters of Colonel Walter Herron Taylor, 1862–1865. Columbia: University of South Carolina Press, 1995.

Townshend, Geo. Alfred. Campaigns of a Non-Combatant, and His Romaunt Abroad During the War. New York: Blelock, 1866.

Trowbridge, J. T. *A Picture of the Desolated States; and the Work of Restoration, 1865–1868.* Hartford, Conn.: L. Stebbins, 1868.

————. *The South: A Tour of Its Battlefields and Ruined Cities, a Journey Through the Desolated States, and Talks with the People . . .* Hartford, Conn.: L. Stebbins, 1866.

Truman, Ben C. "Valuable Relics of the Confederacy." *CV* 16 (1908): 77.

Tucker, Dallas. "The Fall of Richmond," *SHSP* 29 (1901): 152–63.

Turner, Justin G., and Linda Levitt Turner, eds. *Mary Todd Lincoln: Her Life and Letters.* New York: Fromm International Publishing, 1987.

United States Congress. *Report of the Joint Committee on the Conduct of the War, at the Second Session Thirty-eighth Congress.* Washington, D.C.: Government Printing Office, 1865.

————. *Report of the Joint Committee on Reconstruction at the First Session Thirty-ninth Congress.* Washington, D.C.: Government Printing Office, 1866.

United States Navy War Records Office. *Official Records of the Union and Confederate Navies in the War of the Rebellion.* 27 vols. Washington, D.C.: Government Printing Office, 1894–1922.

United States War Department. *The War of the Rebellion: A Compilation of the Official Records of the Union and Confederate Armies.* 128 vols. Washington, D.C.: Government Printing Office, 1880–1901.

Vandiver, Frank E., ed. *The Civil War Diary of General Josiah Gorgas.* University: University of Alabama Press, 1947.

Watehall, E. T. "Fall of Richmond, April 3, 1865." *CV* 17 (1909): 215.

Wheless, John F. "The Confederate Treasure—Statement of Paymaster John F. Wheless." *SHSP* 10 (1882): 137–41.

White, W. S. "Stray Leaves from a Soldier's Journal." *SHSP* 11 (1883): 552–59.

Wiggins, Sarah Woolfolk, ed. *The Journals of Josiah Gorgas, 1857–1878.* Tuscaloosa and London: University of Alabama Press, 1995.

Wiley, Bell Irvin, ed. *A Southern Woman's Story: Life in Confederate Richmond, by Phoebe Yates Pember: Including Unpublished Letters Written from the Chimborazo Hospital.* Jackson, Tenn.: McCowat-Mercer Press, 1959.

Wilson, Joseph T. *The Black Phalanx: A History of the Negro Soldiers of the United States in the Wars of 1775–1812, 1861–'65.* Richmond: United Mfg. Publishing Company, 1903.

Winthrop, Robert Charles. "The Fall of Richmond: A Speech Made at Faneuil Hall, Boston, April 4, 1865." *Addresses and Speeches on Various Occasions from 1852 to 1867, by Robert C. Winthrop.* Boston: Little, Brown, 1867.

Wise, John S. *The End of an Era.* Boston and New York: Houghton Mifflin, 1902.

Wood, H. E. "More of the Last Defense of Richmond." *CV* 16 (1908): 397.

Woods, John L. G. "Last Scenes of War—How I Got Home." *CV* 27 (1919): 140–44.

Woodward, C. Vann, ed. *Mary Chesnut's Civil War.* New Haven and London: Yale University Press, 1981.

Worsham, John H. *One of Jackson's Foot Cavalry.* Ed. by James I. Robertson, Jr. Jackson, Tenn.: McCowat-Mercer Press, 1964.

Younger, Edward, ed. *Inside the Confederate Government: The Diary of Robert Garlick Hill Kean, Head of the Bureau of War.* New York: Oxford University Press, 1957.

Newspapers and Periodicals

American Missionary
Boston Daily Evening Transcript
Chicago Tribune
Cincinnati Daily Gazette
Grant's Petersburg Progress
London *Index*
Lynchburg Virginian
New York Herald
New York Times
New York Tribune
New York World
Philadelphia Christian Recorder
Philadelphia Inquirer
Pittsburgh Post
Richmond Daily Enquirer
Richmond Dispatch and *Richmond Daily Dispatch*
Richmond Examiner
Richmond Religious Herald
Richmond Sentinel
Richmond Times
Richmond Whig and *Richmond Evening Whig*
Washington, D.C., Daily National Republican
Washington Daily National Intelligencer

Selected Web Sites

www.alincolnassoc.com
    Abraham Lincoln Association
    Searchable database of the Collected Works of Abraham Lincoln
carlisle-www.army.mil/usamhi/
    U.S. Army Military History Institute, Carlisle Barracks, Pennsylvania
www.lva.lib.va.us
    Library of Virginia
    Online catalog
www.mdgorman.com
    Michael D. Gorman's Civil War Richmond
    Compilation of photographs of the Confederate capital

www.nara.gov/genealogy/civilwar.html
   National Archives and Records Administration
   Civil War Records
www.itd.nps.gov/cwss/
   National Park Service
   Civil War Soldiers & Sailors System
aa.usno.navy.mil/data/
   U.S. Naval Observatory
   Data on sunrise, sunset, moonrise, moonset
www.iath.virginia.edu/vshadow2/
   The Valley of the Shadow: Two Communities in the American Civil War
www.vahistorical.org
   Virginia Historical Society
   Online catalog

Secondary Sources

Ambler, Charles H. *Francis H. Pierpont: Union War Governor of Virginia and Father of West Virginia.* Chapel Hill: University of North Carolina Press, 1937.

Andrews, J. Cutler. *The North Reports the Civil War.* Pittsburgh: University of Pittsburgh Press, 1955.

———. *The South Reports the Civil War.* Princeton: Princeton University Press, 1970.

Angle, Paul M., and Earl Schenck Miers, eds. *A Documentary History of the American Civil War.* Vol. 2, *Tragic Years, 1860–1865.* New York: Simon & Schuster, 1960.

Armstrong, William H. *A Friend to God's Poor: Edward Parmelee Smith.* Athens and London: University of Georgia Press, 1993.

Ash, Stephen V. *When the Yankees Came: Conflict and Chaos in the Occupied South, 1861–1865.* Chapel Hill: University of North Carolina Press, 1995.

———. "White Virginians Under Federal Occupation, 1861–1865." *VMHB* 98 (1990): 169–92.

Ballard, Michael B. *A Long Shadow: Jefferson Davis and the Final Days of the Confederacy.* Jackson and London: University Press of Mississippi, 1986.

Barber, Edna Susan. " 'Sisters of the Capital': White Women in Richmond, Virginia, 1860–1880." Ph.D. dissertation, University of Maryland, 1997.

Bartholomees, J. Boone, Jr. *Buff Facings and Gilt Buttons: Staff and Headquarters Operations in the Army of Northern Virginia, 1861–1865.* Columbia: University of South Carolina Press, 1998.

Bartlett, A. W. *History of the Twelfth Regiment New Hampshire Volunteers in the War of the Rebellion.* Concord, N.H.: Ira C. Evans, 1897.

Bill, Alfred Hoyt. *The Beleaguered City: Richmond, 1861–1865.* New York: Alfred A. Knopf, 1946.

Black, Robert C. *The Railroads of the Confederacy*. Chapel Hill: University of North Carolina Press, 1952.

Blair, William. *Virginia's Private War: Feeding Body and Soul in the Confederacy, 1861–1865*. New York and Oxford: Oxford University Press, 1998.

Blanton, Wyndham B. *The Making of a Downtown Church: The History of the Second Presbyterian Church, Richmond, Virginia, 1845–1945*. Richmond: John Knox Press, 1945.

Bleser, Carol K. "The Marriage of Varina Howell and Jefferson Davis: 'I gave the best and all my life to a girdled tree.' " *JSH* 65:1 (Feb. 1999): 3–40.

Blight, David W. *Race and Reunion: The Civil War in American Memory*. Cambridge, Mass., and London: Belknap Press of Harvard University Press, 2001.

Boritt, Gabor S., ed., and Norman O. Forness, assoc. ed. *The Historian's Lincoln: Pseudohistory, Psychohistory, and History*. Urbana and Chicago: Illinois University Press, 1996.

Brown, Elsa Barkley. "Uncle Ned's Children: Negotiating Community and Freedom in Postemancipation Richmond, Virginia." Ph.D. dissertation, Kent State University, 1994.

Brubaker, John H. *The Last Capital: Danville, Virginia, and the Final Days of the Confederacy*. Danville: Danville Museum of Fine Arts and History, 1979.

Bruce, Kathleen. *Virginia Iron Manufacture in the Slave Era*. New York and London: Century, 1931.

Brumbaugh, Thomas B. "The Evolution of Crawford's 'Washington.' " *VMHB* 70:1 (Jan. 1962): 3–29.

Brydon, G. MacLaren. "The 'Confederate Prayer Book.' " *Historical Magazine of the Protestant Episcopal Church* 17:4 (Dec. 1948): 339–44.

———. "The Diocese of Virginia in the Southern Confederacy." *Historical Magazine of the Protestant Episcopal Church* 17:4 (Dec. 1948): 384–410.

Callahan, James Morton. *The Diplomatic History of the Southern Confederacy*. Baltimore: Johns Hopkins Press, 1901.

Campbell, R. Thomas. *Academy on the James: The Confederate Naval School*. Shippensburg, Pa.: Burd Street Press, 1998.

Carroll, J. Frank. *Confederate Treasure in Danville*. Danville, Va.: URE Press, 1996.

Chesson, Michael B. *Richmond After the War, 1865–1890*. Richmond: Virginia State Library, 1981.

Christian, W. Asbury. *Richmond: Her Past and Present*. Richmond: L. H. Jenkins, 1912.

Clark, James C. *Last Train South: The Flight of the Confederate Government from Richmond*. Jefferson, N.C., and London: McFarland, 1984.

Clark, Malcolm Cameron. "The First Quarter-Century of the Richmond & Danville Railroad, 1847–1871." M.A. thesis, George Washington University, 1959.

Cole, Garold L. *Civil War Eyewitnesses: An Annotated Bibliography of Books and Articles, 1986–1996*. Columbia: University of South Carolina Press, 2000.

Collier, Malinda W., et al. *White House of the Confederacy*. Richmond: Cadmus, 1993.

Cooper, William J., Jr. *Jefferson Davis, American*. New York: Alfred A. Knopf, 2000.

Cortissoz, Royal. *The Life of Whitelaw Reid*. 2 vols. New York: Charles Scribner's Sons, 1921.

Couper, William. *One Hundred Years at VMI*. 4 vols. Richmond: Garrett & Massie, 1939.

Crandall, Marjorie, comp. *Confederate Imprints: A Check List Based Principally on the Collection of the Boston Athenaeum*. Boston: Boston Athenaeum, 1955.

Cresap, Bernarr. *Appomattox Commander: The Story of General E. O. C. Ord*. San Diego and New York: A. S. Barnes, 1981.

Crofts, Daniel W. "Late Antebellum Virginia Reconsidered." *VMHB* 107 (1999): 253–86.

——. *Reluctant Confederates: Upper South Unionists in the Secession Crisis*. Chapel Hill and London: University of North Carolina Press, 1989.

Crozier, Emmet. *Yankee Reporters, 1861–65*. Westport, Conn.: Greenwood Press, 1956.

Cullum, George W. *Biographical Register of the Officers and Graduates of the U.S. Military Academy, at West Point, N.Y. From Its Establishment, March 16, 1802, to the Army Re-organization of 1866–67*. 2 vols. New York: D. Van Nostrand, 1868.

Dabney, Virginius. *Pistols and Pointed Pens: The Dueling Editors of Old Virginia*. Chapel Hill: Algonquin Books, 1987.

——. *Richmond: The Story of a City*. Garden City, N.Y.: Doubleday, 1976.

——. *Virginia: The New Dominion*. First published in 1971. Charlottesville: University Press of Virginia, 1983.

Davis, William C. *Breckinridge: Statesman, Soldier, Symbol*. Baton Rouge: Louisiana State University Press, 1974.

——. *An Honorable Defeat: The Last Days of the Confederate Government*. New York: Harcourt, 2001.

——. *Jefferson Davis: The Man and His Hour*. Baton Rouge: Louisiana State University Press, 1991.

Dew, Charles B. *Ironmaker to the Confederacy: Joseph Reid Anderson and the Tredegar Iron Works*. New Haven, Conn.: Yale University Press, 1966.

Dillon, William. *Life of John Mitchel*. 2 vols. London: Kegan Paul, Trench, 1888.

Donald, David. *Charles Sumner and the Rights of Man*. New York: Alfred A. Knopf, 1970.

——. *Lincoln*. New York: Simon & Schuster, 1995.

Dormon, James H. "Thespis in Dixie: Professional Theater in Confederate Richmond." *VC* 28:1 (Summer 1978): 4–13.

Dornbusch, E. C., comp. *Military Bibliography of the Civil War*. 4 vols. New York: New York Public Library; Dayton, Ohio: Morningside House, 1961–77.

Dowdey, Clifford. *Experiment in Rebellion*. Garden City, N.Y.: Doubleday, 1946.

——. *Lee*. Boston: Little, Brown, 1965.

Dozier, Graham T., comp. *Virginia's Civil War: A Guide to Manuscript Collections at the Virginia Historical Society*. Richmond: Virginia Historical Society, 1998.

Duggan, Richard M. "The Military Occupation of Richmond, Virginia." M.A. thesis, University of Richmond, 1965.

Duke, Maurice, and Daniel P. Jordan, eds. *A Richmond Reader: 1733–1983*. Chapel Hill and London: University of North Carolina Press, 1983.

Dunaway, Wayland Fuller. *History of the James River and Kanawha Company*. New York: Columbia University, 1922.

Durden, Robert F. *The Gray and the Black: The Confederate Debate on Emancipation*. Baton Rouge: Louisiana State University Press, 1972.

Durkin, Joseph T., S. J. *Stephen R. Mallory: Confederate Navy Chief*. Chapel Hill: University of North Carolina Press, 1954.

Evans, Clement A. *Confederate Military History*. 12 vols. Atlanta: Confederate Publishing Company, 1899.

Evans, Eli N. *Judah P. Benjamin: The Jewish Confederate*. New York: Free Press, 1988.

Ezekiel, Herbert T., and Gaston Lichtenstein. *The History of the Jews of Richmond from 1769 to 1917*. Richmond: Herbert T. Ezekiel, 1917.

Fahrner, Alvin A. "William 'Extra Billy' Smith, Governor of Virginia, 1864–1865." *VMHB* 74:1 (1966): 68–87.

Faust, Patricia L., ed. *Historical Times Illustrated Encyclopedia of the Civil War*. New York: Harper & Row, 1986.

Felt, Jeremy P. "Lucius B. Northrop and the Confederacy's Subsistence Department." *VMHB* 69:2 (1961): 181–93.

Fisher, Geo. D. *History and Reminiscences of the Monumental Church, Richmond, Va., from 1814 to 1878*. Richmond: Whittet & Shepperson, 1880.

Fitzgerald, Oscar Penn. "John M. Daniel and Some of His Contemporaries." *South Atlantic Quarterly* 4 (1905): 13–17.

Flower, Frank Abial. *Edwin McMasters Stanton: The Autocrat of Rebellion, Emancipation, and Reconstruction*. Akron, Ohio, and New York: Saalfield Publishing, 1905.

Foner, Eric, and Olivia Mahoney. *America's Reconstruction: People and Politics After the Civil War*. New York: HarperPerennial, 1995.

Foote, Shelby. *The Civil War: A Narrative*. Vol. 3, *Red River to Appomattox*. New York: Random House, 1974.

Foster, Jack Hamilton. "A Yankee Soldier Writes from Richmond." *Richmond Quarterly* 14:2 (Fall 1991): 43–48.

Frassanito, William A. *Grant and Lee: The Virginia Campaigns, 1864–1865*. New York: Charles Scribner's Sons, 1983.

Freeman, Douglas Southall. *A Calendar of Confederate Papers . . .* Richmond: Confederate Museum, 1908.

———. *Lee's Lieutenants: A Study in Command*. 3 vols. New York: Charles Scribner's Sons, 1942–44.

———. *R. E. Lee: A Biography*. 4 vols. New York: Charles Scribner's Sons, 1935.

Furgurson, Ernest B. *Ashes of Glory: Richmond at War*. New York: Alfred A. Knopf, 1996.

Gaddy, David Winfred. "William Norris and the Confederate Signal and Secret Service." *Maryland Historical Magazine* 70:2 (Summer 1975): 167–88.

Gallagher, Gary W. *The Confederate War.* Cambridge, Mass., and London: Harvard University Press, 1997.

———. "A Widow and Her Soldier: La Salle Corbell Pickett as Author of the George E. Pickett Letters." *VMHB* 94 (1986): 329–44.

Gordon, Lesley J. *General George E. Pickett in Life & Legend.* Chapel Hill and London: University of North Carolina Press, 1998.

Greeley, Horace. *American Conflict: A History of the Great Rebellion in the United States of America, 1850–'65 . . .* Hartford, Conn.: O. D. Case, 1866.

Griffis, William Eliot. *Charles Carleton Coffin: War Correspondent, Traveller, Author, and Statesman.* Boston: Estes & Lauriat, 1898.

Guzman-Stokes, Theresa M. "A Flag and a Family: Richard Gill Forrester, 1847–1906." *VC* 47:2 (Spring 1998): 52–63.

Hall, Virginius C., Jr. *Portraits in the Collections of the Virginia Historical Society.* Richmond: Virginia Historical Society, 1981.

———. "The Virginia Historical Society: An Anniversary Narrative of Its First Century and a Half." *VMHB* 90 (1982): 1–150.

Hallion, Linda B., comp. "The Fall of Richmond, April 2–5, 1865." 2 vols. Unpublished annotated bibliography. Museum of the Confederacy, Richmond, 1994.

Hanchett, William. "The Lincoln Murder Conspiracies: The Assassination in History and Historiography." In Boritt, ed., *The Historian's Lincoln.*

Hanna, A. J. *Flight into Oblivion.* N.p.: Johnson Publishing Company, 1938.

Harris, William C. *With Charity for All: Lincoln and the Restoration of the Union.* Lexington: University Press of Kentucky, 1997.

Harwell, Richard Barksdale. *Brief Candle: The Confederate Theatre.* Worcester, Mass.: American Antiquarian Society, 1971.

Heite, Edward F. "Extra Billy Smith: A Beloved and Eccentric Governor Met Difficult Challenges with Unusual Solutions." *VC* 15:3 (1966): 4–13.

———. "Judge Robert Ould: His Struggle for Justice Continued Long After the War Was Over." *VC* 14:4 (1965): 10–19.

Hettle, Wallace. "The 'Self-Analysis' of John C. Rutherfoord: Democracy and the Manhood of a Virginia Secessionist." *Southern Studies* 5 (Spring and Summer 1994): 81–116.

Hoehling, A. A. and Mary. *The Day Richmond Died.* San Diego: A. S. Barnes, 1971.

Holland, James W. "A Preliminary Study of Chimborazo Hill, Richmond, Virginia." Richmond: Richmond National Battlefield Park, 1956.

Hoole, Wm. Stanley. *Lawley Covers the Confederacy.* Confederate Centennial Studies, No. 26. Tuscaloosa, Ala.: Confederate Publishing Company, 1964.

Irons, Charles F. "And All These Things Shall be Added unto You: The First African Baptist Church, Richmond, 1841–1865." *VC* 47:1 (Winter 1998): 26–35.

Irvine, Dallas D. "The Fate of the Confederate Archives." *American Historical Review* 44 (July 1939): 823–41.

Johns, Frank S., and Anne Page Johns. "Chimborazo Hospital and J. B. McCaw, Surgeon-in-Chief." *VMHB* 62:2 (1954): 190–200.

Jones, Terry L., ed. *Campbell Brown's Civil War: With Ewell and the Army of Northern Virginia*. Baton Rouge: Louisiana State University Press, 2001.

Jordan, Evin L., Jr. *Black Confederates and Afro-Yankees in Civil War Virginia*. Charlottesville and London: University of Virginia Press, 1995.

Jordan, Weymouth T., Jr., comp. *North Carolina Troops, 1861–1865: A Roster*. Vol. 11. Raleigh, N.C.: Division of Archives and History, 1987.

Kimball, Gregg D. *American City, Southern Place: A Cultural History of Antebellum Richmond*. Athens and London: University of Georgia Press, 2000.

King, Joseph Leonard, Jr. *Dr. George William Bagby: A Study of Virginian Literature, 1850–1880*. New York: Columbia University Press, 1927.

Krick, Robert K. *Lee's Colonels: A Biographical Register of the Field Officers of the Army of Northern Virginia*. 4th edition. Dayton, Ohio: Morningside House, 1992.

Krowl, Michelle A. "African American Women and the United States Military in Civil War Virginia." In John Saillant, ed., *Afro-Virginian History and Culture*. New York and London: Garland, 1999.

Lee, Richard M. *General Lee's City: An Illustrated Guide to the Historic Sites of Confederate Richmond*. McLean, Va.: EPM Publications, 1987.

Leech, Margaret. *Reveille in Washington, 1860–1865*. New York and London: Harper & Brothers, 1941.

Litterst, Michael. *He Came as a Peacemaker: Abraham Lincoln in the Confederate Capital*. The Papers of the Blue and Gray Education Society, No. 1. Danville, Va.: BGES, 1995.

Litwack, Leon F. *Been in the Storm So Long: The Aftermath of Slavery*. New York: Alfred A. Knopf, 1979.

Long, E. B., with Barbara Long. *The Civil War Day by Day: An Almanac, 1861–1865*. Garden City, N.Y.: Doubleday, 1971.

Longacre, Edward G. *Army of Amateurs: General Benjamin F. Butler and the Army of the James, 1863–1865*. Mechanicsburg, Pa.: Stackpole Books, 1997.

Love, Richard. *Founded upon Benevolence: A Bicentennial History of the Mutual Assurance Society of Virginia*. Richmond: Valentine Museum, 1994.

Lowe, Richard. *Republicans and Reconstruction in Virginia, 1856–70*. Charlottesville and London: University Press of Virginia, 1991.

Lowry, Thomas P. *The Story the Soldiers Wouldn't Tell: Sex in the Civil War*. Mechanicsburg, Pa.: Stackpole Books, 1994.

McPherson, James M. *Battle Cry of Freedom: The Civil War Era*. New York: Ballantine Books, 1989.

———. "Ulysses S. Grant: The Unheroic Hero." *New York Review of Books* 46:2 (Feb. 4, 1999): 16–19.

McPherson, James M., and William J. Cooper, Jr., eds. *Writing the Civil War: The Quest to Understand*. Columbia: University of South Carolina Press, 1998.

Maddex, Jack P., Jr. *The Reconstruction of Edward A. Pollard: A Rebel's Conversion to Postbellum Unionism*. Chapel Hill: University of North Carolina Press, 1974.

Marvel, William. *A Place Called Appomattox*. Chapel Hill and London: University of North Carolina Press, 2000.

Meade, Robert Douthat. *Judah P. Benjamin: Confederate Statesman*. New York: Oxford University Press, 1943.

Miers, Earl Schenk, editor in chief. *Lincoln Day by Day: A Chronology, 1809–1865*. Vol. 3, *1861–1865*, ed. by C. Percy Powell. Washington, D.C.: Lincoln Sesquicentennial Commission, 1960.

Musselman, Homer D. *47th Virginia Infantry*. Lynchburg, Va.: H. E. Howard, 1991.

Naragon, Michael Douglas. "Ballots, Bullets, and Blood: The Political Transformation of Richmond, Virginia, 1850–1874." Ph.D. dissertation, University of Pittsburgh, 1996.

Narol, Raoul S. "Lincoln and the Sherman Peace Fiasco—Another Fable?" *JSH* 20 (Nov. 1954): 459–83.

Neely, Mark E., Jr. *Southern Rights: Political Prisoners and the Myth of Confederate Constitutionalism*. Charlottesville and London: University Press of Virginia, 1999.

Nelson, Scott Reynolds. *Iron Confederacies: Southern Railways, Klan Violence, and Reconstruction*. Chapel Hill and London: University of North Carolina Press, 1992.

Nicolay, John G., and John Hay. *Abraham Lincoln: A History*. 10 vols. New York: Century, 1890.

———. "Abraham Lincoln: A History. The Fall of the Rebel Capital—Lincoln in Richmond." *Century Magazine* 39:2 (Dec. 1899): 305–13.

O'Brien, John T. "Factory, Church, and Community: Blacks in Antebellum Richmond." *JSH* 44:4 (Nov. 1978): 509–36.

———. "Reconstruction in Richmond: White Restoration and Black Protest, April–June 1865." *VMHB* 89:3 (1981): 259–81.

Parker, Sandra V. *Richmond's Civil War Prisons*. Lynchburg, Va.: H. E. Howard, 1990.

Patrick, Rembert. *The Fall of Richmond*. Baton Rouge: Louisiana State University Press, 1960.

Perry, James M. *A Bohemian Brigade: The Civil War Correspondents—Mostly Rough, Sometimes Ready*. New York: John Wiley & Sons, 2000.

Pfanz, Donald C. *The Petersburg Campaign: Abraham Lincoln at City Point, March 20–April 9, 1865*. Lynchburg, Va.: H. E. Howard, 1989.

———. *Richard S. Ewell: A Soldier's Life*. Chapel Hill and London: University of North Carolina Press, 1998.

Power, J. Tracy. *Lee's Miserables: Life in the Army of Northern Virginia from the Wilderness to Appomattox*. Chapel Hill and London: University of North Carolina Press, 1998.

Preisser, Thomas M. "The Virginia Decision to Use Negro Soldiers in the Civil War, 1864–1865." *VMHB* 83 (1975): 98–113.

Quarles, Benjamin. *The Negro in the Civil War*. Boston: Little, Brown, 1953.

Reck, W. Emerson. *A. Lincoln: His Last 24 Hours*. Columbia: University of South Carolina Press, 1987.

Redkey, Edwin S. "Black Chaplains in the Union Army." *Civil War History* 33: 4 (1987): 331–50.

Riggs, David F. *Embattled Shrine: Jamestown in the Civil War.* Shippensburg, Pa.: White Mane, 1997.

Robertson, James I., Jr. *General A. P. Hill: The Story of a Confederate Warrior.* New York: Random House, 1987.

Robinson, William M., Jr. *Justice in Grey: A History of the Judicial System of the Confederate States.* Cambridge, Mass.: Harvard University Press, 1941.

Ropes, John C. "Memoir of Charles Devens, LL.D." *Proceedings of the Massachusetts Historical Society,* 2nd ser., 8 (1891–92): 104–17.

Royster, Charles. *The Destructive War: William Tecumseh Sherman, Stonewall Jackson, and the Americans.* New York: Alfred A. Knopf, 1991.

Ryan, David D. *Four Days in 1865: The Fall of Richmond.* Richmond: Cadmus, 1993.

Sale, Marian Marsh. "Disaster at the Spotswood." *VC* 12:2 (Autumn 1962): 13–19.

Sanborn, Margaret. *Robert E. Lee: The Complete Man, 1861–1870.* 2 vols. Philadelphia: J. B. Lippincott, 1966–67.

Sanders, Charles W., Jr. "Jefferson Davis and the Hampton Roads Peace Conference: 'To secure peace to the two countries.' " *JSH* 68:4 (Nov. 1997): 802–26.

Saunders, Robert, Jr. *John Archibald Campbell, Southern Moderate, 1811–1889.* Tuscaloosa and London: University of Alabama Press, 1997.

Scott, Mary Wingfield, and Louise F. Catterall. *Virginia's Capitol Square: Its Buildings and Its Monuments.* Richmond: Valentine Museum, 1957.

Scott, W. W., and W. G. Stanard. *The Capitol of Virginia and of the Confederate States . . .* Richmond: James E. Goode, 1894.

Seale, William. *Virginia's Executive Mansion: A History of the Governor's House.* Richmond: Virginia State Library and Archives for the Citizens Advisory Council for Interpreting and Furnishing the Executive Mansion, 1988.

Sibley, F. Ray, Jr. *The Confederate Order of Battle.* Vol. 1, *The Army of Northern Virginia.* Shippensburg, Pa.: White Mane, 1996.

Simpson, Craig M. *A Good Southerner: The Life of Henry A. Wise of Virginia.* Chapel Hill and London: University of North Carolina Press, 1985.

Smith, Gene. *American Gothic: The Story of America's Legendary Theatrical Family—Junius, Edwin, and John Wilkes Booth.* New York: Touchstone Books, 1992.

———. *Lee and Grant: A Dual Biography.* New York: McGraw-Hill, 1984.

Smith, William B. "Recovery of the Great Seal of the Confederacy." *SHSP* 41 (1916): 20–33.

Soley, James Russell. *Admiral Porter.* New York: D. Appleton, 1903.

Sommers, Richard J. *Richmond Redeemed: The Siege at Petersburg.* Garden City, N.Y.: Doubleday, 1981.

Steele, Janet E. *The Sun Shines for All: Journalism and Ideology in the Life of Charles A. Dana.* Syracuse: Syracuse University Press, 1993.

Strode, Hudson. *Jefferson Davis, Tragic Hero: The Last Twenty-five Years, 1864–1889*. New York: Harcourt, Brace & World, 1964.

Stuart, Meriwether. "Colonel Ulric Dahlgren and Richmond's Union Underground: April 1864." *VMHB* 72 (1964): 152–204.

———. "Of Spies and Borrowed Names: The Identity of Union Operatives in Richmond Known as 'The Phillipses' Discovered." *VMHB* 89 (1981): 308–27.

———. "Samuel Ruth and General R. E. Lee: Disloyalty and the Line of Supply to Fredericksburg, 1862–1863." *VMHB* 71 (1963): 35–109.

Takagi, Midori. *"Rearing Wolves to Our Own Destruction": Slavery in Richmond, Virginia, 1782–1865*. Charlottesville and London: University Press of Virginia, 1999.

Thomas, Benjamin, and Harold M. Hyman. *Stanton: The Life and Times of Lincoln's Secretary of War*. New York: Alfred A. Knopf, 1962.

Thomas, Emory M. *The Confederate State of Richmond: A Biography of the Capital*. Austin: University of Texas Press, 1971.

———. *Robert E. Lee: A Biography*. New York: W. W. Norton, 1995.

Tidwell, William A. *April '65: Confederate Covert Action in the American Civil War*. Kent, Ohio, and London: Kent State University Press, 1995.

Tidwell, William A., with James O. Hall and David Winfred Gaddy. *Come Retribution: The Confederate Secret Service and the Assassination of Lincoln*. Jackson and London: University Press of Mississippi, 1988.

Trexler, Harrison A. "The Davis Administration and the Richmond Press, 1861–1865." *JSH* 41:2 (May 1950): 177–95.

Turner, Thomas Reed. "Beware the People Weeping." In Boritt, ed., *The Historian's Lincoln*.

Tyler-McGraw, Marie. *At the Falls: Richmond, Virginia, and Its People*. Chapel Hill and London: University of North Carolina Press, 1994.

Valentine Museum. *Richmond Portraits in an Exhibition of Makers of Richmond, 1737–1860*. Richmond: Valentine Museum, 1949.

Vandiver, Frank. *Ploughshares into Swords: Josiah Gorgas and Confederate Ordnance*. Austin: University of Texas Press, 1952.

Van Liew, Willard Randolph. *Van Liew-Lieu-Lew Genealogical and Historical Record . . .* Revised by Emerio R. Van Liew. Upper Montclair, N.J.: n.p., 1956.

Warner, Ezra J. *Generals in Blue: Lives of the Union Commanders*. Baton Rouge: Louisiana State University Press, 1964.

———. *Generals in Gray: Lives of the Confederate Commanders*. Baton Rouge: Louisiana State University Press, 1959.

Weaver, Jeffrey C. *The Virginia Home Guards*. Lynchburg, Va.: H. E. Howard, 1996.

Weddell, Elizabeth Wright. *St. Paul's Church, Richmond, Virginia: Its Historic Years and Memorials*. Richmond: William Byrd Press, 1931.

Weis, Tracey. "Negotiating Freedom: Domestic Service and the Landscape of Labor and Household Relations in Richmond, Virginia, 1850–1880." Ph.D. dissertation, Rutgers University, 1994.

Weisiger, Benjamin B., III. *Old Manchester and Environs, 1769–1910*. Richmond: B. B. Weisiger, 1993.

Wells, John E., and Robert E. Dalton. *The Virginia Architects, 1835–1955: A Biographical Dictionary*. Richmond: New South Architectural Press, 1997.

Wilson, James Harrison. *The Life of Charles A. Dana*. New York and London: Harper & Brothers, 1907.

Wood, John Sumner. *The Virginia Bishop: A Yankee Hero of the Confederacy*. Richmond: Garrett & Massie, 1961.

Work Projects Administration. *The Negro in Virginia: Compiled by Workers of the Writers' Program of the Work Projects Administration in the State of Virginia*. Sponsored by Hampton Institute. New York: Hastings House, 1940.

Wyatt-Brown, Bertram. *The Shaping of Southern Culture: Honor, Grace, and War, 1760s-1890s*. Chapel Hill and London: University of North Carolina Press, 2001.

INDEX

Page numbers *in italics* refer to maps.